Uncle John's

SIXTH BATHROOM READER

The Bathroom Readers' Institute

Bathroom Reader's Press
Berkeley

Produced and Packaged by Javnarama
Design by Javnarama

Cover Design by Michael Brunsfeld

If you're still reading this, you might want to know that the first shopping center was built in Ardmore, PA, in 1928. We don't know *why* you'd want to know that, but we feel it's our job to tell you.

THANK YOU

*The Bathroom Readers' Institute sincerely
thanks the people whose advice and
assistance made this book possible.*

John Javna
John Dollison
Lenna Lebovich
Alison Macondray
Jack Mingo
Gordon Javna
Eric Lefcowitz
Nenelle Bunnin
Julie Bennett
Penelope Houston
Larry Kelp
Gordon Javna
Michael Brunsfeld
William Cone
Thomas Crapper
Hi, Emily and Molly Bennett

Gordon Javna
Deirdre Carlson
Teresa Buswell
Patricia Flynn
Leo Rosten
Gordon Javna
Andrea Sohn
Julie Roeming
Paul Stanley
Gordo "Deja Vu" Javna
Tom Otrumba
Russel Schoch
Jesse & Sophie, *B.R.I.T.*
...and all the bathroom
readers

CONTENTS

NOTE
Because the B.R.I. understands your reading needs, we've
divided the contents by length as well as subject.
Short—a quick read
Medium—1 to 3 pages
Long—for those extended visits, when something
a little more involved is required.

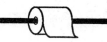

INTRODUCTION

*Well, here we are again, with a sixth volume. It's amusing to
think that in 1987, most New York publishers told us a
Bathroom Reader was a ridiculous idea. But back in
1987, it was a new idea. For those of you who are
curious, Here's how we came up with it.*

B ACKGROUND
• In the mid-'80s, Uncle John wrote (or co-wrote) a number
of books about pop culture—TV, music, the 1960s, etc.

• It seemed as though everyone who read them said they kept the
books in the bathroom...and they meant it as a compliment, not
an insult.

• So Uncle John suggested to an editor that they put a picture of a
toilet in the corner of one of his books, with a *Good Housekeeping*-
type seal that said "Bathroom Approved." The editor thought it
was a pretty dumb idea.

• Uncle John knew it wasn't. For one thing, he reads in the bathroom and knows how valuable a good bathroom-friendly magazine
or newspaper is. For another, there were all these people who obvi-
ously shared his interest.

THE BATHROOM READER

• Gradually, he developed the idea of doing a book specifically for
bathroom reading: easy to read, a wide variety of topics so readers
would never be bored, designed to be read quickly...but with an
option for a longer sitting.

• He took it to all the big New York publishers...and was rejected
by every single one. In fact, he became embarrassed he'd ever
thought of it and refused to talk about it anymore.

• Then one afternoon, he got a call from Stuart Moore, an editor
at St. Martin's Press. Stuart had brought it up at an editorial meeting, and St. Martin's had decided to do it, if it was still available.

• It was...and so the Bathroom Reader's Institute was born. It
wasn't just writers who helped on the project. There was a doctor, a
contractor, an artist, a teacher, and so on.

• The first Bathroom Reader was a lot of fun...and satisfying to get a handle on. We picked subjects we'd always wanted to know about. The ideas just started flowing: Someone wondered about the Edsel, so we did a story on it. Someone came up with the title "Famous for 15 Minutes," so we created a feature with that title, etc. After a while, we could hardly contain ourselves.

BATHROOM EXPLOSION

• We thought we'd created a good book...but we were still bowled over when it sold hundreds of thousands of copies and became a best seller. Shows you how many frustrated bathroom readers there are.

• It was no flush in the pan. Now it's turned into an annual event, and we've got our own company, the Bathroom Reader's Press, which publishes our Readers....And "Bathroom Reading" is a *genre* in a lot of bookstores! We've made our mark.

• To all of you who've been *going* along with us for all these years, thanks! If this is your first Bathroom Reader, we think you're in for an enlightening experience.

Remember, *Go With the Flow!*

Note: *Yes, that's Uncle John on the cover. We wanted to do something different after 5 volumes...and he was elected.*

YOU'RE MY INSPIRATION

It's fascinating to see how many pop characters—real and fictional—are inspired by other characters. Maybe in the next Bathroom Reader, we'll get into that. For now, here's a a handful of examples.

TINKERBELLE. Walt Disney's animators gave her Marilyn Monroe's measurements.

JAFAR, the Grand Vizier. The villain in the 1993 animated film *Aladdin*—described by the director as a "treacherous vizier...who seeks the power of the enchanted lamp to claim the throne for his own greedy purposes"—was inspired by Nancy Reagan. The Sultan, a doddering, kindly leader, was inspired by Nancy's husband.

THE EMPEROR in the *Star Wars* trilogy. In early drafts of the Star Wars scripts, George Lucas portrayed the emperor as "an elected official who is corrupted by power and subverts the democratic process." Lucas modeled him after Richard Nixon.

MICK JAGGER. Studied the way Marilyn Monroe moved, and learned to mimic her onstage.

THE STATUE OF LIBERTY. The face of Miss Liberty, sculpted by Frederic Auguste Bartholdi, was inspired by his mother. Ironically, although the statue has welcomed immigrants to New York City since 1886, Madame Bartholdi was "a domineering bigot."

DR. STRANGELOVE. Dr. Kissinger, I presume? According to Penny Stallings in *Flesh & Fantasy*, "[Director] Stanley Kubrick...made a special trip to Harvard to meet Dr. Henry Kissinger while researching the title role for his screen adaptation of *Dr. Strangelove*."

DR. JEKYL & MR. HYDE. Inspired by Dr. Horace Wells, celebrated inventor of modern anesthesia. He got hooked on ether, and went mad; he was jailed for throwing acid in a woman's face, while under the effects of ether.

William Moulton Marston, creator of Wonder Woman, also invented the polygraph.

FAMILIAR PHRASES

Here are the origins of some well-known sayings.

HE'S (SHE'S) A LOOSE CANNON

Meaning: Dangerously out of control.

Origin: On old-time warships, the cannons were mounted on "wheeled carriages." When they weren't being used, they were tied down. "Now imagine a warship rolling and pitching in a violent gale." A gun breaks loose and starts rolling around the ship—"a ton or so of metal on wheels rolling unpredictably about the deck, crippling or killing any sailor unlucky enough to get in the way and perhaps smashing through the ship's side. Human loose cannons are equally dangerous to their associates and to bystanders." (From *Loose Cannons and Red Herrings*, by Robert Claiborne)

DYED IN THE WOOL

Meaning: Dedicated, committed, uncompromising.

Origin: From the textile trade. "It was discovered that yarn that's dyed 'in the wool'—before being woven—retained its color better than yarn that was dyed 'in the piece,' i.e. after being woven." So if something's dyed-in-the-wool, it's unlikely to change. (From *Getting to the Roots*, by Martin Manser)

GET YOUR DUCKS LINED UP IN A ROW

Meaning: Get organized, ready for action.

Origin: Refers to setting up bowling pins—which were called *duckpins* in early America, because people thought they looked like ducks.

FIRST RATE

Meaning: The very best.

Origin: "In the 1600s a system for rating British naval ships according to their size and strength was developed. There were six different ratings, with a warship of the first rate being the largest and most heavily armed and one of the sixth rate being considerably smaller and having far fewer guns." The general public picked up the phrase right away, using it for anything topnotch. (From *Why You Say It*, by Webb Garrison)

Unemployment stat: Nevada has more out-of-work dancers than any other state.

START YOUR OWN COUNTRY

Ever wondered what it'd be like to be king—or president—
of your own country? Here are some people who found out.

ATLANTIS

Founding Father: J. L. Mott, a Danish sea captain.
History: In 930 A.D. Leif Ericson, a Viking explorer, discovered some Caribbean islands he mistook for remnants of the lost continent of Atlantis. In 1934, claiming to be Ericson's descendant, Mott declared himself the rightful heir to the islands, which he could not locate but believed "were somewhere near Panama." He drafted a 1-page constitution and began issuing passports and triangle-shaped postage stamps.

What Happened: The International Postal Union refused to recognize Mott's postage stamps. Then, in 1936, Mott was almost arrested for trying to enter the United States using an Atlantis passport. By 1954 the elusive country had been renamed the Empire of Atlantis and Lemuria. Despite the country's fancy new name, however, all attempts to actually *locate* it have failed.

GRANBIA

Founding Father: Andrew Richardson, a Liverpool postal worker.
History: In the 1970s Richardson declared his semi-detached flat to be the independent nation of Granbia (the rest of the building remained a part of the United Kingdom).
What Happened: He lost interest, and the apartment reverted to England by default.

NEW ATLANTIS

Founding Father: Leicester Hemingway, little brother of author Ernest Hemingway.
History: In 1964 he built an 8-foot by 30-foot floating bamboo platform 7 miles off the coast of Jamaica, anchoring it to the ocean floor with a Ford engine block. "I can stand on the platform, walk around on it, and salute the flag, all of which I do periodically,"

50's Nostalgia: Howdy Doody's sister's name was Heidi Doody.

Hemingway bragged to reporters. "There are no taxes here, because taxes are for people not smart enough to start their own countries."

What Happened: Part of the country was destroyed by fishermen in search of scrap wood; the rest sank in a storm.

THE HUTT RIVER PROVINCE PRINCIPALITY

Founding Father: "Prince" Leonard George Casely, an Australian wheat farmer.

History: When the Western Australia Wheat Quota Board limited the amount of wheat he could grow in 1969, Casely and his 18,500 acre farm seceded from the union. He designed his own national flag and motto, printed his own money, and set up his own parliament.

What Happened: Australia refused to recognize his sovereignty, and in 1977 he declared war. Nothing came of it—he backed down two days later and re-established diplomatic relations. Casely claims he pays no Australian taxes, but admits he he makes payments to the Australian government as an "international courtesy."

ISLE OF THE ROSES

Founding Father: Giorgio Rosa, an Italian engineering professor.

History: Rosa built a tower in the Adriatic Sea large enough to contain a bar, restaurant, and post office, and declared independence from Italy .

What Happened: The Italian government ignored him at first—but after a while they invaded the tower and blew it up.

THE SOLAR ATLANTIC EMPIRE

Founding Father: David Owen, a writer for The *Atlantic Monthly*.

History: Owen wanted to form his own country but couldn't find any available land. So the took possession of the sun, one of the last unclaimed territories in the solar system. He backed up his claim by writing a letter to the U.S. State Department asking for official recognition. "The sun should now be referred to as the Solar Atlantic Empire," he wrote, "and I, henceforth, will be known as Lord High Suzerain of Outer Space."

What Happened: The State Department wrote back saying that it was unable to consider his application.

The Columbia University football team's mascot, Leo the Lion, became the first MGM lion.

FAMOUS
FOR 15 MINUTES

Here it is again—our feature based on Andy Warhol's prophetic comment that "In the future, everyone will be famous for 15 minutes." Here's how a few people are using up their allotted quarter-hour.

THE STAR: Angelyne (She won't tell anyone her real name)
THE HEADLINE: *Blonde Bimbo's Billboards Bring Big Bonus*
WHAT HAPPENED: In 1981, Angelyne—an out-of-work busty blonde—began posting billboards of herself all over L.A. (they simply said *Angelyne*, and listed a phone number), and distributing hot-pink press releases (describing her as "a living icon, Hollywood billboard queen, the new Love Goddess of the Future!") from her pink Corvette. Later she had an 85-foot-high likeness of herself painted on the side of a building at Hollywood and Vine.

The result: She made more than 250 media appearances, including bit parts in films like *Earth Girls Are Easy* and *L.A. Story.* Her billboard appeared in the opening montage of "Moonlighting," and in an issue of *National Geographic.*

THE AFTERMATH: She never made it as a sex symbol, but has come to represent, as one writer put it, "raw fame, unsullied by any known talent, charm, or accomplishments." She doesn't mind. "I'm the first person in the history of Hollywood to be famous for doing nothing," she says, and adds: "I really don't want to be famous for being an actress. I just want to be famous for the magic I possess."

THE STAR: Larry Villella
THE HEADLINE: *14-year-old Chips in to Cut Deficit*
WHAT HAPPENED: In Feb., 1993, President Clinton was trying to drum up support for his "deficit-reduction plan." So Larry Villella, a 14-year-old from Fargo, North Dakota, sent the White House $1,000 (money he earned watering trees) to help pay it off.

Somehow, the media found out about Larry's check *before* it got to Washington—and every U.S. news service reported it as a major story. Larry was an instant celebrity. He was invited to appear on network TV talk shows, where he told interviewers his story—and

---

General Douglas MacArthur's mother dressed him in skirts until he was 8 years old.

got a chance to plug a tree-watering gizmo he'd invented.

THE AFTERMATH: He inspired people all over the U.S. One San Francisco man even sent the White House 375 lbs. of coins (about $500) he'd been saving. As for Larry's check: Clinton sent it back with a note that said: "I am very impressed with your concern...but I cannot accept your money." (Bonus: Bill Cosby sent Larry $2,000 as "a thank-you on behalf of the American people.")

THE STAR: Keron Thomas, a 16-year-old New York student

THE HEADLINE: *New York Youth Takes A-train on Joyride*

WHAT HAPPENED: On May 8, 1993, a man carrying a set of motorman's tools and a Transit Authority identification signed in at New York City's subway trainyard. "I'm the substitute man," he said. "Got anything for me?" They did—an A train.

The only problem: he wasn't the substitute man—and wasn't even a transit employee. He was Keron Thomas, a high school sophomore.

Thomas drove his train the length of Manhattan and all the way to Queens, carrying an estimated 2,000 passengers and making 85 stops along the way (He was even on *schedule*). The trip was so uneventful that he probably would have gotten away with it...until he took a turn too fast and set off the emergency brakes. He escaped before they learned his true identity, but investigators arrested him two days later.

THE AFTERMATH: He pled guilty to 3 misdemeanors and was sentenced to three years' probation. Why such a light sentence? As the *New York Times* said, authorities were "wary of punishing a folk hero." As he left the courtroom, he declared: "I'm going to be a train engineer."

THE STAR: Don Calhoun

THE HEADLINE: *Lucky Fan Hits $1 Million Shot in Chicago*

WHAT HAPPENED: On April 14, 1993, a 23-year-old office supply salesman named Don Calhoun got a free ticket to an NBA game between the Miami Heat and the Chicago Bulls.

As Calhoun headed for his seat at the game, someone told him he'd been picked to take the "Million Dollar Shot" (a promotion sponsored by Coca-Cola and a local restaurant chain). He'd get to take one shot from the opposite foul line, 73 feet away, and sink a basket. The prize: $1 million. Eighteen people had already tried and failed. (Why was he picked? *Shoes:* the Bulls marketing representative loved his yellow suede hiking boots.)

At first he didn't want to do it—he even suggested that his friend make the shot instead. But the Bulls representative insisted. "I thought she was crazy," Calhoun told reporters. "But she ran after me, so I shrugged and said 'Okay.'" During a time-out early in the third period, he was brought to the floor. He took one dribble, launched the ball, and....Basket!

THE AFTERMATH: Just about every sportscaster in the country carried Calhoun's Cinderella story on the news that night. He also did radio interviews, TV shows, even NBC's "Today" show. But a few days later, the bubble burst: It turned out Calhoun had played 11 games of college basketball, and the rules stipulated that no one who'd played in college could participate. But the ensuing publicity was so bad that Coke, the owner of the Bulls, and the restaurant all assured him he'd get his money anyway.

THE STAR: Holden Hollom
THE HEADLINE: *Frisco Cabbie Nabs Runaway Crook*
WHAT HAPPENED: On a June night in 1989, Hollom, a 51-year-old San Francisco cabbie (and former stunt driver) was driving a fare up Market Street, when he saw someone knock down a woman and steal her purse. He gave chase, yelling to his surprised passenger, "You're riding for free!"

He cornered the purse snatcher (a 212 lb. ex-convict) in an alley. To keep him from running away, he pinned him to the wall with his cab bumper. Newspapers all over the country reported the citizen's arrest as an example of what's *right* about America, and lauded Hollom for getting involved. He appeared on every major talk show, including "Larry King" and "Donahue."

AFTERMATH: The crook had to undergo 3 operations on his legs, and in 1992 sued Hollom for using excessive force. When he won, and was awarded $24,500 by a jury, the verdict got as much attention as the original incident. It generated more than $100,000 from outraged sympathizers who felt the cabbie had been shafted. (The verdict was later overturned.) Fleeting fame: he later ran for the S.F. Board of Supervisors, but came in 19th in a field of 26 candidates.

New Hampshire allows boys to be married at 14 and girls at 13—with parental permission.

WHAT DOES IT SAY?

Here's a game where the position of words and letters is part of the sentence. See if you can figure out what these say. If you need a sample answer, check out the Hints at the end of the last column. Answers on page 224.

1. A letter was addressed to:
WOOD
JOHN
MASS
Who got it; where did they live?

2. I thought I heard a noise outside, but it was
ALL 0

3. Let's have   STANDING
AN

4.   LOOK
LOOK   U   LOOK
LOOK

5. "Remember," she said to the group,
WE   WESTAND   FALL

6. "Why'd he do that?" Jesse asked. "Well, son," I said, he's a DKI

7. Texas? I love
S   P   A   C   E   S

8. "Drat! My watch broke." Time to get it RE-RE

9. "I remember the 1960s," she said, GNIKOOL

10. No, we're not living together anymore. It's a
L   E   G   A   L

11. Haven't seen him in a while. He's
FAR   HOME

12. Careful, I warned my sister. He's a   WOWOLFOL

13. "How do I get out of here?" he asked. I said, "Just calm down and put the
R A C

14. I tried to teach her, but no luck. I guess she's a
DLIHC

15. When it's raining...
AN UMBRELLA
SHEME

HINTS (if you need them):

• The answer to #1 is John Underwood, Andover Mass (JOHN under WOOD and over MASS)

• Answer to #14: I guess she's a *backward child.* (DLIHC is child spelled backward.)

The Great Salt Lake is only 13 feet deep.

A FOOD IS BORN

These foods are fairly common, but you've probably never wondered where they come from, have you? Doesn't matter. We'll tell you anyway.

CAMPBELL SOUP. Arthur Dorrance and his nephew, Dr. John Thompson Dorrance, took over the Campbell canning company when its founder, Joseph Campbell, retired in 1894. A few years later they perfected a method of condensing tomato soup—which made it cheaper to package and ship—but they couldn't decide on a design for the label. That Thanksgiving, company employee Herberton L. Williams went to a football game between Cornell and the University of Pennsylvania. He was impressed with Cornell's new red and white uniforms—and suggested to his bosses that they use those colors on the label. They did.

WHEATIES. Invented in 1921 by a Minneapolis health spa owner who fed his patients homemade bran gruel to keep them regular and help them lose weight. One day he spilled some on the stove, and it hardened into a crust. He was going to throw it out, but decided to eat it instead. To his surprise, the flakes he scraped off the stove tasted better than the stuff in the pot...so he made more and showed them to a friend at the Washburn Crosby Company (predecessor to General Mills). People at the company liked the flakes too, but didn't like the way they crumbled. So they came up with a better one using wheat. Once they had a flake they were satisfied with, they held a company-wide contest to name the product. Jane Bausman, the wife of a company executive, suggested *Wheaties*.

PEPPERIDGE FARM. One of Margaret Rudkin's sons suffered from severe asthma, a condition that became worse when he ate processed food. She couldn't find any bread that didn't make him ill, so in 1935 she started baking him stone-ground whole wheat bread. One day she brought a loaf to the boy's doctor; he liked it so much he began recommending it other patients. After building up a small mail-order business to local asthmatics and allergy-sufferers, she expanded her customer base to include people who *weren't* sick—and named her company after the family's 125 acre farm in Connecticut, *Pepperidge Farm*.

That's progress: Jimmy Carter was the first president born in a hospital.

LOG CABIN SYRUP. Invented in 1887 by P. J. Towle, a St. Paul, Minnesota grocer, who wanted to combine the flavor of maple syrup with the affordability of sugar syrup. He planned to name his creation after his boyhood hero Abraham Lincoln, but there were already so many Lincoln products that he named it after the slain president's birthplace instead. It sold in tin containers shaped like log cabins until World War II, when metal shortages forced the company to switch to glass bottles.

BROWN 'N SERVE ROLLS. Invented accidentally by Joe Gregor, a Florida baker and volunteer firefighter. One morning the fire alarm sounded while Gregor was baking some rolls, and he had to pull them out of the oven half-baked to go fight the fire. He was about to throw them out when he got back, but he decided to finish baking them, to see if they were still good. They were.

SANKA. Dr. Ludwig Roselius was a turn-of-the-century European coffee merchant looking for a way to decaffeinate coffee beans without harming the aroma and flavor. He wasn't having much luck—until someone gave him a "ruined" consignment of coffee beans that had been swamped with seawater while in transit. The damaged beans behaved differently than regular beans, and inspired Roselius to begin a new round of experiments with them. He eventually succeeded in removing 97% of the caffeine without harming the taste. He named his new product *Sanka*, a contraction of the French expression "sans caffeine."

FOLGER'S COFFEE. James Folger and his older brothers, Edward and Harry, planned on joining the California Gold Rush in 1849—but when they got to San Francisco, they only had enough money for two of them to continue on to the gold country. James had to stay behind; he eventually decided to go into the coffee business. Today people take roasted coffee for granted—but in the 1840s most people roasted coffee themselves in their own homes. When Folger thought of his brothers in the gold country and how difficult it was for them to roast their own beans, he decided to roast his beans before selling them.

Random thought: "History is a set of lies agreed upon."
—Napoleon Bonaparte

ACCORDING TO SHAW...

A few thoughts from George Bernard Shaw, the curmudgeon who was considered he greatest English playright since Shakespeare.

"I often quote myself; it adds spice to my conversation."

"Youth is a wonderful thing. What a crime to waste it on children."

"When a stupid man is doing something he is ashamed of, he always declares that it is his duty."

"A perpetual holiday is a good working definition of hell."

"A government which robs Peter to pay Paul can always count on the support of Paul."

"I am a gentleman; I live by robbing the poor."

"England and America are two countries separated by the same language."

"If all economists were laid end to end they would not reach a conclusion."

"Life does not cease to be funny when people die any more than it ceases to be serious when people laugh."

"No man can be a pure specialist without being, in a strict sense, an idiot."

"There may be some doubt as to who are the best people to have in charge of children, but there can be no doubt that parents are the worst."

"We should all be obliged to appear before a board every five years and justify our existence...on pain of liquidation."

"The fickleness of the women whom I love is only equaled by the infernal constancy of the women who love me."

"The power of accurate observation is commonly called cynicism by those who have not got it."

"The trouble with her is that she lacks the power of conversation but not the power of speech."

"There is no satisfaction in hanging a man who does not object to it."

APRIL FOOLS!

Why is April 1 a "fool's day"? The most plausible explanation is one we wrote in the first Bathroom Reader: "Until 1564 it was a tradition to begin the New Year with a week of celebration, ending with a big party. But the calendar was different then: the New Year began on March 25, and the biggest party fell on April 1. In 1564 a new calendar made January 1 the New Year. People who forgot—or didn't realize—what had happened, and still showed up to celebrate on April 1, were called 'April fools.' "
These days, most of the memorable April Fool's jokes are played by radio and TV stations. Here are a few recent classics.

PASTA FARMING

On April 1, 1966, the BBC broadcast a TV documentary on spaghetti-growing in Italy. Among the film's highlights: footage of Italian farmers picking market-ready spaghetti from "spaghetti plants." To the BBC's astonishment, British viewers accepted the news that Italy's "pasta farmers" had been able to fight off the "spaghetti weevil, which has been especially destructive recently."

HE'S BA-A-ACK

In 1992, National Public Radio's "Talk of the Nation" news show announced on April 1 that Richard Nixon had entered the race for president. They actually interviewed the "former president" (played by impressionist Rich Little) on the air. "I never did anything wrong," he announced, "and I won't ever do it again." Listeners actually called the show to comment. "Nixon is more trustworthy than Clinton," one remarked. "Nixon never screwed around with anyone's wife except his own. And according to some accounts, not even with her."

GRAVITATIONAL PULL

On April 1, 1976 a famous British astronomer told BBC radio audiences that since the planet Pluto would be passing close to Jupiter on April 1, the Earth's gravitational pull would decrease slightly for about 24 hours. He explained that listeners would feel the effect most if they jumped into the air at precisely 9:47 a.m. that morning. The BBC switchboard was jammed with listeners calling to say that the experiment had worked.

Gail Borden, inventor of condensed milk, also coined the phrase, "Remember the Alamo!"

COLORFUL BROADCAST

In the '70s, Britain's Radio Norwich announced on April 1st that it was experimenting with "color radio," and that the tests would affect the brilliance of tuning lights on radios at home. Some listeners actually reported seeing results: one complained that the experiment had affected the traffic lights in his area; another asked the station managers how much longer the bright colors he saw would be streaming out of his radio.

ANIMAL BEHAVIOR

On April 1, 1992, TV's Discovery Channel ran a "nature documentary" called "Pet Hates," actually a spoof of nature films by a British humorist posing as an animal expert. In the film the humorist criticized the animals for their "sexual excesses, appalling sense of hygiene and all-around stupidity"—and denounced them as "sex-crazed, bug-awful, foul-breathed, all-fornicating, all-urinating, disease-ridden, half-wit, furry, four-legged perverts."

DRIVING PRANK

One year a Paris radio station announced that from April 1 on, all Europe would begin driving on the left. Some drivers actually started driving on the left side of the road. A number of accidents resulted (no fatalities, though).

NEEDLING PEOPLE

In 1989 a Seattle TV station interrupted its regular April 1 broadcast with a report that the city's famous Space Needle had collapsed, destroying nearby buildings in the fall. The report included fake eyewitness accounts from the scene, which were punctuated with bogus updates from the studio newsroom. The "live" footage was so realistic that viewers jammed 911 lines trying to find out if their loved ones were safe. The station later apologized.

THE JOKE IS RED

Even the media of the former Soviet Union celebrates April Fool's Day. In 1992 the Moscow press printed stories claiming that gay rights activists had crossed the Atlantic Ocean in condoms, and that the Moscow City Council was planning a second subway system "in the interest of competition."

Model Citizen: President Zachary Taylor never voted in a presdential election.

MYTH AMERICA

A few things you probably didn't know about the founding fathers who wrote the U.S. Constitution.

THE MYTH: The men who attended the Constitutional Convention in 1787 were a sober, well-behaved group. They showed up on time, stuck it out 'til the end, and were all business when it came to the important task at hand.

THE TRUTH: Not quite. According to historical documents found by researchers at the National Constitution Center in 1992:

• Nineteen of the 74 people chosen to attend the convention never even showed up. (At least one of them had a good excuse, though—William Blount of New York refused to make the horseback ride to Philadelphia because of hemorrhoids.)

• Of the 55 who *did* show up, only 39 signed the document. Twelve people left early, and 4 others refused to sign. "A lot of them ran out of money and had to leave because they were doing a lot of price gouging here," observes researcher Terry Brent. Besides, he adds, the hot weather and high humidity must have been murder on the delegates, who wore wool breeches and coats. "They must have felt like dying. Independence Hall must have smelled like a cattle barn."

• And how did the Founding Fathers unwind during this pivotal moment in our nation's history? By getting drunk as skunks. One document that survived is the booze bill for a celebration party thrown 2 days before the Constitution was signed on September 17, 1787. According to the bill, the 55 people at the party drank 54 bottles of Madeira, 60 bottles of claret, 8 bottles of whiskey, 22 bottles of port, 8 bottles of cider, 12 bottles of beer, and 7 large bowls of alcoholic punch. "These were really huge punch bowls that ducks could swim in," Brent reports. "The partiers were also serenaded by 16 musicians. They had to be royally drunk—they signed the Constitution on the 17th. On the 16th, they were probably lying somewhere in the streets of Philadelphia."

Important first: Dwight D. Eisenhower was the first president to make a hole-in-one in golf.

Q & A:
ASK THE EXPERTS

Everyone's got a question or two they'd like answered—basic stuff, like "Why is the sky blue?" Here are a few of those questions, with answers from books by some of the nation's top trivia experts.

HOLY QUESTION

Q: *Why are manhole covers round?*

A: "So they can't be dropped *through* the manhole itself. Squares, rectangles, ovals, and other shapes could be positioned so they'd slip into the manhole. Round manhole covers rest on a lip that's smaller than the cover. So the size and shape keeps the manhole cover from falling in." (From *The Book of Answers*, by Barbara Berliner)

SHOE TIME

Q: *How and why did people start shining their shoes?*

A: "A high polish on shoes is a tradition passed down from the Spanish caballero (gentleman on horseback), whose shiny boots served notice that he rode his own horse and didn't walk along dusty roads with lesser men." (From *Do Elephants Swim?*, compiled by Robert M. Jones)

NIPPED IN THE BUD

Q: *Why do men have nipples?*

A: "Males actually have the anatomical equipment in place to provide milk, but it lies dormant unless stimulated by estrogen, the female hormone. Might men have suckled babies in the distant past? No one knows." (From *Why Do Men Have Nipples*, by Katherine Dunn)

PRUNY SKIN

Q: *Why does your skin get wrinkled when you soak for a long time in water?*

Peeping Tom's delight: There are 6,500 windows in the Empire State Building.

A: Normally, skin is water-resistant because of a "protective barrier of keratin," a protein made by the epidermis to keep moisture, bacteria, and other unwanted stuff out. But if skin is immersed in water for a long time, moisture gets through and "the cells in the epidermal layer…absorb water and swell. The enlarged cells cause the skin to pucker and wrinkle."

Luckily, they don't stay that way. "Several minutes after toweling off, the water in the skin cells evaporates, and the cells return to their normal shape and size. Otherwise, we would all be walking around looking like the California raisins." (From *The Book of Totally Useless Information*, by Don Voorhees)

EGGS-ACTLY!

Q: *Why don't people ever eat turkey eggs?*

A: "They don't taste good. More precisely, they don't have as much water in them as chicken eggs. The next time you eat a couple of chicken eggs, think about how wet they are. But a turkey egg, if exposed to high heat, turns rubbery." (From *Why Things Are, Volume II*, by Joel Achenbach)

HALF-WIT?

Q: *Is the old saying true that "we only use 10% of our brains?"*

A: "No—you use every part of your brain. Not every area at the same time, of course; they all do different things at different times. At any given moment, only about 5% of your brain cells are actually firing—that is, working. So in one sense this is actually true. But as far as we know, there are no parts that never do *anything*." (From *Know It All!*, by Ed Zotti)

EAT LIKE A BIRD

Q: *How do birds find worms underground?*

A: "When a bird stands on the ground near a worm that is crawling underneath, it can feel the earth's vibrations with its very sensitive feet. It will also cock its head to put into operation the low-frequency apparatus of its ears. Then, when it zeroes in on the victim, it pierces the earth with a sudden stab of its beak, grabs the worm, and pulls it out." (From *How Do Flies Walk Upside Down?*, by Martin M. Goldwyn)

PEOPLE-WATCHING

It's scary what experts in behavior can predict about us. All it takes is a few studies, and they know more about what we're going to do in a given situation than WE do. Bernard Asbell put the results of hundreds of these studies together in The Book of You. *We've reprinted a small part of the book here.*

STUDIES ABOUT "PERSONAL SPACE" SHOW THAT...

• *"If you observe a stranger in a room gradually moving closer to you:* You'll show symptoms of alertness or anxiety sooner if the ceiling is low than if it's high.

• *"If you're riding in a elevator:*
√ Whether you're a man or a woman, you're likely to stand closer to a stranger if he or she smiles at you...and you'll let a short stranger stand twice as close as a tall stranger.
√ If you're a man, you'll stand closer to a woman than to another man.
√ If you're a woman, you'll let either a man or a woman stand closer to you than a man will...and you'll let a stranger stand closer to your sides than to your front.

• *"If you're a man sitting next to a woman on an airliner:* The odds are an overwhelming 5 to 1 that you'll take over the armrest between you, no questions asked. "

STUDIES ABOUT DATING SHOW THAT...

• *"If you're a man on a first date with a new acquaintance:* You're considerably more likely to be anxious about the date than she is. Your anxiety does not center around sex and intimacy (that comes later), but, more likely, on not knowing what to do or say, and having unrealistic expectations of what occurs on dates. (And by the way, if you are anxious about dating, you're also likely to be anxious in your friendships with other men.)"

STUDIES OF CONVERSATIONS SHOW THAT...

• *"If you're talking with someone and you've been told in advance that the two of you have certain attitudes in common:* You're likely to stand (or sit) closer than if you've been told a person has opposing attitudes."

There are no photographs of Abe Lincoln smiling.

- *"If you're chatting with a friend in a coffee shop:*
  - √ If you're Americans chatting in a coffee shop in Gainesville, Florida, you probably touch each other twice an hour.
  - √ If you're English and chatting in a London coffee shop, you probably do not touch each other at all.
  - √ If you are French and chatting in a Parisian café, you touch each other 110 times an hour.
  - √ If you are Puerto Rico and chatting in a San Juan coffee shop, you touch each other 180 times an hour."

- *"If you're sitting and talking with someone you don't know:*
  - √ If you're a man, the farther you sit from the other person, (within a range of 2-10 feet), the more willing you are to talk intimately about yourself.
  - √ If you're a woman, the closer you sit together (within a range of 2-10 feet) the more willing you are to tell intimate details about yourself.
  - √ Within that range of 1-10 feet (whether you're a man or a woman), you'll talk with a stranger longer and volunteer the most about intimate topics at a distance of 5 feet."

STUDIES ABOUT "NUDE" MAGAZINES SHOW THAT...

- *"If you've been looking at nudes depicted in* Playboy, Playgirl, *or* Penthouse: After perusing the pictures, regardless of whether you are a woman or a man, you are likely to rate your own mate as less attractive sexually than you did a while before you looked, and to report yourself feeling less in love with him or her."

STUDIES ABOUT JOGGERS SHOW THAT...

- *"If you're a male jogger:* When you jog past a park bench where a young woman sits facing your running path, you will speed up your running pace significantly, even though she shows no sign of looking at you. But you'll maintain your accustomed lope if her back is turned to the path."

Thank Goodness: "Things are more like they are now than they ever have been." —*President Gerald Ford*

One bucket of water can make enough fog to cover 105 square miles in 50 ft. of fog.

COLORS

Colors have a lot more impact on our daily lives than you might think. Here are some things researchers have found out about people and color.

BLUE

• Blue has a tranquilizing effect on people. Bridges are often painted blue to discourage suicide attempts. And according to one report: "When schoolroom walls were changed from orange and white to blue, students' blood pressure levels dropped and their behavior and learning comprehension soared."

• Researchers say blue is the #1 color for women's sweaters, because women think men like it. (They're right; it's U.S. men's favorite color.)

RED

• Red is a stimulant that can cause "restlessness and insomnia" if it's used in bedrooms.

• According to marketing studies, red makes people oblivious to how much time is passing. That's why it's "the color of choice for bars and casinos."

• Women tend to prefer blue-toned reds, while men like yellowish reds. Businesses keep this in mind. For example: the Ford Mustang, which is targeted to men, is orange-red (called "Arrest-me" red at Ford); the Probe, targeted to women, is offered in more blue-red shades.

GREEN

• Because it reminds people of fields and foliage, green makes us feel secure. Researchers say it's a good color for bedrooms; and green kitchens reportedly make cooks more creative.

• Studies show that "people working in green environments get less stomachaches than people in areas where other colors predominate."

YELLOW

• It's the color most likely to stop traffic...or sell a house.

• But yellow also represents "caution or temporariness— so car rental agencies and taxis use it, but not banks."

• Too much yellow makes people anxious. "Babies cry more and temperamental people explode more in yellow rooms."

America's favorite colors— #1: Blue. Then red, green, white, pink, purple and orange.

MISS PIGGY

Porcine words of wisdom from America's favorite Pig.

DIET TIPS

"Never eat anything at one sitting that you can't lift."

"Always use one of the new—and far more reliable—elastic measuring tapes to check on your waistline."

ARTICHOKES

"These things are just plain annoying…after all the trouble you go to, you get about as much actual 'food' out of eating an artichoke as you would from licking thirty or forty postage stamps. Have the shrimp cocktail instead."

PERFUME

"Perfume is a subject dear to my heart. I have so many favourites: Arome de Grenouille, Okéfénokée, Eau Contraire, Fume de Ma Tante, Blast du Past, Kermes, Je suis Swell, and Attention S'il Vous Plait, to name but a few."

TIPPING

"There are several ways of calculating the tip after a meal. I find that the best is to divide the bill by the height of the waiter. Thus, a bill of $12.00 brought by a six foot waiter calls for a $2.00 tip."

TRAVEL TIPS

"If you're traveling alone, beware of seatmates who, by way of starting a conversation, make remarks like, 'I just have to talk to someone—my teeth are spying on me' or 'Did you know that squirrels are the devil's oven mitts?' "

"Public telephones in Europe are like our pinball machines. They are primarily a form of entertainment and a test of skill rather than a means of communication."

HOTELS

"Generally speaking, the length and grandness of a hotel's name are an exact opposite reflection of its quality. Thus the Hotel Central will prove to be a clean, pleasant place in a good part of town, and the Hotel Royal Majestic-Fantastic will be a fleabag next to a topless bowling alley."

HATS

"Someone you like is wearing an ugly hat, and she asks you to give her your honest opinion of it: 'What a lovely chapeau! But if I may make one teensy suggestion? If it blows off, don't chase it.' "

Top-rated final TV episodes: 1. "MASH," 2. "The Fugitive," 3. "Family Ties"

STRANGE LAWSUITS

These days, it seems that people will sue each other over practically anything. Here are a few real-life examples of unusual legal battles.

THE PLAINTIFF: Frank Zaffere, a 44-year-old Chicago lawyer.

THE DEFENDANT: Maria Dillon, his 21-year-old ex-fiance.

THE LAWSUIT: In June, 1992—about 2 months before they were supposed to get married—Dillon broke off the engagement. Zaffere responded by suing her for $40,310.48 to cover his "lost courting expenses." In a letter sent to Dillon, he wrote, "I am still willing to marry you on the conditions herein below set forth: 1) We proceed with our marriage within 45 days of the date of this letter; 2) You confirm [that you]...will forever be faithful to me; 3) You promise...that you will never lie to me again about anything." He closed with: "Please feel free to call me if you have any questions or would like to discuss any of the matters discussed herein. Sincerely, Frank."

"He's trying to...make me say 'OK Frank, I'll marry you,' " said Dillon. "But...I can't imagine telling my children as a bedtime story that Mommy and Daddy got married because of a lawsuit."

VERDICT: The case was dismissed.

THE PLAINTIFF: 27-year-old Scott Abrams.

THE DEFENDANTS: The owners and managers of an apartment building.

THE LAWSUIT: During an electrical storm in 1991, Abrams was sitting on the ledge of the apartment-building roof with his feet in a puddle of water. He was hit by lightning and suffered a cardiac arrest; fortunately, he was revived by a rescue squad. But in 1993 he filed a $2 million lawsuit charging the defendants with negligence. His reason: "They should have provided signs and brighter paint."

VERDICT: Pending.

Talk-talk: Americans make 350 billion phone calls a year.

THE PLAINTIFF: Ronald Askew, a 50-year-old banker from Santa Ana, California.

THE DEFENDANT: His ex-wife, Bonnette.

THE LAWSUIT: In 1991, after more than a decade of marriage, Bonnette admitted to her husband that although she loved him, she'd never really found him sexually attractive. He sued her for fraud, saying he "wouldn't have married her had he known her feelings."

VERDICT: Incredibly, he won. The jury awarded him $242,000 in damages.

THE PLAINTIFF: The family of 89-year-old Mimi Goldberg, a Jewish woman who died in 1991.

THE DEFENDANT: The Associated Memorial Group, a Hawaiian firm that ran nine funeral homes.

THE LAWSUIT: In 1993, Goldberg's body was shipped from the Nuuanu Mortuary in Hawaii to California.

When the casket was opened at an Oakland synagogue, "the remains of a dissected fetal pig in a plastic bag" were found resting next to the body. A mortuary representative said the pig had been put there accidentally by an employee "whose wife was taking a class requiring the dissection of fetal pigs." The woman's family, horrified because Jewish religious law specifically bans pork, sued.

VERDICT: The family won $750,000. In addition, the funeral home was ordered to make a donation to the U.S. Holocaust Memorial, and print an apology in leading West Coast newspapers.

THE PLAINTIFF: Dimitri K. Sleem, a 38-year-old Yale graduate.

THE DEFENDANT: Yale University.

THE LAWSUIT: In April 1993, an old college friend called Sleem to read him the entry listed under his name in the 1993 Yale alumni directory. It said: "I have come to terms with my homosexuality and the reality of AIDS in my life. I am at peace."

Sleem—who didn't have AIDS, wasn't gay, and was married with 4 children—filed a $5 million libel suit against Yale.

VERDICT: Still pending. Meanwhile, Yale hired a handwriting expert to find out who submitted the false statement.

In New Orleans, the soil is too wet for regular burials—so the dead are buried above ground.

PRIME TIME PROVERBS

TV comments about everyday life. From Prime Time
Proverbs, *by Jack Mingo and John Javna.*

ON GROWING UP:

Robin [gazing at a female criminal's legs]: "Her legs sort of remind me of Catwoman's."

Batman: "You're growing up Robin, but remember: In crimefighting, always keep your sights high."

—*Batman*

ON LIFE:

[As she folds her son's clothes] "There's got to be more to life that sittin' here watchin' 'Days of Our Lives' and holdin' your Fruit of the Looms."

—*Mama,*
Mama's Family

Coach Ernie Pantusso: "How's life, Norm?"

Norm Peterson: "Ask somebody who's got one."

—*Cheers*

ON PSYCHIATRY:

TV interviewer: "You mean, you ask forty dollars an hour and you guarantee nothing?"

Bob Hartley: "Well, I validate."

—*The Bob Newhart Show*

ON MENTAL HEALTH:

Bob Hartley: "Howard, what do you do when you're upset?"

Howard Borden: "Well, I've got a method—it always works. I go into a dark room, open up all the windows, take off all my clothes, and eat something cold. No, wait a minute, I do that when I'm overheated. When I have a problem I just go to pieces."

—*The Bob Newhart Show*

[To an old flame] "Someday your Mr. Right will come along. And when he does, he's gonna be wearing a white coat and a butterfly net."

—*Louie DePalma,*
Taxi

ON MASCULINITY:

Ward Cleaver: "You know, Wally, shaving is just one of the outward signs of being a man. It's more important to try to be a man inside first."

Wally Cleaver: "Yeah sure, Dad."

—*Leave It to Beaver*

Look out below: An average of 14 people jump off of the Golden Gate Bridge every year.

THE CURSE OF KING TUT

*After Tutankhamen's tomb was unearthed in 1922, a number of
people associated with the discovery died mysterious deaths.
Was it coincidence...or was it a curse?*

BACKGROUND: King Tutankhamen reigned from about
1334 to 1325 B.C., at the height of ancient Egypt's glory.
The "boy king" was only about 9 when he was crowned, and
died mysteriously at the age of 18 or 19. He was buried beside other
pharaohs in the Valley of the Kings, near the Nile River at Luxor,
the capital of ancient Egypt.

THE DISCOVERY

King Tutankhamen's tomb remained undisturbed for more than
three thousand years until it was unearthed in November, 1922 by
Howard Carter, an amateur archeologist commissioned by the English nobleman Lord Carnarvon to find it. Carter's discovery was due
largely to luck; having exhausted a number of other leads, he finally
decided to dig in a rocky patch of ground between the tombs of
three other pharaohs. Three feet under the soil he found the first of
a series of 16 steps, which led down to a sealed stone door. Mark-
ings on the door confirmed that it was a royal tomb. Realizing what
he had discovered, Carter ordered the steps buried again, and wired
Lord Carnarvon in London to join him.

Three weeks later Carnarvon arrived and digging resumed. The
first stone door was opened, revealing a 30-foot-long passage way
leading to a second stone door. Carter opened the second door and,
peeking into the darkness with the light of a single candle, was
greeted by an amazing sight—two entire rooms stuffed with price-
less gold artifacts that had not seen the light of day for more than
30 centuries. The room was so crammed with statues, chariots, furniture, and other objects that it took two full months to catalog and
remove items in the first room alone. Tutankhamen's body lay in a
solid gold coffin in the next room; the gold coffin was itself encased
inside three other coffins, which rested inside a huge golden shrine
that took up nearly the entire room.

The discovery of the site was hailed as "the greatest find in the annals of archeology." Unlike other tombs, Tutankhamen's was almost completely undisturbed by graverobbers; its hundreds of artifacts provided a glimpse of ancient Egyptian cultural life that had never been seen before.

THE CURSE

But unearthing the treasures may have been a dangerous move—soon after the Tut discovery was announced, rumors about a curse on his tomb's defilers began to circulate. They weren't taken seriously—until Lord Carnarvon came down with a mysterious fever and died.

The curse gained credibility when word came from Lord Carnarvon's home in England at 1:50 a.m.—the exact moment of Lord Carnarvon's death—that his favorite dog had suddenly collapsed and died. And at *precisely* the same moment, Cairo was plunged into darkness, due to an unexplainable power failure.

Other Deaths: Over the next several years, a series of people associated with the Tut excavation died unexpectedly, often under mysterious circumstances. The dead in 1923 alone included Lord Carnarvon's brother, Col. Aubrey Herbert; Cairo archaeologist Achmed Kamal, and American Egyptologist William Henry Goodyear.

• The following year, British radiologist Archibald Reed died on his way to Luxor, where he planned to x-ray Tut's still-unopened coffin. Oxford archeologist Hugh Eveyln-White, who had dug in the necropolis at Thebes, also died in 1924.

• Edouard Neville, Carter's teacher, as well as George Jay-Gould, Carnarvon's friend, papyrus expert Bernard Greenfell, American Egyptologist Aaron Ember, and the nurse who attended to Lord Carnarvon, all died in 1926. Ember's death was particularly spooky—he was attempting to rescue from his burning house a manuscript he had worked on for years: The Egyptian Book of the Dead.

• In 1929, Lord Carnarvon's wife, Lady Almina, died, as did John Maxwell, the Earl's friend and executor, and Carter's secretary, Richard Bethell, who was found dead in bed, apparently from circulatory failure, at the age of 35.

If you keep your goldfish in a dark room, they'll turn white.

THE AFTERMATH

Fallout from the rumors of the curse continued for years, as did the string of mysterious deaths.

• As accounts of the deaths circulated, hysteria spread. In England, hundreds of people shipped everything they had that was even remotely Egyptian to the British Museum—including an arm from a mummy.

• The popularity of the curse legend led to a series of classic horror films: "The Mummy" (1932), starring Boris Karloff, and "The Mummy's Hand" (1940) and three sequels starring Lon Chaney, Jr.—"The Mummy's Tomb" (1942), "The Mummy's Ghost" and "The Mummy's Curse" (both 1944).

LAST WORDS

• Was the curse for real? Many prominent people insisted that it wasn't; they argued that the mortality rates of people associated with the Tutankhamen discovery and other finds were no higher than that of the general public. Dr. Gamal Mehrez, Director-General of the Egyptian Museum in Cairo, disputed the curse in an interview made several years after the discovery of Tut's tomb. "All my life," he said, "I have had to deal with pharaonic tombs and mummies. I am surely the best proof that it is all coincidence." Four weeks later he dropped dead of circulatory failure, as workers were moving Tutankhamen's gold mask for transport to London.

• For what it's worth, Lord Carnarvon's son, the sixth Earl of Carnarvon, accepts the curse at face value. Shortly after the fifth Earl's burial, a woman claiming psychic powers appeared at Highclere Castle and warned the sixth Earl, "Don't go near your father's grave! It will bring you bad luck!" The wary Earl heeded the crone's advice, and never visited the grave. In 1977 he told an NBC interviewer that he "neither believed nor disbelieved" the curse—but added that he would "not accept a million pounds to enter the tomb of Tutankhamen."

Profound Thought: "It's a question of whether we're going to go forward with the future, or past to the back." —*Dan Quayle*

(JUNK) FOOD FOR THOUGHT

*Background info on some of the foods you love—
and some you love to hate.*

CHEEZ WHIZ. Invented by Kraft laboratory technicians in 1951. According to *The Encyclopedia of Pop Culture*, they were looking for a cheese product that wouldn't clump or "disintegrate into ugly, oily wads of dairy fat glop," like real cheese did when heated. It was first test-marketed to housewives in 1952; they found 1,304 different uses for it.

TANG. Fresh from the success of its decade-long struggle to get consumers to give instant coffee a try, in 1955, General Foods decided to try the same tactic with orange juice. Its goal: to make a "fruit-flavored breakfast companion to Instant Maxwell House coffee." It took 10 years to perfect the recipe, but one advantage of the delay was that 3 months after it made its nationwide debut in 1965, NASA announced that Tang would be used to feed the Gemini astronauts in space. General Foods played the endorsement for all it was worth. The orangy powder never bit into orange juice sales, but it was still a hit—at least until Americans lost their taste for both the space program and artificial foods in the 1980s.

PRETZELS. According to legend, pretzels were invented by an Italian monk during the Middle Ages because he wanted something he could give to children who memorized their prayers. He rolled dough into a long rope and shaped it so it looked like arms folded in prayer. He called his salty treats *pretioles*, Latin for "little gift."

MACARONI & CHEESE. During the Depression, the Kraft company tried to market a low-priced cheddar cheese powder to the American public—but the public wouldn't buy it. One St. Louis salesman, looking for a way to unload his allotment of the stuff, tied individual packages to macaroni boxes and talked grocers on his route into selling them as one item, which he called "Kraft Dinners." When the company found out how well they were selling, it made the Dinners an official part of its product line.

Bathroom news: Franklin Roosevelt thought up the name *United Nations* in the shower.

THE GODZILLA QUIZ

Here's a multiple-choice quiz to find out how much you really know about filmdom's most famous dinosaur. Answers are on page 225.

1 Godzilla first lumbered out of the ocean in a 1954 film titled *Gojira*. The dino-monster was awakened from a million-year ◆ slumber by A-bomb testing underseas and went on a rampage, destroying Tokyo, wreaking havoc with his radioactive breath. In 1956, the movie was brought to the U.S. as *Godzilla, King of Monsters* ("Makes King Kong Look Like a Midget!"). How did they adapt it for American audiences?

> **A)** They made it seem as though Godzilla was fighting for the U.S. during World War II.
>
> **B)** They inserted footage of Godzilla destroying New York City and Washington, D.C. as well.
>
> **C)** They added Raymond Burr, casting him as a hospitalized reporter who remembers the whole incident as a flashback.

2. The first Japanese sequel to *Gojira* was made in 1955. But when this flick finally made it to the U.S. in 1959, it didn't mention Godzilla in the title. What was it called, and why?

> **A)** *The Monster vs. the Maiden*; the studio tried to make it sexier.
>
> **B)** *The Rockin' Monster*; rock 'n' roll movies were hot.
>
> **C)** *Gigantis*; it was illegal to use the name Godzilla.

3. In the 1964 flick, *Godzilla Vs. Megalon*, Godzilla saves the world from the Seatopians, an evil alien race that plans to take over using two secret weapons—Gaigan and Megalon. How would you describe this evil pair?

> **A)** A King Kong-like ape and a giant poisonous frog.
>
> **B)** A giant cockroach and a robot with a buzz saw in his stomach.
>
> **C)** A giant pickle and a Richard Nixon look-alike.

4. *Godzilla vs. the Thing* was released in 1964. What Thing did Godzilla fight?

> **A)** A giant rabbit.
>
> **B)** A giant moth.
>
> **C)** A giant spider.

Breakfast treat: In Colonial America, kids ate popcorn with cream and sugar for breakfast.

5. How did Godzilla celebrate his 20th anniversary in 1974?

   A) He fought a Godzilla robot from outer space.

   B) He saved the world from a giant alien grasshopper.

   C) He made an appearance on the Johnny Carson Show.

6. *Godzilla on Monster Island* was released in 1971. The plot: Earth is invaded again. This time it's giant cockroaches from outer space, using monsters to do their dirty work. They've got Gaigan (the monster in *Godzilla Vs. Megalon*) and Ghidrah. Who's Ghidrah?

   A) Godzilla's mother-in-law.

   B) A giant anteater.

   C) A three-headed dragon.

7. In 1972, a scientist discovers a growing mass in a polluted lake. He wonders if it's a giant tadpole...but no! It's a new monster named Hedora! What will Godzilla be fighting this time?

   A) The Smog Monster—a 400-foot blob of garbage.

   B) The Phlegm Monster—a 2-ton ball of mucus.

   C) The Sludge Monster—A 60-foot-wide hunk of waste.

8. In *Godzilla's Revenge*, released in 1969, Godzilla returns for what purpose?

   A) To settle a score with another monster named Gorgo.

   B) To show a little kid how to fight bullies.

   C) To get revenge on Raymond Burr.

9. In the 1966 epic, *Godzilla vs. the Sea Monster*, Godzilla fights for the Free World against Red Bamboo, an evil totalitarian group. Their secret weapon is Ebirah. Who is he?

   A) A hypnotist who can brainwash Godzilla.

   B) A mechanical jellyfish.

   C) A giant lobster.

10. In 1969, Godzilla reappeared with Minya. What was special about this new monster?

   A) It was Godzilla's mother.

   B) It was Godzilla's cousin.

   C) It was Godzilla's son.

SILLY BRITISH VILLAGE NAMES

People often ask how we find the material for our Bathroom Readers. *This one was easy—Uncle John was doing some leisurely bathroom reading one morning, checking out the 6 newspapers he gets, when he found himself laughing at an article in the* Wall Street Journal. *So here it is.*

L ITTLE SNORING, England — Residents of this sleepy crossroads are tired of jokes about their village. And no one finds the jibes more wearisome than Little Snoring's most famous son.

"I'm very active, always have been," says Eric Gotobed, leaving home at dawn to cut weeds in his pasture. "And I don't snore. Ask my wife."

His wife peers warily from behind half-drawn curtains. The elderly couple has long endured phone calls from children ("Mr. Gotobed, are you sleeping?") and from mail-order houses, which have doubts about checks from one "E. Gotobed, Little Snoring." Then there are nosy travelers, who hear about Mr. Gotobed at a nearby pub and come to see if the locals are pulling their leg.

"I wish people would give the whole business a rest," Mr. Gotobed says.

ROADMAP AS COMIC BOOK

New York has Flushing. Maryland has Boring. Pennsylvania, of course, has Intercourse. But probably no territory in the English-speaking world can match Britain's wealth of ludicrous place names: Crackpot, Dorking, Fattahead, Goonbell, Giggleswick, Nether Poppleton, Wormelow Tump, Yornder Bognie. The litany, which swells with each page of the atlas, sounds like a Monty Python gag.

So does life in some of these villages. Irene Camp is secretary of the Ugley Women's Institute, a group that holds scholarly lectures and afternoon teas. It meets every month at the Ugley Village Hall. Emerging from a recent meeting, Ms. Camp says that 75 years of tea, scones and speeches haven't quelled snickers about the group's name.

"We try to call ourselves the Women's Institute of Ugley," she says. "But it never sticks." The name proves most awkward at national conferences, when women's institutes gather from across Britain—and are identified by their village names. "We have to walk around all day saying, 'We're Ugley,' " Ms. Camp complains. Ugley is actually an attractive village of thatch-roofed cottages. Its name derives from an Anglo-Saxon phrase that means, "Ucga's clearing." The nearby hamlet of Nasty—also picturesque—gets its name from Middle English for "place at the east settlement." Snoring refers to an ancient settler, as does Seething....

MORE SILLY NAMES

Britain's rural past also has sown the map with silly names that reek of fields and barnyards: Horsey, Bunny, Corney, Swine Sty, Pig Street, Dog Village, Donkey Town, Toad's Mouth, Maggots End. Other names evoke Britain's sodden landscape: Foulbog, Dull, Muck, Mold, Moss of Barmuckity. Digestion seems another theme: Belchford, Burpham, Lickey End, Spital in the Street.

Over time, many villages also have subdivided, with silly consequences: Great Snoring and Little Snoring, Middle Wallop and Nether Wallop, Helions Bumpstead and Steeple Bumpstead, Sheepy Magna (Latin for "big") and Sheepy Parva (Latin for "small"). Then there is the English habit of designating "upper" and "lower" ends of villages, which may grow into communities of their own. Optimists, for instance, will feel at home in the hamlet of Upperup—which is reached, appropriately, via High Street.

"If the hamlet grows any more, we'll have to call one end of it Upper Upperup," jokes Charles Hadfield, a local historian.

Roger Radcliffe [is] an official in Cornwall whose parish includes Goonbell, Goongumpus, Goonearl, Goonown and Gooninnis ("goon" is a Cornish word for pasture). "It's true we have a lot of Goons here," he says, "but I've never thought that was funny." He pauses, then chuckles and adds: "What about Piddle. Now that's amusing, isn't it?"

Not if you live there. Ian Curthoys, a pig farmer in North Piddle, gripes that passersby often pose for snapshots beside signs for the village—usually while piddling. Other travelers steal the signs, a common nuisance in villages with silly names. Asked about the origin of Piddle's name, Mr. Curthoys replies: "It's a wet place, isn't it?" Sloshing through the mud to feed his sows, he smiles, adding: "There was a South Piddle once, but it dried up."...

Back in Little Snoring...folks have chosen to lie low. [Some Gotobed] family members have changed their name to Gottabed. And when a bed company, Slumberland, asked Eric Gotobed to appear in advertisements, he decided to sleep on it. Later, he turned down the offer.

"Our name's enough of a nightmare already," he says, "without going out and telling the whole world about it."

...And Now For Some Health Info from the BRI

Skin cancer has become the most common form of cancer in the U.S. today...and nine times out of ten it's caused by too much exposure to the sun.

Know Your Risk

• If you sunburn easily and have a hard time getting tan, you're especially vulnerable to skin cancer. If you have fair skin, red or blonde hair, and light-colored eyes, you are at higher risk.

• If you got a severe, blistering sunburn during childhood, you're more likely to get the most deadly form of skin cancer later in life.

• If a member of your immediate family had skin cancer, you're at risk. About 10% of skin cancer cases run in families.

Protect Yourself

• Cut back on how much sun you get. Be most careful between 10 a.m. and 3 p.m., when the sun's UV rays are most intense.

• Wear a hat to protect your face and head (especially if you're bald). If possible, cover your arms and legs. Be careful on overcast days; as much as 85% of the sun's ultraviolet rays can penetrate clouds.

• Use sunscreen, even if you're not on the beach. Apply it 30-45 minutes before exposure. Experts recommend a Sun Protection Factor (SPF) of at least 15. A higher rating isn't necessary, as long as you apply sunscreen liberally. An average adult should use about an ounce per application. Apply evenly to all exposed skin.

• Note: Sunscreens are formulated today to protect against UVB. But sunscreens rated SPF 15 or higher contain ingredients that provide some protection against UVA.

Camel's-hair brushes are made with squirrel hair. They got their name

THE WORLD'S MOST POPULAR TWINS

To most people, all twins are fascinating.
Here are three sets of twins who are famous as well.

CHANG AND ENG BUNKER

Claim to Fame: The original "Siamese twins."

Background: Chang and Eng—"left" and "right" in Thai—were born at Meklong, Siam (Thailand) on May 11, 1811, permanently attached at the chest by a fleshy band of skin. They were discovered by an American sea captain who put them on display in Europe and America—where P.T. Barnum bought out their contract.

The Bunkers became world-famous as "Siamese twins." They managed to live relatively normal lives, becoming American citizens, marrying (unattached) sisters Adelaide and Sarah Yates in 1864, and somehow fathering 22 children between them. They spent their entire lives looking for a doctor who'd guarantee they'd both survive an operation to separate them, but never found one. They died hours apart in 1874.

Gossip: Chang and Eng hated each other—and fought constantly. According to an 1874 article in the *Philadelphia Medical Times*, "Eng was very good-natured, Chang cross and irritable....Chang drank pretty heavily—at times getting drunk; but Eng never drank. They often quarreled; and, of course, under the circumstances their quarrels were bitter. They sometimes came to blows, and on one occasion came under the jurisdiction of the courts."

ESTHER PAULINE AND PAULINE FRIEDMAN

Claim to Fame: The most popular advice columnists in America.

Background: Esther Pauline (Eppie) and Pauline Esther (Popo) Friedman were born 17 minutes apart on July 4th, 1918, in Sioux City, Iowa. They were inseparable throughout their youth; they dressed identically, double-dated, slept in the same bed until their wedding nights, and married on the same day in a double wedding.

Eppie got her start as Ann Landers in 1955 when she entered and won a *Chicago Sun-Times* contest to succeed the original Ann Landers. In the first weeks of the column, Eppie mailed some of the Landers column's letters to California, where Popo apparently helped answer them. But when the *Sun-Times* editors found out about it, they prohibited her from sending any more letters out of the office. The twins had to stop working together.

A few weeks later, Popo walked into the office of the *San Francisco Chronicle* and complained about the paper's advice columnist. The editor gave her a stack of past columns, and told her to fill in her own answers. She did—and the editor hired her the next day. Popo chose Abigail Van Buren as her pen name (from President Martin Van Buren), and her column became Dear Abby.

Gossip: When Eppie found out about her sister's column, she was furious. "I got into this work first," she told a reporter. "She saw what a great time I was having. And she got into it. I felt it was mine, something that I did. It was a serious problem." They didn't speak to each other for 8 years, but eventually buried the hatchet.

JOAN AND JANE BOYD

Claim to Fame: TV's first "Doublemint Twins."

Background: In 1959, the 21-year-old sisters were singing advertising jingles at CBS radio. One day they were asked if they wanted to audition to be the first live Doublemint twins. (Wrigley's Gum had used illustrated twins since the '20s.) They were taken to meet the boss—P.K. Wrigley—who hired them on the spot. That was the only time they ever saw him.

The girls became American icons and made Doublemint the #1 gum. But the magic ended in 1963, when Wrigley learned that Joan—recently married—was pregnant...and fired them. (Their contract prohibited pregnancy, even within marriage.) Since then there have been more than 20 different sets of Doublemint twins—but none as popular as the originals.

Gossip: Wrigley never gave the twins free gum—even though fans were always walking up to them and asking for it. "We never got a free pack of chewing gum in our lives," Jane remembers. "So we'd buy our own gum to give to people on the street." They were also never allowed to chew gum in their commercials. According to Joan, "We were told that Mr. Wrigley had said, 'I never want to see gum in the mouths of the Doublemint Twins. My girls do not chew gum on-camera.' "

FAMILIAR NAMES

Some people become famous because their names become commonly associated with an item or activity. You know the names, now here are the people:

Andre Marie Ampere. 19th-century French physicist. His work on electricity and magnetism "laid the groundwork for modern electrodynamics." The standard unit of electrical current—the *ampere*, or *amp*—was named after him.

Fitzherbert Batty. A Jamaican lawyer. "In 1839," writes an English etymologist, "he was certified as insane, which attracted considerable interest in London." His surname became "an affectionate euphemism to describe someone who is harmlessly insane."

William Beukel. 14th-century Dutchman. Invented the process "by which we shrink and sour cucumbers." The result was originally called a *beckel* or *pekel*, after him. It eventually became known as a *pickle*.

Mr. Doily (or Doyley). A 17th-century London merchant whose first name has been forgotten. "He became prosperous," says *Webster's Dictionary*, "by selling various summer fabrics trimmed with embroidery or crochet work, and, being a good businessman, used up the remnants by making ornamental mats for the table called *doilies*."

Hans Geiger. German physicist. In 1920, he perfected a device for measuring radioactivity—the *Geiger counter*.

John McIntosh. A Canadian farmer. In 1796, he found a wild apple tree on his Ontario property and cultivated it. The *McIntosh apple* is now America's favorite variety.

Colonel E.G. Booz (or Booze). 18th-century Philadelphia distiller. who sold his Booz Whiskey in log cabin-shaped bottles. His product helped make the Old English term *booze* (from *bouse*, "to drink") slang for alcohol.

Sotheby's auction house sold a 200-year-old piece of Tibetan cheese for $1,513 in 1993.

Archibald Campbell, the 3rd Duke of Argyll. Powerful Scottish noble in the early 1700s. Had the Campbell clan tartan woven into his *argyle* socks.

Enoch Bartlett. 19th-century businessman. Distributed a new kind of pear developed by a Massachusetts farmer. Eventually bought the farm and named the pear after himself.

Brandley, Voorhis, and Day. Owners of an underwear manufacturing company. Known by their initials: BVDs.

Robert Wilhelm Bunsen. German chemist in the mid-1800s. Invented the gas burner used in chemistry labs.

Lambert de Begue. A monk whose 12th-century followers were wandering mendicants. His name—pronounced *beg*—became synonymous with his followers' activities.

Rudolph Boysen. California botanist. In 1923, he successfully crossed blackberries and raspberries to create *boysenberries*.

Charles F. Richter. 20th-century American seismologist. In 1935, he came up with a scale for measuring the "amplitude of the seismic waves radiating from the epicenter of an earthquake." The *Richter scale* is now used worldwide to understand the magnitude of shock waves.

Thomas "Jim Crow" Rice. A white "blackface" comedian. In 1835 he came up with a typically racist song and dance routine that went: "Wheel about, turn about / Do just so / Every time I wheel about / I jump 'Jim Crow." For some reason, this phrase came to refer to all discrimination by whites against blacks.

TOTALLY IRRELEVANT THOUGHT:

The faces on today's U.S. banknotes have been unchanged since 1929. No one knows for sure why each coin or banknote ended up with the face it did: According to the Bureau of Engraving and Printing, "Records do not reveal the reasons that portraits of certain statesmen were chosen in preference to those of other persons of equal importance and prominence."

Don't call me: 66% of Las Vegas phone numbers are unlisted—the most of any city in the U.S.

THE GOODYEAR BLIMP

No major sporting event is complete without it. In fact, it's probably the best-known lighter-than-air ship ever (except maybe the Hindenburg, which is famous for blowing up). Here's the story of the Goodyear blimp. Contributed by BRI member Jack Mingo.

In 1909 Charles Goodyear, a hardware merchant from Connecticut, saw that rubber had tremendous commercial potential—but only if it could be made less sticky and would hold a shape better than it already did.

So he obtained a large quantity of latex, and tried mixing it with everything in his desk, cellar, and pantry—including witch hazel, ink, and cream cheese—with no luck. One day he tried mixing rubber with sulfur. Then, while working on something else, he accidentally knocked the sulfurized rubber mixture onto a hot stove. He found that the rubber had changed form; it was no longer sticky and snapped back to its original shape when stretched. He named the process *Vulcanizing* after Vulcan, the Roman god of fire.

THE GOODYEAR COMPANY

Goodyear didn't get rich from his discovery—he died penniless in 1860. But when Frank A. Seiberling started a rubber company in Akron, Ohio in 1898, he decided to name it after the inventor. It's likely he hoped to profit from the confusion created by having a name similar to another Akron rubber company, B.F. Goodrich.

Goodyear's first products were bicycle and horse carriage tires, rubber pads for horseshoes, rubber bands, and poker chips. The company produced its first auto tires in 1901, airplane tires in 1909, and, using a Scottish process for rubberized fabric, the skins for airplanes in 1910. (This was back when airplanes were based on kite designs and made mostly of wood and cloth.)

The same rubberized fabric turned out to be useful for lighter-than-air craft, and Goodyear flew its first dirigible in 1922.

THE MILITARY CONNECTION

The military used Goodyear blimps for observation and reconnaissance during World War I and World War II. After World War II, Goodyear bought five of its blimps back from the armed forces.

The distance between a Boeing 747's wing tips is longer than the Wright Brothers' first flight.

It painted them and began using them for promotional purposes. But the company's executives didn't see the value of having blimps. In 1958, they tried to ground the airships permanently, to save the operating and maintenance expenses.

The plan was stalled at the last minute by a plea from Goodyear's publicity director, Robert Lane. To demonstrate the blimps' worth to the company, he scheduled a six-month marathon tour that sent the airship *Mayflower* barnstorming the Eastern Seaboard. It generated so much favorable press that the executives were convinced to keep it.

The blimps' first TV coverage was an Orange Bowl game in the mid-1960s. Now they're used in about 90 televised events a year. Goodyear doesn't charge TV networks; the publicity generated makes the free service worthwhile.

BLIMP FACTS

• Each blimp is equipped with a crew of 23, consisting of 5 pilots, 17 support members who work on rotating schedules, and one public relations representative. The blimps cruise at a speed of 45-50 miles per hour (max 65 mph unless there's a really good wind).

• Each blimp can carry 9 passengers along with the crew. The seats have no seatbelts.

• The camera operator shoots from the passenger compartment through an open window from about 1200 feet up, where he or she can see everything, read a scorboard, and hear the roar of a crowd. The hardest sport for the pilots to film is golf, because they have to be careful not to disturb a golfer's shot with engine noise or by casting a sudden shadow over the green.

• If punctured, the worst that will happen is that the blimp will slowly lose altitude. Good thing, too, since the company reports that a blimp is shot at in the air abut 20 times a year.

• Each blimp is 192 feet long, 59 feet high, and holds 202,700 cubic feet of helium. The helium does leak out, like a balloon, and has to be "topped off" every four months or so.

• The word *blimp* is credited to Lt. A. D. Cunningham of Britain's Royal Navy Air Service. In 1915, he whimsically flicked his thumb against the inflated wall of an airship and imitated the sound it made: "Blimp!"

Creative naming: "Booker" T. Washington got the nickname Booker because he loved books.

GO ASK ALICE

Alice In Wonderland and Through the Looking Glass aren't just for kids. They're great reading for grown-ups, too. Especially in the bathroom. Here are some sample quotes.

"Dear, dear! How queer everything is today! I wonder if I've been changed in the night? Let me think: was I the same when I got up this morning? I almost think I can remember feeling a little different. But if I'm not the same, the next questions is, 'Who *am* I?' Ah, that's the puzzle!"
—Alice, *Alice in Wonderland*

"Cheshire Puss," began Alice, "would you tell me, please, which way I ought to go from here?"

"That depends a good deal on where you want to get to," said the Cat.

"I don't much care where—" said Alice.

"Then it doesn't matter which way you go," said the Cat.

"—so long as I get *somewhere*," Alice added as an explanation.

"Oh, you're sure to do that," said the Cat, "if only you walk long enough."

—*Alice in Wonderland*

Alice laughed. "There's no use in trying," she said. "One can't believe impossible things."

"I daresay you haven't had much practice," said the Queen. "When I was your age, I always did it for half-an-hour a day. Why, sometimes I've believed as many as six impossible things before breakfast."

—*Through the Looking Glass*

"You should say what you mean," said the March Hare.

"I do," Alice hastily replied; "at least—I mean what I say—that's the same thing, you know."

"Not the same thing a bit!" said the Hatter. "Why, you might

Before he was nicknamed "Stonewall," Thomas Jackson was known as "Fool Tom."

just as well say that 'I see what I eat' is the same as 'I eat what I see'!"

"You might as well say," added the March Hare, "that 'I like what I get' is the same thing as 'I get what I like'!"

"You might just as well say," added the Dormouse, "that 'I breathe when I sleep' is the same thing as 'I sleep when I breathe'!"

"It *is* the same thing with you," said the Hatter.

—*Alice in Wonderland*

"It's no use going back to yesterday, because I was a different person then."

—Alice, *Alice in Wonderland*

"Be what you would seem to be—or, if you would like it put more simply—Never imagine yourself not to be otherwise than what it might appear to others that what you were or might have been was not otherwise than what you had been would have appeared to them to be otherwise."

—The Duchess, *Alice in Wonderland*

"Take some more tea," the March Hare said to Alice, very earnestly.

"I've had nothing yet," Alice replied in an offended tone: "So I can't take more."

"You mean you can't take less," said the hatter: "It's very easy to take *more* than nothing."

—*Alice in Wonderland*

"If everybody minded their own business," the Duchess said in a hoarse growl, "the world would go round a deal faster than it does."

"Which would not be an advantage," said Alice. "Just think what work it would make with the day and night! You see, the earth takes twenty-four hours to turn round on its axis—"

"Talking of axes," said the Duchess, "chop off her head!"

—*Alice in Wonderland*

Believe it or not: The U.S. Congress was so unpopular during the American Revolution that its

WEDDING SUPERSTITIONS

If this book was Modern Bride, we'd probably call these wedding "traditions" rather than superstitions. But think about it—most of them were started by people who believed in evil spirits and witches and talismans.

THE BRIDAL VEIL: The veil has served a number of purposes throughout history, including: (1) protecting the bride from the "evil eye," (2) protecting her from jealous spinsters (who might also be witches) and (3) protecting the groom, his family, and other wedding guests from the bride's psychic powers—just in case she has any.

THE WEDDING KISS: A toned-down but direct throwback to the days when the couple was required to consummate their marriage in the presence of several witnesses, to insure that the consummation actually took place.

THE BRIDE'S GARTER AND GARLAND OF FLOWERS: Originally the groomsmen fought with each other to see who would get the bride's garter, which was supposed to bring good luck to the person who possessed it. But the Catholic Church frowned on the rowdy practice, and it was eventually replaced by a milder custom: the bride throwing a garland of flowers to her bridesmaids. Today the customs exist side by side.

WEDDING RINGS: One of the most ancient wedding practices The Egyptians, Romans, and Greeks all exchanged rings during their wedding ceremonies. Because a circle is a round, unending shape, it came to symbolize the ideal love that was supposed to come from marriage: it flowed from one person to the other and back again, forever. The ring has always been worn on the left hand—and was originally worn on the thumb. It was later moved to the index finger and then to the middle finger, and eventually ended up on the third, or "medical," finger. Reason: the third finger was believed to lead straight to the heart, via a single nerve.

HONEYMOON: This European tradition dates back hundreds of years and gets its name from the fact that newlyweds were expected to drink honey (believed to be an aphrodisiac) during the period of one full cycle of the moon (about a month).

THROWING RICE OR CONFETTI: Originally a fertility ritual. Wedding guests threw wheat at the bride only, in the hope that she would bear children the same way that wheat produced bread.

WEDDING CAKE: Guests originally gave "bride-cakes" to a just-married woman to encourage fertility.

JUNE WEDDING: It was customary for Romans to marry in June to honor the queen of the gods, Juno—who was also the goddess of women. They hoped to win her favor to make the marriage last, and make childbirth easier.

CARRYING THE BRIDE OVER THE THRESHOLD: Romans thought good and evil spirits hung around at the entrance of a home. As we mentioned in our Left-handed Pages, they also believed that if you walked into your house left foot first, the evil spirits won. So to be sure the bride—whom Romans figured was "in a highly enotional state and very apt to be careless"—didn't accidentally step into her new home with the wrong foot, the groom just picked her up and carried her.

THE RECEPTION SPEECH: In pre-Christian Rome, newlyweds hired an "official joker" to tell dirty stories to guests during the reception. The Romans believed that "unclean" thoughts in the minds of guests turned the attention of vengeful gods away from the newlyweds, which helped protect them from evil.

DECORATING THE WEDDING CAR. In medieval France, when a couple was unpopular, people derided them publicly by banging on pots, kettles, etc. This was a *charivari*, or "rough serenade." In America it became a *shivaree*, and people got the treatment from friends. This gave way to a new custom—trying to keep a couple from consummating their marriage by making noise at their window. When newlyweds began leaving weddings by car, the only way to harass them was to deface the vehicle.

LIMERICKS

Limericks have been around since the 1700s. Here are some that readers have sent us over the years.

There once was a spinster
from Wheeling,
Endowed with such
delicate feeling,
That she thought any chair
Should not have its legs bare,
So, she kept her eyes fixed
on the ceiling.

There was a young lady
of Kent,
Who always said just what
she meant;
People said, "she's a dear—
So unique—so sincere—"
But they shunned her by
common consent.

There once was a pious
young priest,
Who lived almost wholly
on yeast;
"For," he said, "it is plain
We must all rise again,
And I want to get started
at least."

I sat next to the Duchess
at tea,
Distressed as a person
could be.
Her rumblings abdominal
Were simply phenomenal—
And everyone thought
it was me!

A rocket explorer
named Wright
Once traveled much faster
than light.
He set out one day
In a relative way,
And returned
on the previous night.

There once was an old man
of Boolong
Who frightened the birds
with his song.
It wasn't the words
Which astonished the birds
But the horrible
dooble ontong.

A classical scholar
from Flint
Developed a
curious squint.
With her left-handed eye
She could scan the whole sky
While the other was reading
small print.

There was a young girl
from Detroit
Who at kissing was
very adroit;
She could pucker her lips
Into total eclipse,
Or open them out
like a quoit.

FAMILIAR PHRASES

Here are the origins of a few common phrases.

TO CLOSE RANKS

Meaning: To present a united front.

Origin: "In the old-time European armies, the soldiers were aligned side by side, in neat rows, or ranks, on the battlefield. When the enemy attacked, officers would order the troops to close ranks; that is, to move the rows close together, so that the enemy faced a seemingly impregnable mass of men." (From *Fighting Words*, by Christine Ammer)

FOR THE BIRDS

Meaning: Worthless.

Origin: According to Robert Claiborne in *Loose Cannons and Red Herrings*, it refers to city streets before cars. "When I was a youngster on the streets of New York, one could both see and smell the emissions of horse-drawn wagons. Since there was no way of controlling these emissions, they, or the undigested oats in them, served to nourish a large population of English sparrows. If you say something's for the birds, you're politely saying that it's horseshit."

BEYOND THE PALE

Meaning: Socially unacceptable.

Origin: "The pale in this expression has nothing to do with the whitish color, but comes originally from Latin *palus*, meaning a pole or stake. Since stakes are used to mark boundaries, a pale was a particular area within certain limits." The pale that inspired this expression was the area around Dublin in Ireland. Until the 1500s, that area was subject to British law. "Those who lived beyond the pale were outside English jurisdiction and were thought to be uncivilized." (From *Getting to the Roots*, by Martin Manser)

I'VE GOT A FROG IN MY THROAT

Meaning: I'm hoarse from a cold.

Origin: Surprisingly, this wasn't inspired by the croaking sound of a

---

Man is the only animal that sleeps on its back.

cold-sufferer's voice, but a weird medical practice. "In the Middle Ages," says Christine Ammer in *It's Raining Cats and Dogs*, "throat infections such as thrush were sometimes treated by putting a live frog head first into the patient's mouth; by inhaling, the frog was believed to draw out the patient's infection into its own body. The treatment is happily obsolete, but its memory survives in the 19th century term *frog in one's throat*."

KEEPING UP WITH THE JONESES

Meaning: Trying to do as well as your neighbors.

Origin: "Keeping Up with the Joneses" was the name of a comic strip by Arthur R. 'Pop' Momand that ran in the *New York Globe* from 1913 to 1931. At first, Momand planned to call it "Keeping Up with the Smiths," but his real-life neighbors were named Smith, and a lot of his material came from observing them. So he picked another common surname. (From *Why Do We Say It?*, by Nigel Rees)

X X X

Meaning: A kiss, at the end of a letter.

Origin: In medieval times, when most people were illiterate, "contracts were not considered legal until each signer included St. Andrew's cross after his name." (Or instead of a signature, if the signer couldn't write.) To prove his sincerity, the signer was then required to kiss the X. "Through the centuries this custom faded out, but the letter X [became associated] with a kiss." This is also probably where the phrase "sealed with a kiss" comes from. (From *I've Got Goose Pimples*, by Martin Vanoni)

READ BETWEEN THE LINES

Meaning: To perceive or understand a hidden meaning.

Origin: In the 16th century, it became common for politicians, soldiers, and businessmen to write in code. "To a person ignorant of the code, a secret paper was meaningless. Ordinary folk fascinated with this mystery concluded that the meaning was not in lines of gibberish, but in the space between them." (From *Why You Say It*, by Webb Garrison)

Q. Who was the first person to put *Frankenstein* on film?   A. Thomas Edison.

CAFFEINE FACTS

What's America's favorite drug? You guessed it—caffeine. We use more caffeine than all other drugs—legal or illegal—combined. Want to know what the stuff is doing to you? Here's a quick overview.

B ACKGROUND. If you start the day with a strong cup of coffee or tea, you're not alone. Americans ingest the caffeine equivalent of 530 million cups of coffee *every day*. Caffeine is the world's most popular mood-altering drug. It's also one of the oldest: according to archaeologists, man has been brewing beverages from caffeine-based plants since the Stone Age.

HOW IT PICKS YOU UP

Caffeine doesn't keep you awake by supplying extra energy; rather, it fools your body into thinking it isn't tired.

• When your brain is tired and wants to slow down, it releases a chemical called *adenosine*.

• Adenosine travels to special cells called *receptors*, where it goes to work counteracting the chemicals that stimulate your brain.

• Caffeine mimics adenosine; so it can "plug up" your receptors and prevent adenosine from getting through. Result: Your brain never gets the signal to slow down, and keeps building up stimulants.

JAVA JUNKIES

• After a while, your brain figures out what's going on, and increases the number of receptor cells so it has enough for both caffeine *and* adenosine.

• When that happens, caffeine can't keep you awake anymore... unless you *increase* the amount you drink so it can "plug up" the new receptor cells as well.

• This whole process only takes about a week. In that time, you essentially become a caffeine addict. Your brain is literally restructuring itself to run on caffeine; take the caffeine away and your brain has too many receptor cells to operate properly.

Humans and elephants are the only animals that can stand on their heads.

• If you quit caffeine "cold turkey," your brain begins to reduce the number of receptors right away. But the process takes about two weeks, and during that time your body sends out mild "distress signals" in the form of headaches, lethargy, fatigue, muscle pain, nausea, and sometimes even stiffness and flu-like symptoms. As a result, most doctors recommend quitting caffeine gradually.

CAFFEINE'S EFFECTS

• **Good:** Caffeine has been scientifically proven to temporarily increase alertness, comprehension, memory, reflexes, and even the rate of learning. It also helps increase clarity of thought.

• **Bad:** Too much caffeine can cause hand tremors, loss of coordination or appetite, insomnia—and in extreme cases, trembling, nausea, heart palpitations, and diarrhea.

• Widely varying the amount of caffeine you ingest can put a strain on your liver, pancreas, heart, and nervous system. And if you're prone to ulcers, caffeine can make your situation worse.

• If you manage to consume the equivalent of 70-100 cups of coffee in one sitting, you'll experience convulsions, and may even die.

CAFFEINE FACTS

• The average American drinks 210 milligrams of caffeine a day. That's equal to 2-3 cups of coffee, depending on how strong it is.

• How you make your coffee has a lot to do with how much caffeine you get. Instant coffee contains 65 milligrams of caffeine per serving; coffee brewed in a percolator has 80 milligrams; and coffee made using the "drip method" has 155 milligrams.

• Top 4 sources of caffeine in the American diet: coffee, soft drinks, tea, and chocolate, in that order. The average American gets 75% of his or her caffeine from coffee. Other sources include over-the-counter pain killers, appetite suppressants, cold remedies—and some prescription drugs.

• What happens to the caffeine that's removed from decaf coffee? Most of it is sold to soda companies and put into soft drinks. (Cola contains some caffeine naturally, but they like to add even more.)

• Do you drink more caffeine than your kids do? If you correct for body weight, probably not. Pound for pound, kids often get as much caffeine from chocolate and soft drinks as their parents get from coffee, tea, and other sources.

Read all about it: 28% of Americans go to a library at least once a month; 27% never go at all.

CHEVY CHASE'S "HOW TO DO A PRATFALL"

This article by Chevy Chase is from Jerry Dunn's book, Tricks of the Trade. *You can apply these valuable tips to falling down in the bathroom—especially if you're visiting a friend and want to try to collect some quick insurance money.*

Although it may look cloddish, an actor on stage needs finely tuned skills to fall flat on his face in a way that looks real, looks funny, and doesn't cause bodily injury. Offstage, too, there's no social occasion that can't be improved by a thunderous crash over the coffee table followed by an understated "whoops."

MY RULES:

STAY IN MOTION. I learned how to fall when I played college soccer: we were taught to roll whenever we fell on the field. And that's the basic principle behind any pratfall—you never land. You're always in motion, so no one portion of your body (particularly pointed portions!) hits without the force being absorbed by other points along the anatomy. It helps to be tall, because you can put your arms and legs out and roll over them in a series of moves to absorb the shock.

On the other hand, John Belushi felt that because of the way he was built, he could just go fall on anything....For that type of build, it's good to have a lot of mass and fat (and a lot of hair on your back). These are shock absorbers a tall, skinny guy like me doesn't have....

FALL THROUGH OBSTACLES. I used to go to dinner with Paul Simon and "Saturday Night" producer Lorne Michaels. We'd be walking across the street in the Village to a Chinese restaurant, and I'd hit the curb with my foot, which gave me enough momentum so I'd stumble forward. But I was always careful to fall *through* something, like trash cans. And whenever I did a pratfall on Saturday Night, I made sure to arrange some tables and chairs to crash

---

Per capita, North Carolinians drink more soda than people in any other state.

through. These things help break your fall. The idea is that you never quite hit the floor without hitting a number of little floors first....

NOISE IMPROVES A PRATFALL. I always find it advantageous to grab on to as many things as possible that will break away throughout the fall. This way you make noise, and the more noise, the worse the fall seems to be. Glass is good, metal objects—anything that clatters. I think a pratfall is better in direct proportion to the noise level....

MAKE THE FALL LOOK REAL. To be funny, a pratfall has to look real. It's a strange thing, but if the fall looks at all fake, you generally hurt yourself.

FALL WHEN IT IS LEAST EXPECTED. ...I think the best kind of pratfall is totally unexpected: You're just walking along, then you trip over or through something.

HAVE NO FEAR. The first really funny pratfall I did was in college at the dorm, mindlessly falling down some stairs and then out a door, through a series of rocks and bramble bushes—with no fear whatsoever that I would get hurt. And the "no fear" concept works because you *don't* get hurt. Football coaches teach you this when you're blocking and tackling: Go all out, and don't hold back.

BE AWARE OF YOUR ENVIRONS. You must be totally on your toes. It's like understanding the size of your car if you're driving between a couple of buses at top speed: You just *feel* the width of your car and know you'll make it, although there may be only an inch on each side. Well, you have to feel that same thing with your body. It's kind of instinctual, but it's also something you can learn.

One of the better pratfalls I enjoyed taking was off the top of the Christmas tree as Gerald Ford on "Saturday Night." We had Ford decorating the tree and singing "Easter Parade." I was at least fifteen feet off the ground; I simply held on to the top branches, leaned forward, and let myself go. I knew that as the tree hit the floor, it would break my fall.

The fox uses its tail to balance when it runs.

KNOW WHERE YOU'RE GOING TO FINISH. You must think *before* you make the moves. You can't just say, "I'm gonna go for it!" without knowing where you'll end up—and that means within an inch.

LAND IN THE "CLASSIC POSITION." It's almost invariably funnier to end a pratfall on your back, with your legs up and spread in the air. A good facial expression to use is "pain."...If you say anything at the end, I think understatement is funniest, like, "No problem!"

It's something only the great minds can handle.

ANYONE (?) CAN LEARN THIS ONE

Here's a great move anybody can learn. You're going into a restaurant. The person in front of you opens the door, they hear a bang and an "OOoooph!" and then you're pretending to hold your nose and spit out teeth.

It's simple: The door hits your *toe*. That causes the noise and stops the door, which never touches your face: it barely grazes it, like the wind.

Some fine points: Be close enough to the door so that from any angle it looks as if it hit you; you almost have to *feel* it hit your face. (If you stay too far from the door, people will see the air.) To pull off this stunt, you have to know that your foot is going to stop the door at the perfect place. You can't be scared; you have to feel it; out and just do it. Also, if you want to spit out "teeth," try using Chiclets. All in all, it's a delicate maneuver—but a great one.

...AND FOR THE HEADACHE AFTER A PRATFALL

Aspirin (acetylsalicylic acid) was discovered in 1853 by Charles Frederick von Gerhardt, a French chemist. But von Gerhart didn't think it was an improvement over existing pain remedies, so he forgot about it. 40 years later, a chemist working for the German drug company Farbenfabriken Bayer made a batch to test on his father, who was suffering from rheumatoid arthritis. It killed the pain almost completely. In 1899 Bayer began selling the acid in powder form as *Aspirin* (a combo of acetylsalicylic acid and the Latin name for the meadowsweet plant, *Spiraea ulmaria*, which was used to make the product). Aspirin *pills* were introduced in 1915.

Q. Who invented swim fins?   A. Benjamin Franklin.

ENGLISH / JAPANESE WORDS

Purists in the Land of the Rising Sun don't like it, but the Japanese language is becoming more Americanized. A number of words that commonly appear in Japanese pop culture have been loosely adapted from English. Here are some of the words, written phonetically. See if you can tell what they mean. Answers are at the bottom of the page.

1. Biiru
2. Terebi
3. Nyusu
4. Supotsu
5. Basu
6. Rajio
7. Gasu
8. Hoteru
9. Resutoran
10. Sabisu
11. Memba
12. Peji

13. Kappu
14. Bata
15. Sekkusu
16. Bitami
17. Dezain
18. Pantsu
19. Supu
20. Dorama
21. Sosu
22. Burausu
23. Sutecchi
24. Bonasu

25. Kado
26. Pointo
27. Makudonarudo
28. Sungurasu
29. Sunobbari
30. Caresu
31. Weta
32. Tawa
33. Sumato
34. Boru
35. Gorufu
36. Sumoggu

ANSWERS

1. beer; 2. TV; 3. news; 4. sports; 5. bus; 6. radio; 7. gas; 8. hotel; 9. restaurant; 10. service; 11. member; 12. page; 13. cup; 14. butter; 15. sex; 16. vitamin; 17. design; 18. pants; 19. soup; 20. drama; 21. sauce; 22. blouse; 23. stitch; 24. bonus; 25. card; 26. point; 27. McDonald's; 28. sunglasses; 29. snobbery; 30. caress; 31. waiter; 32. tower; 33. smart; 34. ball; 35. golf; 36. smog

---

Malaysians wash their babies in beer to protect them from disease.

BASKETBALL NAMES

In the Second Bathroom Reader, *we did the origins of baseball and football names. Here's what we could dig up about origins of pro basketball names.*

Seattle Supersonics. Named after a supersonic jet proposed by Seattle-based Boeing in the late '60s. (The jet was never built.)

Washington Bullets. Originally the Baltimore Bullets, they were named in honor of a nearby ammunition factory that had supplied American troops during World War II.

Los Angeles Lakers. There are no lakes in L.A. The team was originally the Minneapolis Lakers; Minnesota is the "Land of 1,000 lakes."

Detroit Pistons. Not named for the auto industry. The team's founder, Fred Zollner, owned a piston factory in Fort Wayne, Indiana. In 1957, the Zollner Pistons moved to Detroit.

New Jersey Nets. Originally called the New York Nets to rhyme with N.Y. Mets (baseball) and N.Y. Jets (football).

Houston Rockets. Ironically, it has nothing to do with NASA. They began as the San Diego Rockets—a name inspired by the theme of a "City in motion" and its "space age industries."

Orlando Magic. Inspired by Disney's Magic Kingdom.

New York Knicks. Short for knickerbockers, the pants that Dutch settlers in N.Y. wore in the 1600s.

Indiana Pacers. Owners wanted to "set the pace" in the NBA.

Los Angeles Clippers. Started out in San Diego, where great sailing boats known as Clipper Ships used to land a hundred years ago.

Sacramento Kings. When the Cincinnati Royals moved to the Kansas City-Omaha area in 1972, they realized both cities already had Royals baseball teams. They became the K.C. Kings, then Sacramento Kings.

Atlanta Hawks. Started in 1948 as the Tri-Cities Blackhawks (Moline and Rock Island, Illinois and Davenport, Iowa), they were named after Sauk Indian chief Black Hawk, who fought settlers of the area in the 1831 Black Hawk Wars. In 1951 the team moved to Milwaukee and shortened the name to Hawks.

In case you were wondering: In general, frogs hop faster than toads.

OOPS!

*Everyone's amused by tales of outrageous blunders—probably because it's
comforting to know that someone's screwing up even worse that
we are. So here's an ego-building page from the BRI. Go
ahead and feel superior for a few minutes.*

A PUBLISHING BOMB

"In 1978 Random House issued a cookbook that contained
a potentially lethal mistake. *Woman's Day Crockery Cuisine*
offered a recipe for caramel slices that inadvertently left out one
simple ingredient—water. It was soon discovered that if the recipe
was followed exactly, a can of condensed milk called for in the
book could explode. Random House had to recall 10,000 copies of
the book" to correct the potentially lethal recipe.

—From *The Blunder Book*, by M.L. Ginsberg

TAKE THAT!

"In 1941 the British warship *Trinidad* sighted a German destroyer
and fired a torpedo at it. The icy Arctic waters apparently affected
the torpedo's steering mechanism—it began to curve in a slow arc.
As the crew watched in horror, it continued curving slowly around
until it was speeding right back at them at forty knots. The *Trinidad*'s torpedo slammed into the *Trinidad* and caused so much damage that it put the warship out of action for the rest of the war. "

—From *The Emperor Who Ate the Bible*, by Scott Morris

SOLID PLANNING

"In 1974 the Nigerian government decided to initiate a 'Third National Nigerian Development Plan,' intended to bring the country
in a single leap into line with most developed Western nations.

"The planners calculated that to build the new roads, airfields,
and military buildings which the plan required would call for some
20 million tons of cement. This was duly ordered and shipped by
freighters from all over the world, to be unloaded at Lagos docks.

"Unfortunately, the Nigerian planners had not considered the
fact that the docks were only capable of handling two thousand

tons a day. Working every day, it would have taken 27 years to unload just the ships that were at one point waiting at sea off Lagos. These contained a third of the world's supply of cement—much of it showing its fine quality by setting in the hold of the freighters."

—From *David Frost's Book of the World's Worst Decisions*

CALLING ALL CARS

In 1977, carmakers actually recalled more vehicles than they produced. 9.3 million cars were made in America that year; 10.4 million were recalled.

RAISING THE DEAD

"A mixup at a company that makes compact disks resulted in rock music with lines like 'God told me to skin you alive' being shipped to radio stations labeled as religious music.

"The Southern Baptist Radio-TV Commission, which markets a weekly religious radio program called *Powerline*, is calling more than 1,200 radio stations across the country to warn them that some CDs it sent out for religious broadcasts are mislabeled.

"The CDs are supposed to contain inspirational talks and music. They are actually the alternative rock band Dead Kennedys' album, 'Fresh Fruit for Rotting Vegetables.' "

—Reported in the *Chicago Tribune*, June 22, 1993

HAPPY BIRTHDAY

"Festivities marking the centennial of organized soccer in Hereford, England, were canceled abruptly when officials discovered the league was only 90 years old."

—From *News of the Weird*

USING HIS HEAD

"On May 26, 1993, Texas Rangers outfielder Jose Canseco went back for a fly ball hit by Carlos Martinez of the Cleveland Indians. It missed his glove, bounced off his head, and ricocheted into the stands for a home run. 'I thought I had it,' Canseco explained later. 'Now I'll be on ESPN for a month.' "

—The *San Francisco Chronicle*

A restaurant in Mississippi called *Hello, I'm...Jello* serves over 400 dishes made from Jell-O.

FABULOUS FLOPS

Next time you see the hype for some amazing "can't-miss" phenomenon, hold on to a healthy sense of skepticism by remembering these duds.

ESPERANTO

Glorious Prediction: "Where will Esperanto be tomorrow as a world language? (1) Everyone will *learn* Esperanto; (2) Everyone will *use* Esperanto; (3) It will be the international *neutral* language; and (4) It will be a major step toward *world peace and prosperity*."

Background: Esperanto was created in 1887 by Lazarus Ludwig Zamenhof, an idealistic 28-year-old Polish ophthalmologist. According to one account, "Zamenhof's neighbors—Poles, Russians, Estonians, Latvians, and Germans, profoundly misunderstood and mistrusted each other in a multitude of tongues. It was his dream to fashion a new language they could share, and through which they could learn to coexist." Drawing on nearly all the romance languages, Zamenhof created a simplified, hybrid version with only 16 rules of grammar, no irregular verbs (English has 728), and words that could be changed from nouns to adjectives, adverbs, or verbs by changing the vowel at the end of the word. He published his language under the pseudonym Dr. Esperanto, which translates "one who hopes."

What Happened: Despite more than 100 years of lobbying by Esperanto devotees, the language has never taken hold. Still, today there are thousands of Esperanto devotees organized into clubs in 100 countries around the world—including special interest chapters for vegetarians and nudists.

THE COMET KAHOUTEK

Glorious Prediction: "Kahoutek will be the greatest sky show of the century, with a brilliance fifty times that of Halley's comet and a tail extending across a sixth of the sky." One Harvard astronomer even predicted that the comet's tail length "might reach 36 times the apparent diameter of the full moon."

Background: The comet, "a grimy lump of chemical ice some three miles in diameter" was discovered by German astronomer Lubos Kahoutek in 1973.

What Happened: Nothing. On January 15, 1974, the comet came as close to the earth as it would get in 80,000 years—and no one on Earth could see it. One astronomer described the spectacle as "a thrown egg, that missed." Where was Dr. Kahoutek? He and 1,692 other passengers were on the Queen Elizabeth 2, which had been specially chartered for the event. As *Newsweek* magazine put it, "The weather turned out rough and overcast, and Dr. Kahoutek spent much of the voyage too seasick to leave his cabin." Two weeks later the comet did emit a burst of explosive color—but by then it was so close to the sun that only three people saw it—the astronauts aboard Skylab.

THE WORLD FOOTBALL LEAGUE

Glorious Prediction: The W.F.L would become a successful alternative to the N.F.L. by 1978. "The National Football League has grown arrogant and complacent," announced the W.F.L.'s founder, in 1973. "The doors are open to a rival....The war is on!"

Background: In October 1973 Gary Davidson, a Newport Beach lawyer, announced he had formed the World Football League. The league started with 12 domestic teams but predicted it would become the first international football league, with franchises in Tokyo, Madrid, London, Paris, and other cities within 5 years.

What Happened: The W.F.L. went broke in its first season, and collapsed 12 weeks into its second season more than $20 million in debt. Nearly all the teams in the league were bankrupt. The Florida franchise was so broke that the coach had to pay for the team's toilet paper out of his own pocket, and the Philadelphia team had to fire its cheerleaders because it couldn't come up with enough cash to pay them their $10-per-game salary.

But perhaps the worst embarrassment came after the 1974 championship "World Bowl" game between the Birmingham Americans and the Florida Blazers. Americans owner Bill Putnam owed the IRS money, and according to *Sports Illustrated*, "After the game, sheriff's deputies moved right into the locker room to repossess the uniforms as soon as the champions took them off."

Thomas Jefferson wrote the Declaration of Independence in only 18 days.

MYTH-CONCEPTIONS

Little bits of info that blow holes in "common knowledge" are especially fun to include in our Bathroom Readers. Think about it: How did we "learn" these lies? And why do we still believe them? These two pages are from You Know What They Say, by Alfie Kohn.

MORE PEOPLE COMMIT SUICIDE DURING THE HOLIDAYS

"Data from the National Center for Health Statistics make it clear that April, not December, is the cruelest month. Daily suicide reports from 1950 through 1978, as reviewed by many statisticians, show that suicides peak in the spring. In some years, there's a second, less impressive, rise in the late summer and early fall. But year after year, Americans—and Canadians, too, incidentally—are least likely to end it all in December and January."

CARROTS ARE GOOD FOR YOUR EYES

"Carrots contain carotene, which your body turns into vitamin A. A complete deprivation of this vitamin, which is needed by the cells in your retina, would cause night blindness. But the human body has immense reserves of carotene stored in the liver, which are replenished from any number of foods. There is no real danger of running low, at least for people in the developed world. Ingesting vitamin A above the minimum you need doesn't do your eyes a bit of good. Practically speaking, then, there is no vision-related benefit to eating carrots."

CHOCOLATE CAUSES ACNE

"This myth was laid to rest back in 1969 by James Fulton, dermatologist, and his colleagues. Every day for four weeks, he fed sixty-five acne-prone teenagers and young adults either a megachocolate bar (containing ten times the chocolate of an ordinary candy bar) or a dummy bar that looked and tasted like chocolate without containing any of the real thing. Then they switched to the other bar.

"None of the subjects knew what they were eating. But could their skin tell the difference? Nope. For most of the young men and women, there was very little change in complexion, regardless of whether or not they were eating real chocolate. Nor was there any difference in the amount or type of oily secretion that their glands were churning out. Two decades later Fulton, a research scientist at the Research Institute in Newport Beach, California, hasn't seen anything to change his mind. He's not willing to state flatly that diet, including sugar consumption, is totally unrelated to complexion, but chocolate is still off the hook…at least for [most] people."

READING IN THE DARK WILL RUIN YOUR EYES

"Tell your mother she was wrong. As a pamphlet prepared by the American Academy of Ophthalmology puts it, 'Reading in dim light can no more harm the eyes than taking a photograph in dim light can harm the camera.' "

BREAKFAST: MOST IMPORTANT MEAL OF THE DAY

"The idea that something dreadful will befall us unless we eat in the morning owes much of its popularity to the frequently cited (but rarely read) *Iowa Studies,* most of which were published in the late 1940s and early 1950s. Blow the dust off them and you'll get a good lesson in how not to conduct research. First, the major measure of performance, referred to as 'maximum work rate,' was how hard people pedaled a bicycle—not a terribly relevant skill in most workplaces and classrooms. Second, each study was conducted with only six to ten subjects. Third, all of the experiments were funded by the Cereal Institute, a group that just possibly could have benefited from positive findings."

DON'T SWIM FOR AN HOUR AFTER EATING

"Every child learns that going swimming right after lunch is about as smart as accepting candy from strangers. Summer camp schedules are arranged so as to avoid this appalling possibility. Some parents even instruct their children to wait for food to digest before taking a shower.

"Solemn believers of this bit of folk wisdom had better brace themselves because it's absolutely false. It got started half a century ago when the Red Cross published a booklet on water safety that claimed stomach cramps and possibly death awaited the foolhardy swimmer who went straight from table to pool. A gruesome illustration accompanied this warning and for years no one thought to question it."

No Surprise: Airlines in America spend an average of $5.73 on food for each passenger.

BARNUM'S HISTORY LESSON

P.T. Barnum said, "There's a sucker born every minute"…then he proved it with his side shows and circuses. He also wrote about it. In a book called Humbugs of the World, published in 1866, he delightedly catalogued some of the great hoaxes in history. This excerpt was one of his favorites. It took place in 1667 in France, when an ambassador from Persia arrived at the pampered court of Louis XIV.

THE AMBASSADOR ARRIVES

T
It was announced formally, one morning, to Louis XIV, that His Most Serene Excellency, Riza Bey, with an interminable tail of titles, hangers-on and equipages, had reached the port of Marseilles to lay before the great "King of the Franks" brotherly congratulations and gorgeous presents from his own illustrious master, the Shah of Persia.

The ambassador and his suite were lodged in sumptuous apartments in the Tuileries, under the care and guidance of King Louis's own assistant majordomo and a guard of courtiers and regiments of Royal Swiss. Banqueting and music filled up the first evening; and the next day His Majesty sent the Duc de Richelieu to announce that he would receive them on the third evening at Versailles.

THE AMBASSADOR IS WELCOMED

Meanwhile the most extensive preparations were made for the audience; when the time arrived, the entire Gallery of Mirrors was crowded with the beauty, the chivalry, the wit, taste, and intellect of France at that dazzling period. Louis the Great himself never appeared to finer advantage. His royal countenance was lighted up with pride and satisfaction as the Envoy of the haughty Oriental king approached the splendid throne on which he sat. As he descended a step to meet him, the Persian envoy bent the knee, and with uncovered head presented the credentials of his mission.

A grand ball and supper concluded this night of splendour, and Riza Bey was launched at the French court; every member of the illustrious court tried to outdo his peers with the value of the books, pictures, gems, etc. which they heaped upon the illustrious Persian.

"The more outrageous a subject can get, the more I like it." —Alfred Hitchcock

The latter gentleman very quietly smoked his pipe and lounged on his divan before company—and diligently packed up the goods when he and his jolly companions were left alone. The presents of the Shah had not yet arrived, but were daily expected, and from time to time the olive-coloured suite was diminished by the departure of one of the number with his chest on a special mission to England, Austria, or other European powers. In the meantime, the Bey was feted in all directions...and it was whispered that the fair ones of the court were, from the first, eager to bestow their favours.

THE AMBASSADOR'S PLANS

The King favoured his Persian pet with numerous personal interviews, at which, in broken French, the Envoy unfolded the most imposing of schemes of conquest and commerce that his master was willing to share with his great brother of France. At one of these téte-à-tétes, the magnificent Riza Bey, upon whom the King had already conferred his own portrait set in diamonds, and other gifts worth several millions of francs, placed in the Royal hand several fragments of opal and turquoise said to have been found near the Caspian sea, which teemed with limitless treasures of the same kind, and which the Shah of Persia proposed to divide with France for the honour of her alliance. The King was enchanted.

THE AMBASSADOR DISAPPEARS

At length, word was sent to Versailles that the gifts from the Shah had come, and a day was appointed for their presentation. The day arrived, and the Hall of Audience was again thrown open. All was jubilee; the King and the court waited, but no Persian—no Riza Bey—and no presents from the Shah!

That morning three men had left the Tuileries at daylight with a bag and a bundle, never to return. They were Riza Bey and his last bodyguards; the bag and the bundle were the smallest in bulk but the most precious in value of a month's plunder. The turquoises and opals bestowed upon the King turned out, on close inspection, to be a new and very ingenious variety of coloured glass.

Of course, a hue and cry was raised—but totally in vain. It was afterward believed that a noted barber and suspected bandit, who had once really travelled in Persia, was the perpetrator of this pretty joke. But no one was sure—no one ever heard from him again.

WORD ORIGINS

We use them, and we understand them. But where do familiar words come from? Probably not where you'd guess. Here are a few examples.

Debonair
French for "of good air." In the Middle Ages, people's health was judged partly by how they smelled. A person who gave off "good air" was presumed healthier and happier.

Gymnasium
Meant "to train naked" in ancient Greece, where athletes wore little or nothing.

Carnival
Literal meaning: "Flesh, farewell." Refers to traditional pre-Lenten feast (like Mardi Gras) after which people usually fasted.

Daisy
Comes from "day's eye." When the sun comes out, it opens its yellow eye.

Ukelele
In the 1800s, an English sailor gave such enthusiastic performances with this instrument that he was nicknamed *Ukelele*—"little jumping flea" in Hawaiian. He went on to popularize it around the world.

Gung Ho
Means "work together" in Chinese. After a group called Carlson's Raiders used it as their motto in WW II, it became a term for an enthusiastic soldier.

Ballot
Italian term for "small ball or pebble." Origin: Italian citizens once voted by casting a small pebble or ball into one of several boxes.

Jiggle
Refers to the jig (a dance).

Genuine
Originally meant "placed on the knees." In Ancient Rome, a father legally claimed his newborn child by sitting in front of his family and placing the child on his knee.

Cab
Old Italian term for goat. The first carriages "for public hire" bounced so much they reminded people of goats romping on a hillside.

Spectator sports: 38% of Americans say they enjoy football on TV; only 16% like baseball.

THE WHOLE TOOTH

*Some info to give you a little historical perspective
when you're brushing your teeth.*

TOOTH BRUSHES. People have been cleaning their teeth for thousands of years, but the implements they used weren't much like toothbrushes. Many cultures used "chew sticks," pencil-sized twigs with one end frayed into soft bristles; they've been found in Egyptian tombs dating back to 3,000 B.C.

The first toothbrush to resemble modern ones originated in China around 1498. The bristles were plucked from hogs and were set into handles of bone or bamboo. But animal hair is porous and water-absorbent, which makes it a breeding ground for bacteria; so brushing often did more harm than good. Nevertheless, by the 19th century, hogshair brushes were the standard for people who brushed.

Toothbrushing didn't become widely popular in the U.S. until the late 1930s. Two reasons for its spread: with the invention of nylon bristles by DuPont chemists in 1938, Americans finally had a hygienic substitute for hogshair; and every soldier who fought in World War II was instructed in oral hygiene and issued a brush—when the war ended they brought the habit home to their families.

TOOTHPASTE. History's first recorded toothpaste was an Egyptian mixture of ground pumice and strong wine. But the early Romans brushed their teeth with human urine...and also used it as a mouthwash. Actually, urine was an active component in toothpastes and mouthwashes until well into the 18th century—the ammonia it contains gave them strong cleansing power.

Fluoridated toothpaste came about as the result of a discovery made in Naples, Italy in 1802, when local dentists noticed yellowish-brown spots on their patients' teeth—but no cavities. Subsequent examination revealed that high levels of fluoride in the water caused the spots *and* prevented tooth decay, and that less fluoride protected teeth without causing the spots. It took a while for the discovery to be implemented; the first U.S. fluoridated water tests didn't take place until 1915, and Crest, the first toothpaste with fluoride in it ("Look, Ma...") didn't hit stores until 1956.

SANDBURGISMS

*Thoughts from Carl Sandburg, one of America's
most celebrated poets and authors.*

"Even those who have read books on manners are sometimes a pain in the neck."

"Put all your eggs in one basket and watch the basket."

"Everybody talks about the weather and nobody does anything about it."

"Blessed are they who expect nothing for they shall not be disappointed."

"Those who fear they may cast pearls before swine are often lacking in pearls."

"May you live to eat the hen that scratches on your grave."

"A lawyer is a man who gets two other men to take off their clothes and then he runs away with them."

"Six feet of earth make us all one size."

"I want money in order to buy the time to get the things that money will not buy."

"Many kiss the hands they wish to see cut off."

"Time is the storyteller you can't shut up..."

"We asked the cyclone to go around our barn but it didn't hear us."

"Someday they'll give a war and nobody will come."

"Who swindles himself more deeply than the one saying, 'I am holier than thou?'"

"There are dreams stronger than death. Men and women die holding these dreams."

"If there is a bedbug in a hotel when I arrive he looks at the register for my room number."

"Why is the bribe-taker convicted so often and the bribe-giver so seldom?"

"Liberty is when you are free to do what you want to do and the police never arrest you if they know who you are and you got the right ticket."

After the birth: New parents spend about 50% more on health care, and 34% less on alcohol.

TWISTED TITLES

California Monthly, *the magazine for alumni of the University of California at Berkeley, features a game called* Twisted Titles. *They ask readers to send the title of a book, film, play, etc., with just one letter changed—and include a brief description of the new work they envision. Here are excerpts from* Twisted Titles XII.

LITTLE RED HIDING HOOD
Marxist midget shelters Hoffa.

DON'T FIT UNDER THE APPLE TREE
The Andrews Sisters experience middle-age spread.

JUNE THE OBSCURE
Wally and the Beaver's reclusive mom tells all.

THE CAT IN THE CAT
Dr. Seuss introduces toddlers to the facts of life.

MY LIFE AS A LOG
Pinocchio reflects on his childhood.

THE NOW TESTAMENT
Bible of the "Me" generation.

DUNCES WITH WOLVES
Western epic starring the Three Stooges.

PATRIOT DAMES
The DAR does the IRA.

'TIL DEATH DO US PARK
Vows exchanged in New York City gridlock.

NEVER THE TWAIN SHALL MEAT
Sam Clemens becomes a vegetarian.

CANTERBURY TALKS
Phil, Oprah, Geraldo, and now, GEOFF!

CLUB TED
High jinks at Hyannisport.

MY LEFT FOOD
Politically correct chow.

GOYZ 'N THE HOOD
Jews and blacks unite to drive the KKK out of Beverly Hills.

THE WINNER OF OUR DISCONTENT
I'm more dysfunctional than you are.

SLEEPING WITH THE ENEMA
A tragedy in one act.

World record: In 1993, Japan became the 1st country with 1/5 of its population age 65 or older.

GIVE YOURSELF SOME CREDIT

Did you use a credit card to buy this book? Credit cards are a way of life to Americans. In fact, you could argue that those little pieces of plastic are actually the backbone of the American economy. How's that for a scary thought?...And they haven't even been around that long. Here is a brief history.

B ACKGROUND. By the 1950s gasoline companies, department stores and major hotels had developed their own credit cards—small pieces of cardboard or metal plates they gave their best customers to use instead of cash (allowing holders to pay for purchases at the end of the month). But these early cards were different than the ones we use today—they were only accepted at the business that had issued them.

THE FIRST SUPPER

That all changed in one night in 1950, when businessman Robert X. McNamara finished his dinner in a posh New York restaurant— and realized that he didn't have enough cash to pay for the meal. His wife had to drive across town to pay for it, which embarrassed him deeply. But it also gave him an idea: why not issue a "diners' card" that people could use to pay for meals when they were short of cash?

McNamara proposed his idea to a number of restaurants around town. In exchange for honoring his new "Diners Club" card, he would pay for the meal of anyone who presented the card. Diners Club would absorb the risk of non-payment; the restaurant got the money even if the cardholder was a deadbeat. How the card made its money: it paid the restaurants 90-95¢ on the dollar, billed the cardholder $1.00, and kept the difference in the form of a "discount." The restaurants balked at this arrangement at first, but McNamara convinced them that people with cards would spend more money—and more often—than people without them. By the end of the year he had signed up 27 New York restaurants and 200 cardholders. The age of the credit card as we know it had begun.

The Danish flag, used since the 13th century, is the oldest unchanged national flag in existence.

CREDIT CARD FACTS

• The average American holds 2.9 Visas or MasterCards; even so, credit card companies send out more than 1 billion new credit card offers every year.

• Why do merchants like credit cards? On average, consumers spend 23% more money when they pay with credit cards than when they pay cash.

• Had you signed up for Sears' Discover card when it premiered in 1986, you would have been entitled to meal discounts at Denny's restaurants and 50% off psychiatric exams.

• Today more than 31 million of the 211 million Visa and Mastercard cards in circulation are "affinity cards"—cards that donate a portion of each purchase to the charity shown on the card. One popular version, the Elvis card, features a picture of the King on it. (Elvis is dead, so the bank gets to keep most of the money; even so, the card has more than 10,000 subscribers.) One of the least popular: the Muscular Dystrophy Association Card, which has a picture of Jerry Lewis on it. It bombed so badly that it was taken off the market.

• It's illegal now, but credit card companies used to mail credit cards to people who hadn't even applied for them. It wasn't always good business: In 1966, five Chicago banks banded together and mailed 5 million credit cards to people who hadn't asked for them. But "the banks had been less than cautious in assembling their mailing lists. Some families received 15 cards. Dead people and babies got cards. A dachshund named Alice was sent not one but four cards, one of which arrived with the promise that Alice would be welcomed as a 'preferred customer' at many of Chicago's finest restaurants."

• In 1972, Walter Cavanagh and a friend bet a dinner to see who could accumulate the most credit cards. Eight years later he won the bet—and broke the world record—by applying for and getting 1,003 credit cards, weighing 34 pounds and entitling him to $1.25 million in credit. He's still applying for credit cards, and has set a goal of 10,000 cards.

• In 1987, aspiring moviemaker Robert Townsend paid for his first film, _Hollywood Shuffle_, by charging $100,000 on his fifteen personal credit cards. Luckily, the movie made enough money for him to pay back the money.

According to one study, the "average American" is a 32.7-year-old woman who likes potato

SCRATCH 'N' SNIFF

*No, this is not a scratch 'n' sniff page—it's about
the scratch 'n' sniff phenomenon.*

BACKGROUND. For years advertisers understood that scents can help sell products, but they couldn't find a way to include smells in printed advertisements. The first attempt came in the '50s, when newspaper companies tried printing with scented ink. The experiment flopped—either the smells dissipated rapidly, or they mixed with the newspaper's smell, spoiling the effect.

In 1969 the 3-M Corp. and National Cash Register Co. (NCR) each developed a way to impregnate printed advertisements with fragrances. They called the technique "microencapsulation," because it literally sealed the smells in the surface of the ad until the consumer released them by scratching the page. For the first time in history, products as diverse as bananas, bourbon, shaving cream, dill pickles, pine trees—and, of course, perfume, could be advertised using their scents.

HOW IT WORKS

• The printing company takes a product like perfume or food, and extracts its aromatic oils.

• The oils are mixed with water, which breaks them up into tiny droplets—an average of 1 million drops per square inch.

• The droplets are sprayed onto paper or some other surface, and are covered with a layer of plastic resin or gum arabic.

• The scent remains fresh beneath the resin until someone scratches the surface. This bursts the layer of resin or gum that holds the droplets, and the smell escapes.

SCRATCH 'N' SNIFF FACTS

• Scratch 'n' sniff pages and scented pages aren't just novelties; they're big business. According to a study commissioned by Ralph Lauren Fragrances, 76% of women who buy new perfumes are introduced to the fragrances through scented inserts in magazines.

• On average, scented pages cost twice as much as "scent-free" ads.

• A lot of people hate perfume strips, despite their popularity with

chips, weighs 134 lbs., and believes in the devil. She has sex about 5 times a month.

perfume and ad companies. In fact, they can actually make sensitive people ill. In June 1991, a man wrote to *The New Yorker* complaining that "A very noxious and pervacious [sic] odor invaded this house with the mail today. Much to our surprise, it came from the arriving copy of *The New Yorker*....I am an elderly asthmatic, allergic to perfume, and although I have retched occasionally at some material in *The New Yorker*, I have never vomited on it before." As a result of his and other complaints, many magazines now offer scented and unscented editions.

• Another problem was that magazines were running more and more ads with perfume strips. Magazines got so smelly that perfume companies had to limit the number that could appear—and the post office itself began regulating scented inserts.

WEIRD USES

• In 1989 the English National Opera produced a scratch 'n' sniff version of Prokofiev's "Love For Three Oranges." Audience members received a special "fragrance panel" at the beginning of the play, along with instructions telling them when to sniff. The card even contained a scent for an unpleasant character named Farfarello, who has "bad breath and emits gasses." His smell was supposed to be "a cross between bad eggs and body odor," but the stench was so overpowering that it made the entire fragrance panel stink. In later performances of the play, his scent was left out.

• In 1990 the rock group Swamp Zombies released *Scratch and Sniff Car Crash*, an album whose cover smelled like burnt rubber. Weird inspiration: the band members got the idea after two of them narrowly escaped serious injury in automobile accidents.

• In 1989 the RJ Reynolds Tobacco company test-marketed Chelsea cigarets, a brand targeted at women. Its major selling point: the smokes were rolled in a paper that gave off a sweet smell when it burned. They promoted the brand with scratch 'n' sniff newspaper ads showing off the scented papers. The ads smelled great—but cigaret sales stank, and the brand was dropped.

• In 1989 BEI Defense Systems, a Dallas missile manufacturer, ran a scratch 'n' sniff ad in *Armed Forces Journal* touting the company's "extraordinarily lethal" Flechette rocket. The ad smelled like cordite (the explosive contained in the warhead), an aroma the company called "the smell of victory."

FAMILIAR PHRASES

Here are more origins of common phrases.

BORN WITH A SILVER SPOON IN HIS/HER MOUTH
Meaning: Pampered; lucky; born into wealth or prosperous circumstances.

Origin: At one time, it was customary for godparents to give their godchild a silver spoon at the baby's christening. These people were usually well-off, so the spoon came to represent the child's good fortune.

BITE THE BULLET

Meaning: Get on with a difficult or unpleasant task.

Origin: "Although one can find other explanations, it seems most plausible that the term originated in battlefield surgery before the days of anesthesia. A surgeon about to operate on a wounded soldier would urge him to bite on a bullet of soft lead to distract him from the pain; at least it would minimize his ability to scream and thus divert the surgeon." (From *The Dictionary of Clichés*, by James Rogers)

SOMETHING FITS TO A "T"

Meaning: It fits perfectly.

Origin: Commonly thought of as a reference to the T-square, which is used to draw parallel lines and angles. But this phrase was used in the 1600s, before anyone called it a T-square. "A more likely explanation is that the expression was originally 'to a tittle.' A tittle was the dot over the "i", so the phrase meant 'to a dot' or 'fine point.' "(From *Why Do We Say It*, by Nigel Rees)

THINGS WILL PAN OUT/ HAVEN'T PANNED OUT

Meaning: Optimistic view that things will work out / things haven't worked out.
Origin: When prospectors look for gold they kneel by a river or stream and wash dirt from the bed in a shallow pan. This is called *panning*. Traditionally, when prospectors were sure they'd find gold,

they said things would "pan out." When they didn't find it, they said things didn't "pan out." (From *Gold!*, by Gordon Javna)

YOU'RE NO SPRING CHICKEN

Meaning: You're not young anymore; you're past your prime.

Origin: "Until recent generations, there were no incubators and few warm hen houses. That meant chicks couldn't be raised during winter. New England growers found that those born in the spring brought premium prices in the summer market places." When these Yankee traders tried to pass off old birds as part of the spring crop, smart buyers would protest that the bird was 'no spring chicken.' " (From *Why You Say It*, by Webb Garrison)

TO CLEAR THE DECKS

Meaning: Prepare for action; Take care of minor matters, so you can focus on important ones.

Origin: A battle order in the days of sailing ships. "A crew prepared for battle by removing or fastening down all loose objects on deck that might otherwise get in the way of the guns or be knocked down and injure a sailor." (From *Fighting Words*, by Christine Ammer)

TRYING TO MAKE BOTH ENDS MEET

Meaning: Trying to stretch your income to live within your means.

Origin: On sailing ships of the 1400s and 1500s, sails "were raised and lowered separately, and the rigging involved hundreds of ropes. Some were permanently fixed. When such a rope broke, most preferred to replace it rather than attempt a repair job." But ship owners who were low on cash often told their captains "to pull broken rope ends together and splice them." So "a piece of rigging was stretched to the limit in order for both ends to meet." Gradually, the term moved from ship to shore, and came to mean stretching things to the limit because of a shortage of funds. (From *I've Got Goose Pimples*, by Martin Vanoni)

Important thought: "If you're killed, you've lost a very important part of your life."　　　　　　　　　　　　　　—*Brooke Shields*

In 1970, the U.S. collected $84 billion in personal income tax. By 1990, it was $447 billion.

BY GEORGE!

Wisdom from our first president, George Washington.

"Associate with men of good quality if you esteem your own reputation; for it is better to be alone than in bad company."

"Discipline is the soul of an army. It makes small numbers formidable, procures success to the weak, and esteem to all."

"Cursing and swearing is a vice so mean and low that every person of sense and character detests and despises it."

"Let us rise to a standard to which the wise and honest can repair."

"I have always given it as my decided opinion that...everyone had a right to form and adopt whatever government they liked best to live under themselves."

"It is only after time has been given for cool and deliberate reflection that the real voice of the people can be known."

"To be prepared for war is one of the most effectual means of preserving peace."

"A great and lasting war can never be supported on [patriotism] alone. It must be aided by a prospect of interest, or some reward."

"Few men have virtue to withstand the highest bidder."

"Do not conceive that fine clothes make fine men, any more that fine feathers make fine birds."

"In a free and republican government, you cannot restrain the voice of the multitude."

"The preservation of the sacred fire of liberty, and the destiny of the republican model of government, are...staked, on the experiment entrusted to the hands of the American people."

"Our cruel and unrelenting enemy leaves us only the choice of brave resistance, or the most abject submission. We have, therefore, to resolve to conquer or die."

"It is well I die hard, but I am not afraid to go."

Poll results: 59% of married men and 61% of married women say sex gets better after marriage.

BY GEORGE, TOO

*Words of wisdom from George Carlin, one
of America's most popular wise guys.*

"Energy experts have announced the development of a new fuel made from human brain tissue. It's called assohol."

"I think I am. Therefore, I am...I think."

"The only good thing to come from religion is the music."

"When I was real small I heard about this thing called the decline of civilization... and I decided that it was something I would like to become involved in."

"I hope that someday a Pope chooses the name Shorty."

"If God really made everything, I'd say he had a quality control problem."

"People are okay taken two or three at a time. Beyond that number they tend to choose up sides and wear armbands."

"I am not a complete vegetarian. I eat only animals that have died in their sleep."

"If you want to really test a faith healer, tell him you want a smaller shoe size."

"Remember: dishonesty is the second best policy."

"I wonder why prostitution is illegal. Why should it be illegal to sell something that's perfectly legal to give away?"

"I say live and let live. Anyone who can't accept that should be executed."

"Just when I found the meaning of life, they changed it."

"I never thought I'd grow old. I always thought it was something that would happen to the other guy."

"Scientists announced today that they have discovered a cure for apathy. However, they claim no one has shown the slightest bit of interest in it."

"I don't mind a little government regulation, but requiring people to wear helmets during intercourse is going too far."

FAMOUS TRIALS:
THE WITCHES OF SALEM

Here's a bit of American history we're all familiar with…but know almost nothing about. The BRI wants to change that, because we don't want witch trials—or witch hunts—in our era. After all, someone just might decide that reading in the bathroom is a sign of demonic possession.

BACKGROUND. The trouble at Salem, Massachusetts began with two young girls acting oddly. It exploded into one of the strangest cases of mass hysteria in American history. In the 6-month period between March and September 1692, 27 people were convicted on witchcraft charges; 20 were executed, and more than 100 other people were in prison awaiting trial.

CHILD'S PLAY

In March, 1992, 9-year-old Betty Parris and her cousin Abigail Williams, 12, were experimenting with a fortune-telling trick they'd learned from Tituba, the Parris family's West Indian slave. To find out what kind of men they'd marry when they grew up, they put an egg white in a glass…and then studied the shape it made in the glass.

But instead of glimpsing their future husbands, the girls saw an image that appeared to be "in the likeness of a coffin." The apparition shocked them…and over the next few days they exhibited behavior that witnesses described as "foolish, ridiculous speeches," "odd postures," "distempers," and "fits."

Reverend Samuel Parris was startled by his daughter's condition and took her to see William Griggs, the family doctor. Griggs couldn't find out what was wrong with the girl, but he suspected the problem had supernatural origins. He told Mr. Parris that he thought the girl had fallen victim to "the Evil Hand"—witchcraft.

The family tried to keep Betty's condition a secret, but rumors began spreading almost immediately—and within two months at least 8 other girls began exhibiting similar forms of bizarre behavior.

The average engagement ring costs $2,025; the average wedding costs $13,310.

THE PARANOIA GROWS

The citizens of Salem Village demanded that the authorities take action. The local officials subjected the young girls to intense questioning, and soon the girls began naming names. The first three women they accused of witchcraft were Tituba, and two other women from Salem Village, Sarah Good and Sarah Osborne.

The three women were arrested and imprisoned for questioning. A few weeks later two more suspects, Martha Cory and Rebecca Nurse, were arrested on similar charges. And at the end of April a sixth person—the Reverend George Burroughs, a minister that Abigail Williams identified as the leader of the witches—was arrested and imprisoned. The girls continued to name names. By the middle of May, more than 100 people had been arrested for witchcraft.

THE TRIALS

On May 14, 1692, the newly appointed governor, Sir William Phips, arrived from England. He immediately set up a special court, the Court of Oyer and Terminer, to hear the witchcraft trials that were clogging the colonial legal system.

• The first case heard was that against Bridget Bishop. She was quickly found guilty of witchcraft, sentenced to death, and then hung on June 10.

• On June 19 the court met a second time, and in a single day heard the cases of five accused women, found them all guilty, and sentenced them to death. They were hung on July 19.

• On August 5 the court heard 6 more cases, and sentenced all 6 women to death. One woman, Elizabeth Proctor, was spared because she was pregnant—and the authorities didn't want to kill an innocent life along with a guilty one. The remaining 5 women were executed on August 19.

• 6 more people were sentenced to death in early September (Only 4 were executed: one person was reprieved, and another woman managed to escape from prison with the help of friends). The remaining sentences were carried out on September 22.

• On September 17th, the court handed down 9 more death sentences. (This time 5 of the accused "confessed" in exchange for a commutation of the death sentence and were not hung.) The remaining 4 were hung on September 22.

- Two days later the trials claimed their last victim when Giles Cory, an accused wizard, was executed by "pressing" (he was slowly crushed to death under heavy weights) after he refused to enter a plea.

REVERSAL OF FORTUNE

By now the hysteria surrounding the witch trials was at its peak. 19 accused "witches" had been hung, about 50 had "confessed" in exchange for lenient treatment; more than 100 people accused of witchcraft were under arrest and awaiting trial—and another 200 people had been accused of witchcraft but had not yet been arrested. Despite all this, the afflicted girls were still exhibiting bizarre behavior. But public opinion began to turn against the trials. Community leaders began to publicly question the methods that the courts used to convict suspected witches. The accused were denied access to defense counsel, and were tried in chains before jurors who had been chosen from church membership lists.

The integrity of the girls then came under question. Some of the adults even charged that they were faking their illnesses and accusing innocent people for the fun of it. One colonist even testified later that one of the bewitched girls had bragged to him that "she did it for sport."

As the number of accused persons grew into the hundreds, fears of falling victim to witchcraft were replaced by an even greater fear: that of being falsely accused of witchcraft. The growing opposition to the proceedings came from all segments of society: common people, ministers, etc.—even from the Court itself.

THE AFTERMATH

Once the tide had turned against the Salem Witchcraft Trials, many of the participants themselves began having second thoughts. Many of the jurors admitted their errors, witnesses recanted their testimony, and one judge on the court of Oyer and Terminer, Samuel Sewall, publicly admitted his error on the steps of the Old South Church in 1697. The Massachusetts legislature made amends as well; in 1711 it reversed all of the convictions issued by the Court of Oyer and Terminer (and did it a second time in 1957), and made financial restitution to the relatives of the executed, "the whole amounting unto five hundred seventy eight pounds and twelve shillings."

What's an ermine? A weasel whose coat has turned white for the winter.

THE COOLEST MOVIE LINES EVER

Here's an entry inspired by the Captain of Cool,
Gene Sculatti, and his book Too Cool.

THE WILD ONE
Girl to Brando: "Hey Johnny, what are you rebelling against?"
Brando: "Whaddaya got?"

THE KILLERS
Claude Akens: "You said Johnny North died. How'd he die?"
Clu Gulager: "Questions . . . he asked one too many."

HIGH SCHOOL CONFIDENTIAL
(*Teenage interpretation of Queen Isabella's reaction to Columbus*)
"Christy, what is this jazz you puttin' down 'bout our planet being round? Everybody's hip that it's square!"

THE COURT JESTER
Mildred Natwick: "The pellet with the poison's in the flagon with the dragon. The chalice from the palace holds the brew that is true."
Danny Kaye: "What about the vessel with the pestle?"

OCEANS 11(*To doc examining X-Rays*) "So tell me, doc. Is it the big casino?"

I WAS A TEENAGE FRANKENSTEIN
"I know you have a civil tongue in your head. I sewed it there myself."

THE BIG CARNIVAL
"I've met some hard-boiled eggs in my time, but you—you're 20 minutes."

MIDNIGHT RUN
Dennis Farina (*to henchman*): "I want this guy taken out and I want him taken out fast. You and that other dummy better start gettin' more personally involved in your work, or I'm gonna stab you through the heart with a f------ pencil. You understand?"
Henchman: "You got it, Jimmy."

THE SWEET SMELL OF SUCCESS
(*Hustler Tony Curtis, about to go into action*) "Watch me make a hundred-yard run with no legs."

GOODFELLAS
"I'm an average nobody. I get to live the rest of my life like a schnook."

---

5 most persuasive words in the English language: *discover, easy, guarantee, health,* and *results.*

THREE MEMORABLE SALES PROMOTIONS

Companies are always trying to get our attention—and our money—with catchy slogans, free stuff, discounts, and so on. But occasionally a promotion stands out for ineptitude...or cleverness. Here are three examples.

A PENNY SAVED

The Company: *Reader's Digest*

The Promotion: For years the *Digest* solicited subscriptions with a letter that began, "An ancient Persian poet once said, 'If thou hast two pennies, spend one for bread and the other to buy hyacinths for the soul...' " In 1956, someone decided to give it a new twist by including two pennies with each letter. The point: People could keep one, and send the other back with their subscription order to get the "soul-satisfying" *Digest*.

What Happened: The magazine planned to send out 50 million letters, which meant they needed 100 million coins—enough to deplete the entire New York area of pennies. The U.S. Mint intervened, forcing *Reader's Digest* to make quick arrangements to ship in 60 million more pennies from all over the country. Then, when the company finally got all the pennies it needed, it stored them all in one room—and the floor collapsed under the weight. In the end, though, it was worth the effort—the promo drew a record number of responses.

HOOVERGATE

The Company: Hoover Europe, England's most prestigious manufacturer of vacuum cleaners.

The Promotion: In 1992 Hoover tried to put a little life into the British vacuum market by offering an incredible deal: Any customer who bought at least 100 British pounds' (about $150) worth of Hoover merchandise got two free round-trip plane tickets to a European destination. Customers who bought 250 pounds' worth ($375) qualified for two tickets to either New York or Orlando, Florida.

Rampant technophobia: 70% of VCR owners say they've never used the timer.

What Happened: It was one of the biggest marketing fiascos in history. Customers realized the obvious—vacuum cleaners are cheaper than airline tickets—and snapped up every available Hoover. An estimated 200,000 customers—roughly 1 in every 300 people in Great Britain and Ireland—claimed they qualified for free flights.

The company sold so many vacuums that the factory switched to a 7-day work week to meet the demand—which made it, as one obeserver noted, "a classic case of mispricing a promotion so that the more products the company sold, the more money it lost." The promotion caused such a run on airline tickets that Hoover had to charter entire planes to meet the demand.

The promotion cost the company $48.8 million more than it expected—and cost 3 top executives their jobs. The parent company, Maytag, had to take a $10.5 million loss in the first quarter of 1993.

NORTH TO ALASKA

The Company: Quaker Oats.

The Promotion: Quaker was the long-time sponsor of "Sergeant Preston of the Yukon," a popular kids' TV series. In 1955, they decided to create a tie-in between the show and some cereals that weren't selling too well—Quaker Puffed Rice and Quaker Puffed Wheat. Their ad agency came up with an unusual plan: Buy up a parcel of land on the Yukon River in Alaska, then subdivide it into 21 million one-inch-square parcels and give away a real deed to one of the parcels in each box of cereal.

What Happened: According to *Getting it Right the Second Time*, "[Quaker's ad exec] and a company lawyer flew to Dawson, Alaska, selected a 19.11-acre plot of ice on the Yukon River from the air, and bought it for $10,000. [The ad man] wanted to go home, but the Quaker lawyer insisted on investigating the land close up by boat. As it turned out, the boat developed a leak in the middle of the half-frozen river, and the passengers were forced to jump overboard. They paddled back to shore, only to find they'd missed their dogsled connection back to the airstrip. As darkness fell, the Quaker contingent was forced to walk six miles in subzero weather to meet the aircraft and go home."

Was it worth the aggravation? Quaker thought so. They sold more than 21 million boxes of Puffed Rice/ Wheat; and it has been cited as one of the 3 most successful cereal promotions ever.

LEFT-HANDED FACTS

We've considered doing something about left-handedness for several years, but the question always comes up—are there enough left-handed bathroom readers to make it worthwhile? After six years, we finally don't care; we just want to use the information. So here's a section for southpaws.

A re you left-handed? If so, you're not alone—but you're definitely outnumbered; lefties make up only 5-15% of the general population. If you're a female southpaw, you're even more unusual—there are roughly 50% more left-handed males than females. For centuries scientists have tried to figure out what makes people left- or right-handed, and they still aren't sure why. (They're not even sure if all lefties are that way for the same reason.) Here are some theories:

WHAT MAKES A LEFTIE?

√ Scientists used to think that left- and right-handedness was purely a genetic trait, but now they have doubts. Reason: In 20% of all sets of identical twins, one sibling is left-handed, and the other is right-handed.

√ Some scientists think the hand you prefer is determined by whether you're a "right-brained" person or a "left-brained" person. The right half of the brain controls the left side of the body, as well as spatial / musical / aesthetic judgement and perception; the left half controls the right side of the body, plus communication skills. Lefties are generally right-brained.

Support for this theory: Most children begin demonstrating a preference for one hand over the other at the same time their central nervous system is growing and maturing. This leads some scientists to believe the two processes are linked.

√ According to another theory, before birth all babies are right-handed—which means that the left side of their brain is dominant. But during a stressful or difficult birth, oxygen deficiency can cause damage to the left side of the brain, making it weaker and enabling the right side to compete against it for dominance. If the right side wins out, the baby will become left-handed.

This theory also explains, researchers claim, why twins, any child born to a smoker, or children born to a mother more than 30 years old are more likely to be left-handed: they are more prone to stressful births. Children of stressful births are also more likely to stammer and suffer dyslexia, traits that are more common in lefties.

LEFT-HANDED HISTORY

No matter what makes southpaws what they are, they've been discriminated against for thousands of years—in nearly every culture on Earth. Some examples:

• The artwork found in ancient Egyptian tombs portrays most Egyptians as right-handed. But their enemies are portrayed as left-handers, a sign they saw left-handedness as an undesirable trait.

• Ancient Greeks never crossed their left leg over their right, and believed a person's sex was determined by their position in the womb—with the female, or "lesser sex," sitting on the left side of the womb.

• The Romans placed special significance on right-handedness as well. Custom dictated that they enter friends' homes "with the right foot forward"…and turn their heads to the right to sneeze. Their language showed the same bias: The Latin word for left was *sinister* (which also meant evil or ominous); and the word for right was *dexter* (which came to mean skillful or adroit). Even the word ambidextrous literally means "right-handed with both hands."

• The Ango-Saxon root for left is *lyft*, which means "weak," "broken," or "worthless." *Riht* means "straight," "just," or "erect."

BIBLICAL BIAS

• The Bible is biased in favor of right-handed people. Both the Old and New Testament refer to "the right hand of God." One Old Testament town, Nineveh, is so wicked that its citizens "cannot discern between their right hand and their left hand."

• The saints also followed the right-hand rule; according to early Christian legend, they were so pious even as infants that they refused to nurse from their mother's left breast.

• The distinction is made even in religious art: Jesus and God are nearly always drawn giving blessings with their right hand, and the Devil is usually portrayed doing evil with his left hand.

MTV FACTS

These pages were contributed by Larry Kelp, whose picture has been on the back cover since the first Bathroom Reader. He's a music writer in the Bay Area in California, and Uncle John's neighbor.

I WANT MY MTV!

In 1981, Robert Pittman, a 27-year-old vice president in charge of new programming at Warner Amex, came up with an idea for "Music Television," an all-music channel that would play almost nothing but rock videos. The gimmick: free programming—the videos would be supplied by record companies at no charge. "The explicit aim," explains one critic, "was to deliver the notoriously difficult-to-reach 14-34 demographic segment to the record companies, beer manufacturers, and pimple cream makers."

Based on that appeal, Pittman talked Warner into investing $30 million in the idea. Four years later, Warner-Amex sold MTV to Viacom for $550 million. And in 1992 its estimated worth was $2 billion. Today it broadcasts in more than 50 different countries.

GETTING STARTED

• Pittman planned to call the channel TV-1, but immediately ran into a problem: "Our legal department found another business with that name. The best we could get was TV-M....and TV-M it was, until our head of music programming said, "Don't you think MTV sounds a little better than TV-M?"

• The design for the logo was another fluke. "Originally," Pittman recalls, "We thought MTV would be three equal-size letters like ABC, NBC and CBS. But... three 'kids' in a loft downtown, Manhattan Design, came up with the idea for a big M, with TV spray-painted over it. We just cut the paint drips off the TV, and that's the logo. We paid about $1,000 for one of the decade's best-known logos."

• MTV originally planned to use Astronaut Neil Armstrong's words, "One small step for man, one giant leap for mankind," with its now-famous "Moon Man" station identification. "But a few days before we launched," Pittman says, "an executive came flying into my office. We had just received a letter from Armstrong's lawyer threatening to sue us if we used his client's voice. We had no time

---

Long live the King: 13 countries around the world have issued Elvis Presley postage stamps.

and, worse, no money to redo this on-air ID. So we took his voice off and used the ID with just music. Not at all what we had envisioned, yet, fortunately, it worked fine."

MTV DATA

• MTV went on air at midnight, August 1, 1981. Its first video was the Buggles' prophetic "Video Killed the Radio Star."

• The average MTV viewer tunes in for 16 minutes at a time.

• MTV's VJ's have a short shelf life. Once they start looking old, they're retired.

• Not all of the music channel's fans are teenagers. One unusual audience: medical offices. *Prevention* magazine says MTV in the doctor's office helps relieve women's tension before medical exams.

• MTV reaches 75% of those households inhabited by people 18 to 34 years old and 85% of the households with one teenager.

• While many countries served by MTV Europe have local programming with their own VJs, most are in English, the official global language of rock. In Holland, a Flemish language show was dropped because viewers complained that it wasn't in English.

YO, MTV!

It took constant badgering by 25-year-old former intern Ted Demme (nephew of film director Jonathan) to get MTV to air a rap show, "Yo! MTV Raps," in 1989. He argued that white suburban kids wanted rap. The execs gave him one shot at it. "Yo !" was aired on a Saturday. By Monday the ratings and calls were so impressive that "Yo!" got a daily slot, and quickly became MTV's top-rated show.

UNPLUGGED

In 1990 MTV first aired "Unplugged," which went against everything music videos had stood for. Instead of stars lip-synching to prerecorded tracks, "Unplugged" taped them live in front of a studio audience, and forced them to use acoustic instruments, making music and talent the focus. What could have been a gimmick turned into a trend when Paul McCartney released his "Unplugged" appearance as an album, and it became one of his best-selling albums. Two years later Eric Clapton did the same with his MTV performance, which made "Layla" a hit song all over again, and earned him Grammy Awards as well as platinum records.

More than 50% of Americans believe in the devil; 1 in 10 say they've talked to him personally.

PRIMETIME PROVERBS

TV comments about everyday life. From Prime Time Proverbs, by Jack Mingo and John Javna

ON AMBITION:

"I'm tired of being an object of ridicule. I wanna be a figure of fear, respect, and SEX!"

—**Radar O'Reilly,**
M*A*S*H

ON AMERICA:

George Jefferson: "It's the American dream come true. Ten years ago, I was this little guy with one store. And now look at me—"

Louise Jefferson: "Now your're the little guy with seven stores."

—*The Jeffersons*

ON THE ARTS:

"You know, if Michelangelo had used me as a model, there's no telling how far he could have gone."

—**Herman Munster,**
The Munsters

ON DATING:

"Randy, there are three reasons why I won't go out with you: one, you're obnoxious; two, you're repulsive; and three, you haven't asked me yet."

—**Julianne,**
Van Dyke

ON MEN:

"A good man doesn't happen. They have to be created by us women. A guy is a lump like a doughnut. So, first you gotta get rid of all the stuff his mom did to him. And then you gotta get rid of all that macho crap that they pick up from the beer commercials. And then there's my personal favorite, the male ego."

—**Roseanne,**
Roseanne

ON COURAGE:

"Wanna do something courageous? Come to my house and say to my mother-in-law, 'You're wrong, fatso!' "

—**Buddy Sorrell,**
The Dick Van Dyke Show

ON BANKERS:

"Why do they call them tellers? They never tell you anything. They just ask questions. And why do they call it interest? It's boring. And another thing—how come the Trust Department has all their pens chained to the table?"

—**Coach Ernie Pantusso,**
Cheers

Claim to Fame: Grand Rapids, Michigan was the first city to fluoridate its water supply.

AUNT LENNA'S PUZZLES

Some adventures with my favorite aunt. Answers are on p. 226.

MURDER AT THE BIG HOTEL
My Aunt Lenna loves puzzles. Not complicated ones—just the kind people call *brain teasers*.
"I don't like those puzzles where you have to be a genius at math," she often says. "I want simple puzzles of logic."

One day she was reading a mystery, and she began musing out loud: "It was a very large, fancy hotel. The hotel detective was making his rounds, walking in the hallway…when suddenly he heard a woman cry, 'Please! Don't shoot me, Steve!' And a shot rang out!"

"Sounds original, Aunt Lenna."

"Well now, hold on, Nephew. The detective ran as fast as he could to the room the shot came from, and pushed his way in. The body of a woman who'd been shot lay in a corner of the room; the gun that had been used to kill her was on the floor near her. On the opposite side of the room stood a postman, an accountant, and a lawyer. For a moment, the detective hesitated as he looked at them. Then he strode up to the postman and said—'You're under arrest for murder.'

"A little hasty, wasn't he? Or was there some evidence you're not mentioning?"

"He wasn't hasty, and there was no other evidence…and the detective made the right choice."

"Well, how did he know?"

How did he?

Aunt Lenna likes word games, too. Some are real groaners. Like she once asked me, "What word is it that when you take away the whole, you still have some left?" Another time she asked, "Can you make one word out of the letters D R E N O O W?"

Got the answers?

Costly mistake: The fine for parking illegally overnight in Tokyo is the equivalent of $1,400.

THE ART OF THE GETAWAY

Chuck Shepherd is already known for his News of the Weird *books and column. Now he's off on a new tangent with a volume called* America's Least Competent Criminals. *Here's a brief excerpt from it.*

I n many crimes, the trickiest part is the getaway, for two reasons:

√ First, only some of the circumstances can be controlled; traffic patterns, for example, may be unpredictable.

√ Second, compared to an insular criminal act, the getaway presents a vastly expanded array of opportunities in which to screw up.

The purpose of the getaway should be to exit the crime scene quickly with minimum chances for detection, so that the criminal can get home as soon as possible, jump into bed, and pull the covers up real tight. To assist the crimino-American, herewith is a list of "Getaway Do's:"

1. Even if you are very stupid, you still have a better chance of success if you try to control your getaway than if you allow others to control it....Therefore, try to avoid making your getaway on a municipal bus. We can appreciate the pro-environment use of mass transit, but jails have housed many civic-minded souls, such as Richard Stowell, then twenty-seven, charged with robbing the Chase Lincoln First Bank in Syracuse, New York, in 1991. (He was on parole for a 1988 bank robbery, from which he also tried to escape on a municipal bus.)...

2. Try to use a vehicle that can go really fast. Jack Kelm of Greeley, Colorado, wanted in a string of robberies in 1989, is just one of several who have embarked on robbery careers using a bicycle as the getaway vehicle. Without exception, they have been short careers....

Randall Marlow at one point had a fast vehicle, a motorcycle, but he gave it up for something less speedy. California highway patrolmen in Los Angeles chased his motorcycle—only because they

---

Not just for kids: Nintendo estimates that 42% of the people who use its games are over 18.

wanted to ticket him for equipment deficiencies—but he continued to outrun them, weaving in and out of traffic on a freeway. Then, for some reason, Marlow pulled off into a neighborhood, abandoned the motorcycle near a golf course and commandeered a golf cart. He was easily apprehended.

Marlow doesn't look that stupid next to the twenty-two-year-old man who tried to make his break in a five-foot-high wheeled arc-welder in Hutchinson, Kansas, in 1990. In addition to its being slow and fairly easy to spot, an arc-welder makes large, ugly marks in the street, so that even if the cops stop off for a half hour at the 7-Eleven, they can still pick up the chase. Raul Camargo was arrested at his home, which was easy to distinguish because it was the only one in the neighborhood with an arc-welder parked outside.

3. Try not to be conspicuous. Raul violated this one, too, as did James Richardson, then thirty-two, and Jeffrey Defalco, then eighteen, who tried to steal a three-ton safe in Canoga Park, California, in 1990. They dragged it home behind their car, believing that it contained several thousand dollars. In fact, it was empty, but it still weighed three tons. Not only did the safe prevent the driver from going fast (see Rule Number 2), it scarred the pavement (see Arc-Welder Principle). It also made such a deafening noise, and the metal scraping on the rock of the pavement created such a shower of sparks, that people were drawn to it from blocks away. Said one witness, "It looked like they were towing a Roman candle." The two men said they planned to break it open with a crowbar....

Douglas Eric "Dougie" Girard, then thirty-two, and his buddy were being chased by police in connection with the robbery of a children's clothing store in La Verne, California. They ducked into a nearby McDonald's and got in line, trying to blend in with the crowd. When police walked into the McDonald's, they saw thirty suburbanites waiting to buy their Big Macs, along with two heavily tattooed guys, both with money bulging out of their socks and one carrying a gun in his back waistband...

4. If you have a getaway vehicle, remember to take the keys. Otherwise, in an urban area, someone might steal it while it's parked out front, as happened to William McNellis, then forty-three, while he was inside robbing a New Haven, Connecticut, bank in 1985. Or, as apparently has happened to other forgetful

---

McDonalds hired 45 Ph.D. scientists to help it develop "carrot sticks" in 1991.

criminoids, they'll lock the keys inside the getaway car, as Paul C. Benier, then twenty-three, did in Swansea, Massachusetts, as he was knocking off the Lafayette Cooperative Bank.

Two seventeen-year-old boys robbed the Seafirst Bank in Des Moines, Washington, a suburb of Seattle, in 1991. Their first mistake was not taking the car in for a full inspection the day before. As they emerged from the bank with money in hand, they discovered that the battery was dead. They got out to check underneath the hood, but the doors locked behind them, with the key still in the ignition and the loot in the front seat. They panicked and started to run away, but dashed smack into a police car responding to the call about the bank robbery.

5. If you're worried about all the details of the robbery, hire accomplices, but try to find people whose I.Q. is at least in the "dull normal" range.

Drivers below that I.Q. are less likely to think of basic considerations, such as whether the car has automatic or manual transmission, which is a crucial distinction for those who can't drive the latter. Below that I.Q. level, also, they might decide, as one fellow did, that while you're in the bank pulling off the heist, this sure would be a good time to get the car washed across the street; be back in just a minute....

6. Bone up on local geography and traffic patterns. Rory Johnson made a really bad decision after knocking off The Liquor Station in Elkhart, Indiana. With a choice of two roads to exit by, he picked the wrong one. He had parked in back of the store to facilitate his getaway, but by the time he drove off, the road on that side of the building had developed a huge bottleneck because of construction; he was quickly sandwiched in by other gridlocked motorists. Five minutes after the robbery, as liquor-store employees emerged from the store, they spotted Johnson sitting in his car, which had moved only a few feet.

Stephen Le, then eighteen, and two companions didn't have a car, but they could have used a map. They were attempting a burglary in Larkspur, California, in 1989 when police broke in on them. Two ran off together, and when they passed a tall chain-link fence with barbed wire atop it, running parallel to the road, over they went because police were on their tails. The fence happened to be the outer perimeter of the San Quentin Prison.

SHAKESPEARE SAYETH…

Here's the "high culture" section of the Bathroom Reader.

"The first thing we do, let's kill all the lawyers."

"Neither a borrower, nor a lender be; For oft loses both itself and friend."

"He is well paid that is well satisfied."

"What's in a name? That which we call a rose / By any other name would smell as sweet."

"Some are born great, some achieve greatness, and some have greatness thrust upon them."

"Though this be madness, yet there is method in it."

"When Fortune means to men most good, she looks upon them with a threatening eye."

"Remuneration! O! that's the Latin word for three farthings."

"Words pay no debts."

"You taught me language; and my profit on't is, I know how to curse."

"Talkers are not good doers."

"The saying is true, the empty vessel makes the loudest sound."

"My words fly up, my thoughts remain below: Words without thoughts never to heaven go."

"If all the year were playing holidays / To sport would be as tedious as to work."

"The fault, dear Brutus, is not in our stars / But in ourselves."

"A politician…One that would circumvent God."

"When my love swears that she is made of truth / I do believe her, though I know she lies."

"Let me have no lying; it becomes none but tradesmen."

"If it be a sin to covet honor, I am the most offending soul."

"One may smile, and smile, and be a villan."

"Time is come round, and where I did begin, there shall I end."

In the average film, male actors utter 10 times as many profanities as female actors.

EVERYDAY ORIGINS

Some quick stories about the origins of everyday objects.

SCOTCH TAPE. Believe it or not, the sticky stuff gets its name from an ethnic slur. When two-toned paint jobs became popular in the 1920s, Detroit carmakers asked the 3-M Company for an alternative to masking tape that would provide a smooth, sharp edge where the 2 colors met. 3-M came up with 2-inch wide cellophane tape, but auto companies said it was too expensive. So 3-M lowered the price by only applying adhesive along the sides of the strip. That caused a problem: the new tape didn't stick—and company painters complained to the 3-M salesman, "Take this tape back to your stingy 'Scotch' bosses and tell them to put more adhesive on it!" The name—and the new tape—stuck.

BRASSIERES. Mary Phelps Jacob, a teenage debutante in 1913, wanted to wear a rose-garlanded dress to a party one evening. But as she later explained, her corset cover "kept peeping through the roses around my bosom." So she took it off, pinned two handkerchiefs together, and tied them behind her back with some ribbon. "The result was delicious," she later recalled. "I could move much more freely, a nearly naked feeling." The contraption eventually became known as a *brassiere*—French for "arm protector"—a name borrowed from the corset cover it replaced. (Jacob later became famous for riding naked through the streets of Paris on an elephant.)

DINNER KNIVES. Regular knives first had their points rounded and their sharp edges dulled for use at the dinner table in 1669. According to Margaret Visser, author of *The Rituals of Dinner,* this was done "apparently to prevent their use as 'toothpicks,' but probably also to discourage assassinations at meals."

WRISTWATCHES. Several Swiss watchmakers began attaching small watches to bracelets in 1790. Those early watches weren't considered serious timepieces, and remained strictly a women's item until World War I, when armies recognized their usefulness in battle and began issuing them to servicemen instead of the traditional pocket watch.

"Smut" gets its name from a fungus that lives on corn kernels.

FORKS. Before forks became popular, the difference between refined and common people was the number of fingers they ate with. The upper classes used three; everyone else used five. This began to change in the 11th century, when tiny, two-pronged forks became fashionable in Italian high society. But they didn't catch on; the Catholic Church opposed them as unnatural (it was an insult to imply that the fingers God gave us weren't good enough for food) and people who used them were ridiculed as effeminate or pretentious. Forks weren't generally considered polite until the 18th century—some 800 years after they were first introduced.

FLIP-TOP BEER CANS. In 1959 a mechanical engineer named Ermal Cleon Fraze was at a picnic when he realized he'd forgotten a can opener. No one else had one either, so he had to use the bumper guard of his car to open a can of soda. It took half an hour, and he vowed he'd never get stuck like that again. He patented the world's first practical pull-top can later that year, and three years later, the Pittsburgh Brewing Company tried using it on its Iron City Beer. Now every beer company does.

REFRIGERATOR MAGNETS. Mass-produced magnets *designed* for refrigerators didn't appear until 1964. They were invented by John Arnasto (son of the guy who invented Eskimo Pies) and his wife Arlene, who sold a line of decorative wall hooks. Arlene thought it would be cute to have a hook for refrigerator doors, so John made one with a magnet backing. The first one had a small bell and was shaped like a tea kettle; It sold well, so the Arnastos added dozens of other versions to their lines. Believe it or not, some of the rare originals are worth more than $100.

TOOTHPASTE TUBES. Toothpaste wasn't packaged in collapsable tubes until 1892, when Dr. Washington Wentworth Sheffield, a Connecticut dentist, copied the idea from a tube of oil-based paint. Increasing interest in sanitation and hygiene made it more popular than jars of toothpaste, which mingled germs from different brushes. Toothpaste tubes became the standard almost overnight.

Believable Quote: "I was not lying. I said things that later on seemed to be untrue."
　　　　　　　　　　　　　　　　　　　　　　　—Richard Nixon

Top 4 presidential religions: Episcopal (12), Presbyterian (9), Baptist and Unitarian (tied at 4).

REEFER MADNESS

After being widely cultivated for 10,000 years, marijuana was suddenly outlawed in America in 1937. Was it because it was a threat to the American public—or only to certain business interests?

For thousands of years, hemp (*cannabis sativa*) has been one of the most useful plants known to man. Its strong, stringy fibers make durable rope and can be woven into anything from sails to shirts; its pithy centers, or "hurds," make excellent paper; its seeds, high in protein and oil, have been pressed for lighting and lubricating oils and pulped into animal feed; and extracts of its leaves have provided a wide range of medicines and tonics.

HEMP & AMERICA

• Hemp also has a notable place in American history:

√ Washington and Jefferson grew it.

√ Our first flags were likely made of hemp cloth.

√ The first and second drafts of the Declaration of Independence were written on paper made from Dutch hemp.

√ When the pioneers went west, their wagons were covered with hemp canvas (the word "canvas" comes from *canabacius*, hemp cloth).

√ The first Levis sold to prospectors were sturdy hemp coveralls.

√ Abraham Lincoln's wife, Mary Todd, came from the richest hemp-growing family in Kentucky.

• After the Civil War, however, hemp production in the States declined steeply. Without slave labor, hemp became too expensive to process. Besides, cotton ginned by machines was cheaper. Still, hemp fabric remained the second most common cloth in America.

• The plant's by-products remained popular well into this century. Maple sugar combined with hashish (a resin from hemp leaves) was sold over the counter and in Sears Roebuck catalogs as a harmless candy. Hemp rope was a mainstay of the navy. Two thousand tons of hemp seed were sold annually as birdfeed. The pharmaceutical

---

Which George Washington portrait is more accurate: the $1 bill or the quarter? The quarter.

industry used hemp extracts in hundreds of potions and vigorously fought attempts to restrict hemp production. And virtually all good paints and varnishes were made from hemp-seed oil and/or linseed oil.

WHAT HAPPENED

• In the 1920s and '30s, the American public became increasingly concerned about drug addiction—especially to morphine and a "miracle drug" that had been introduced by the Bayer Company in 1898 under the brand name "Heroin." By the mid-1920s, there were 200,000 heroin addicts in the U.S. alone.

• Most Americans were unaware that smoking hemp leaves was intoxicating; however, until William Randolph Hearst launched a campaign of sensational stories that linked "the killer weed" to jazz musicians, "crazed minorities," and unspeakable crimes. Hearst's papers featured headlines like:

√ MARIJUANA MAKES FIENDS OF BOYS IN 30 DAYS: HASHEESH [SIC] GOADS USERS TO BLOOD-LUST

√ NEW DOPE LURE, MARIJUANA, HAS MANY VICTIMS

• In 1930, Hearst was joined in his crusade against hemp by Harry J. Anslinger, commissioner of the newly organized Federal Bureau of Narcotics (FBN). Hearst often quoted Anslinger in his newspaper stories, printing sensational comments like: "If the hideous monster Frankenstein came face to face with the monster marijuana he would drop dead of fright."

• Not everyone shared their opinion. In 1930, the U.S. government formed the Siler Commission to study marijuana smoking by off-duty servicemen in Panama. The commission found no lasting effects and recommended that no criminal penalties apply to its use.

• Nonetheless, Hearst and Anslinger's anti-hemp campaign had results. By 1931, twenty-nine states had prohibited marijuana use for nonmedical purposes. In 1937, after two years of secret hearings—and based largely on Anslinger's testimony—Congress passed the Marijuana Tax Act, which essentially outlawed marijuana in America.

• Because Congress wasn't sure that it was constitutional to ban hemp outright, it taxed the plant prohibitively instead. Hemp

The original Gotham City was a mythical English town whose residents were extremely stupid.

growers had to register with the government; sellers and buyers had to fill out cumbersome paperwork; and, of course, it was a federal crime not to comply.

• For selling an ounce or less of marijuana to an unregistered person, the federal tax was $100. (To give some sense of how prohibitive the tax was, "legitimate" marijuana was selling for $2 a pound at the time. In 1992 dollars, the federal tax would be roughly $2,000 per ounce.)

• The Marijuana Tax Act effectively destroyed all legitimate commercial cultivation of hemp. Limited medical use was permitted, but as hemp derivatives became prohibitively expensive for doctors and pharmacists, they turned to chemically derived drugs instead. All other nonmedical uses, from rope to industrial lubricants, were taxed out of existence.

• With most of their markets gone, farmers stopped growing hemp, and the legitimate industry disappeared. Ironically, though, hemp continued to grow wild all over the country, and its "illegitimate" use was little affected by Congress.

WAS IT A CONSPIRACY?

Was a viable hemp industry forced out of existence because it was a threat to people's health or because it was a threat to a few large businesses that would profit from banning it?

THE HEARST CONSPIRACY

• Hemp was outlawed just as a new technology would have made hemp paper far cheaper than wood-pulp paper.

• Traditionally, hemp fiber had to be separated from the stalk by hand, and the cost of labor made this method uncompetitive. But in 1937—the year that hemp was outlawed, the *decorticator* machine was invented; it could process as much as 3 tons of hemp an hour and produced higher-quality fibers with less loss of fiber than wood-based pulp. According to some scientists, hemp would have been able to undercut competing products overnight. Enthusiastic about the new technology, *Popular Mechanics* predicted that hemp would become America's first "billion-dollar crop." The magazine pointed out that "10,000 acres devoted to hemp will produce as much paper as 40,000 acres of average [forest] pulp land."

Coney Island was once full of rabbits, which New York's colonists called "coneys."

• According to Jack Herer, an expert on the "hemp conspiracy," Hearst, the du Ponts, and other "industrial barons and financiers knew that machinery to cut, bale, decorticate (separate fiber from the stalk) and process hemp into paper was becoming avail-able in the mid-1930s." (*The Emperor Wears No Clothes*)

• Hearst, one of the promoters of the anti-hemp hysteria, had a vested interest in protecting the pulp industry. Hearst owned enor-mous timber acreage; competition from hemp paper might have driven the Hearst paper-manufacturing division out of business and caused the value of his acreage to plummet. (ibid.)

• Herer suggests that Hearst slanted the news in his papers to protect his pulp investments. "In the 1920s and '30s," he writes, "Hearst's newspaper chain led the deliberate…yellow journalism campaign to have marijuana outlawed. From 1916 to 1937, as an example, the story of a car accident in which a marijuana cigarette was found would dominate the headlines for weeks, while alcohol-related car accidents (which outnumbered marijuana-related acci-dents by more than 1,000 to 1) made only the back pages." (ibid.)

• Herer says that Hearst was even responsible for popularizing the term "marijuana" in American culture. In fact, he suggests, popu-larizing the word was a key strategy of Hearst's efforts: "The first step [in creating hysteria] was to introduce the element of fear of the unknown by using a word that no one had ever heard of be-fore…'marijuana.' " (ibid.)

THE DU PONT CONSPIRACY

• The Du Pont Company also had an interest in the pulp industry. At this time, it was in the process of patenting a new sulfuric acid process for producing wood-pulp paper. According to the compa-ny's own records, wood-pulp products ultimately accounted for more than 80% of all of Du Pont's railroad car loadings for the next 50 years. (ibid.)

• But Du Pont had even more reasons to be concerned about hemp. In the 1930s, the company was making drastic changes in its business strategy. Traditionally a manufacturer of military explo-sives, Du Pont realized after the end of World War I that develop-ing peacetime uses for artificial fibers and plastics would be more profitable in the long run. So it began pouring millions of dollars into research—which resulted in the development of such synthetic fibers as rayon and nylon.

√ Two years before the prohibitive hemp tax, Du Pont developed a new synthetic fiber, nylon, that was an ideal substitute for hemp rope.

√ The year after the hemp tax, Du Pont was able to bring another "miracle" synthetic fabric onto the market—rayon. Rayon, which became widely used for clothing, was a direct competitor to hemp cloth.

√ "Congress and the Treasury Department were assured, through secret testimony given by Du Pont, that hemp-seed oil could be replaced with synthetic petrochemical oils made principally by Du Pont." These oils were used in paints and other products. (ibid.)

• The millions spent on these products, as well as the hundreds of millions in expected profits from them, could have been wiped out if the newly affordable hemp products were allowed onto the market. So, according to Herer, Du Pont worked with Hearst to eliminate hemp.

• Du Pont's point-man was none other than Harry Anslinger, the commissioner of the FBN. Anslinger was appointed to the FBN by Treasury Secretary Andrew Mellon, who was also chairman of the Mellon Bank, Du Pont's chief financial backer. But Anslinger's relationship to Mellon wasn't just political; he was also married to Mellon's niece.

• Anslinger apparently used his political clout to sway congressional opinion on the hemp tax. According to Herer, the American Medical Association (AMA) tried to argue for the medical benefits of hemp. But after AMA officials testified to Congress, "they were quickly denounced by Anslinger and the entire congressional committee, and curtly excused."

FOOTNOTES

• Five years after the hemp tax was imposed, when Japanese seizure of Philippine hemp caused a wartime shortage of rope, the government reversed itself. Overnight, the U.S. government urged hemp cultivation once again and created a stirring movie called "Hemp for Victory"—then, just as quickly, it recriminalized hemp after the shortage had passed.

• While U.S. hemp was temporarily legal, however, it saved the

---

Cincinnati was so famous for its hog industry in the 1830s that it was nicknamed "Porkopolis."

life of a young pilot named George Bush, who was forced to bail out of his burning airplane after a battle over the Pacific. At the time, he didn't know that:

√ Parts of his aircraft engine were lubricated with hemp-seed oil.

√ 100% of his life-saving parachute webbing was made from U.S.-grown cannabis hemp.

√ Virtually all the rigging and ropes of the ship that rescued him were made of cannabis hemp.

√ The fire hoses on the ship were woven from cannabis hemp.

Ironically, President Bush consistently opposed decriminalizing hemp grown in the United States.

• Does the hemp conspiracy continue? In March 1992, Robert Bonner, the chief of the Drug Enforcement Agency, effectively rejected a petition to permit doctors to prescribe marijuana for patients as medication for chronic pain. Bonner said: "Beyond doubt the claims that marijuana is medicine are false, dangerous and cruel." But, according to a federal administrative law judge, Francis Young, "the record clearly shows that marijuana has been accepted as capable of relieving the distress of great numbers of very ill people and doing so with safety under medical supervision." (*The New York Times*)

RECOMMENDED READING

• This article was excerpted from *It's A Conspiracy*, by the National Insecurity Council (as is the one on Marilyn's death on p. 218). It's highly recommended by the BRI. In fact, some of the BRI members worked on it, so it's just as much fun to read.

• If you'd like a copy (and we know you would), send a check for $10 to EarthWorks Press, 1400 Shattuck Ave. #25, Berkeley, CA 94709. Or ask for it at your local bookstore.

Q & A:
ASK THE EXPERTS

More random questions and answers from America's trivia experts.

ON THE SPOT

Q: *What causes freckles?*

A: "Except in the case of albinos, every person's skin has cells called *melanocytes*, which produce a certain amount of melanin, a dark pigment that absorbs ultraviolet light. These cells produce melanin at increasing rates when the skin is exposed to sunlight—hence the sunbather's tan. Some melanocytes are more active than others. Thus when groups of active melanocytes are surrounded by groups of less active melanocytes, the results are islands of pigment known as freckles." (From *Do elephants Swim?*, compiled by Robert M. Jones)

INFLATED WITH PRIDE

Q: *Why is Chicago called the windy city?*

A: Chicago is pretty windy (with a 10.3 mph wind average), but that's not where the nickname comes from. It comes from the 1893 Chicago World's Columbia Exposition—which was supposed to commemorate the 400th anniversary of Columbus's discovery of the New World, but ended up being used by city politicos to hype Chicago. "So boastful and overblown were the local politicians' claims about the exposition and the city that a New York City newspaper editor, Charles A. Dana, nicknamed Chicago 'the windy city.' "(From *The Book of Totally Useless Information*, by Don Voorhees)

EVERYTHING'S RELATIVE

Q: *Is it true that Einstein's parents once thought he was retarded?*

A: Believe it or not, yes. "It took Einstein so long to learn to speak (he didn't become fluent in his mother tongue of German until age nine) that his parents suspected he was 'subnormal.' His teachers agreed: according to legend, when Einstein's father ask his schoolmaster which profession young Albert should adopt, the schoolmaster replied, 'It doesn't matter; he'll never make a success of anything.' Actually, though, historians don't know all that much about his childhood. The reason: Einstein's memory for personal things was so bad that even *he* couldn't remember what happened to him as a kid. 'You are quite right,' he said when a friend commented this was hard to believe. 'My bad memory for personal things [is] really quite astounding.' "

"Interesting note: Even as an adult Einstein's genius was not immediately recognized. As late as 1910, more than five years after he published his famous papers on statistical mechanics, quantum mechanics, and the special theory of relativity, he was still only an associate professor at the University of Zurich earning just 4,500 francs a year. The meager salary wasn't enough to live on; he was forced to supplement his income with lecture fees and by taking in student boarders. He once told a colleague: 'In my relativity theory, I set up a clock at every point in space, but in reality I find it difficult to provide even one clock in my room.' " (From *Late Night Entertainment*, by John Dollison)

HAIRY THOUGHTS

Q: *Why do people get goose bumps?*

A: "Goose bumps are a vestige from the days when humans were covered with hair. When it got cold, the hairs were stood on end, creating a trap for air and providing insulation. The hairs have long since disappeared, but in the places where they used to be, the skin still bristles, trying to get warm." (From *The Book of Answers*, by Barbara Berliner)

SLICK QUESTION

Q: *Why is ice so slippery?*

A: "Ice has several unusual properties, one of them being that it melts when subjected to pressure. Your foot on ice is such pressure, and a film of melted ice—water—reduces the amount of friction and thus sliding can occur." (From *Science Trivia*, by Charles Cazeau).

FIRST REPORTS

Over the years, we've collected "First Reports"—newspaper articles that gave readers their first glimpse of something that eventually became important in some way. Here are a few examples.

SPACED OUT

Most people don't know it was one incident—and one short newspaper story—that started the UFO craze. Here's the story, sent out over the AP wire from the Pendleton East Oregonian *on June 25, 1947.*

Pendleton, Ore. June 25 (AP)—"Nine bright saucer-like objects flying at 'incredible speed' at 10,000 feet altitude were reported here today by Kenneth Arnold, a Boise, Idaho, pilot who said he could not hazard a guess as to what they were.

"Arnold, a United States Forest Service employee engaged in searching for a missing plane, said he sighted the mysterious objects yesterday at three p.m. They were flying between Mount Rainier and Mount Adams, in Washington State, he said, and appeared to weave in and out of formation. Arnold said that he clocked and estimated their speed at 1200 miles an hour.

"Enquiries at Yakima last night brought only blank stares, he said, but he added he talked today with an unidentified man from Ukiah, south of here, who said he had seen similar objects over the mountains near Ukiah yesterday.

" 'It seems impossible,' Arnold said, 'but there it is.' "

This story was picked up by papers all over the world. At that moment, according to the UFO Encyclopedia, *"the age of flying saucers began."*

THE XEROX MACHINE

When this article appeared in 1948, Xerox was still known as the Haloid Company.

Rochester, N.Y. Oct. 23—"A revolutionary process of inkless printing has been developed that might completely change all the operations of the printing and publishing industry. This was announced yesterday by Joseph C. Wilson, presidential the Haloid Company of Rochester, New York.

"Known as 'Xerography,' this basic addition to the graphic arts reproduces pictures and text at the speed of 1,200 feet a

---

In case you were wondering: The little flap in the back of your throat is called a *uvula*.

minute, on any kind of surface.

"Although there is no immediate prospect of applying the method to general photography, the process will be available within about six months for copying uses. Wilson said it will be in the form of a compact Xerocopying machine for reproducing letters, documents, and line work...

"Looking farther ahead, he said he foresaw incorporating the entire process in a portable Xerocamera. 'With such a camera, the picture taker can snap the shutter and within a few seconds pull out a finished Xeroprint. If he doesn't like the picture, he can discard it and try again, using the same Xeroplate.' "

DEAR ABBY

Dear Abby's first columnn appeared in the San Francisco Chronicle *on January 9, 1956. She answered 4 letters. Here's one. It shows how things have changed.*

"Dear Abby: I am sweet 16 and truly never have been kissed. I have plenty of dates and the boys seem to enjoy my company, but when it comes time to say goodnight, all they do is just say 'goodnight.' Please tell me how I can become irresistible.

—Hopeful Ann

"Dear Ann: If you become 'irresistible' at 16, you'll need police protection by the time you reach 20. If you are longing for a goodnight kiss...which would melt a glacier, it's too early."

INTRODUCING THE CD

This article appeared in the New York Times, *March 18, 1983*

"Five years ago, the electronics industry brought out the videodisk, heralded as the future of home entertainment systems. This month, the digital compact disk audio system will make its way into American homes, making similar promises. But marketers of the audiodisk play down the kinship, with good cause; sales of videodisks have been dismal. The compact audiodisk system, meanwhile, is expected to replace stereo turntables and albums as the industry standard within the decade.

"Some question whether the audiodisk will succeed. Players now cost $800-$900, and disks are $16-20 each, far too expensive for a popular market.

"Even if prices come down ...some analysts doubt whether consumers will be willing to sacrifice substantial investments in turntables and stacks of traditional recordings."

Women have Adam's apples, too. Men's are larger to accommodate longer vocal cords.

FAMOUS TRIALS:
THE CADAVER SYNOD

*Here's the story of a trial that's stranger than anything you'll
ever see on "Court TV" or "The People's Court."*

B ACKGROUND. The late ninth century was a difficult period in the history of the Catholic Church. The Holy Roman
Empire was disintegrating and as the empire's power slipped
away, so did the authority of the Church; not strong enough mili-
tarily to survive on its own, it had to depend on powerful European
nobles for protection.

HERE COMES GUIDO

In 891, Pope Stephen V turned to Duke Guido III of Spoleto for
protection. To cement the relationship, Stephen adopted him as
his son and crowned him Holy Roman Emperor.

...AND POPE FORMOSUS

That relationship didn't last long. Pope Stephen V died a few
months later and a new pope, Formosus I, was elected to head the
Church. Guido was suspicious of the new pope's loyalty. So in 892,
he forced Formosus to crown him emperor a second time. He also
insited that Formosus name his son Lambert "heir apparent."

When Guido died in 894, Formosus backed out of the deal.
Rather than crown Lambert emperor, he called on King Arnulf of
the East Franks to liberate Rome from Guido's family.

...AND ARNULF

A year later Arnulf conquered Rome...and Formosus made him
emperor. This relationship didn't last long either: within a few
months, Arnulf had suffered paralysis and had to be carried back to
Germany; a few months after *that*, Pope Formosus died.

...AND LAMBERT AGAIN

Lambert, who had retreated back to Spoleto, used the crisis to rally
his troops and march on Rome. He reconquered the city in 897.

Who's the St. Pauli Girl? Hint: The German beer is named for Hamburg's red light district.

The new pope, Stephen VI, quickly switched sides and crowned Lambert emperor.

THE TRIAL

What followed was one of the most peculiar episodes in the history of the Catholic Church. Eager to prove his loyalty to the Spoletos, Pope Stephen convened the "cadaver synod," in which he literally had Pope Formosus's 9-month-old, rotting corpse put on trial for perjury, "coveting the papacy," and a variety of other crimes. On Stephen's orders the cadaver was disinterred, dressed in papal robes, and propped up on a throne for the trial. Since the body was in no condition to answer the charges made against it, a deacon was appointed to stand next to it during the proceedings and answer questions on its behalf.

Not surprisingly, the cadaver was found guilty on all counts. As punishment, all of Formosus's papal acts were declared null and void. The corpse itself was also desecrated: the three fingers on the right hand used to confer blessings were hacked off, and the body was stripped naked and dumped in a cemetery for foreigners. Shortly afterwards it was tossed in Tiber River, where a hermit fished it out and gave it a proper burial.

WHAT GOES AROUND...

Stephen VI himself survived the cadaver synod by only a few months. While the gruesome synod was still in session, a strong earthquake struck Rome and destroyed the papal basilica. Taking this as a sign of God's anger with the upstart pope, and encouraged by rumors that Formosus's corpse had begun performing miracles, Formosus's supporters arrested Stephen and threw him into the papal prison, where he was later strangled.

TIME FLIES

According to recent studies, in a lifetime the average American spends...

√ 8 months opening mail

√ 5 years waiting on line

√ 2 years returning phone calls

√ A year looking for misplaced items

Government stats: The poorest county in the U.S. is Shannon County, South Dakota.

DAVE BARRY'S EMBARRASSING MOMENTS

*Here's a column written by Dave Barry, one of America's most popular
humorists. Maybe when he sees that we've included one of his
pieces in a* Bathroom Reader, *he'll write about us in his column.
In fact, why not write to him, care of the* Miami Herald *and suggest it?
We're sure he'd love to hear from you.*

Have you ever really embarrassed yourself? Don't answer
that, stupid. It's a rhetorical question. Of course you've embarrassed yourself. Everybody has. I bet the pope has. If you
were to say to the pope: "Your Holy Worshipfulness, I bet you've
pulled some blockheaded boners in your day, huh?" he'd smile that
warm, knowing, fatherly smile he has, and then he'd wave. He
can't hear a word you're saying, up on that balcony.

But my point is that if you've ever done anything humiliating,
you've probably noticed that your brain never lets you forget
it. This is the same brain that never remembers things you
should remember. If you were bleeding to death and the emergen-
cy-room doctor asked you what blood type you were, you'd say: "I
think it's B. Or maybe C. I'm pretty sure it's a letter." But if your
doctor asked you to describe the skirt you were wearing when you
were doing the Mashed Potatoes in the ninth-grade dance competition in front of 350 people, and your underwear, which had holes
in it, fell to your ankles, you'd say, without hesitating for a millisec-
ond, "It was gray felt with a pink flocked poodle."

Your brain cherishes embarrassing memories. It likes to take
them out and fondle them. This probably explains a lot of un-
explained suicides. A successful man with a nice family and a
good career will be out on his patio, cooking hamburgers, seemingly without a care in the world, when his brain, rummaging through
its humiliating-incident collection, selects an old favorite, which it
replays for a zillionth time, and the man is suddenly so overcome by
feelings of shame that he stabs himself in the skull with his barbe-
cue fork. At the funeral, people say how shocking it was, a seeming-

---

Lee Harvey Oswald's body tag sold at auction for $6,600 in 1991.

ly happy and well-adjusted person choosing to end it all. They assume he must have had a terrible dark secret involving drugs or organized crime or dressing members of the conch family in flimsy undergarments. Little do they know he was thinking about the time in Social Studies class in 1963 when he discovered a hard-to-reach pimple roughly halfway down his back, and he got to working on it, subtly at first, but with gradually increasing intensity, eventually losing track of where he was, until suddenly he realized the room had become silent, and he looked up, with his arm stuck halfway down the back of his shirt, and he saw that everybody in the class, including the teacher, was watching what he was doing, and he knew they'd give him a cruel nickname that would stick like epoxy cement for the rest of his life, such as when he went to his 45th reunion, even if he had been appointed Chief Justice of the U.S. Supreme Court, the instant his classmates saw him, they'd shriek: "Hey look! It's ZIT!"

Everybody has incidents like this. My mother is always reliving the time she lost her car in a shopping-center parking lot, and she was wandering around with several large shopping bags and two small children, looking helpless, and after a while other shoppers took pity on her and offered to help. "It's a black Chevrolet," she told them, over and over. And they searched and searched and searched for it. They were extremely nice. They all agreed that it can be darned easy to lose your car in these big parking lots. They had been there for an hour, some of them, searching for this black Chevrolet, and it was getting dark, when my mother remembered that several days earlier we had bought a new car. "I'm sorry!" she told the people, smiling brightly so they would see what a humorous situation this was. "It's not a black Chevrolet! It's a yellow Ford!" She kept on smiling as they edged away, keeping their eyes on her.

My own personal brain is forever dredging up the time in 11th grade when I took a girl, a very attractive girl on whom I had a life-threatening crush, to a dance. I was standing in the gym next to her, holding her hand, thinking what a sharp couple we made—Steve Suave and His Gorgeous Date—when one of my friends sidled up to me and observed that, over on the other side, my date was using her spare hand to hold hands with another guy. This was of course a much better-looking guy. This was Paul Newman, only taller.

Several of my friends gathered to watch. I thought: What am I supposed to do here? Hit the guy? That would have been asking for a lifetime of dental problems. He was a varsity football player; I was on the Dance Committee. I also had to rule out hitting my date. The ideal move would have been to spontaneously burst into flames and die. I have read that this sometimes happens to people. But you never get a break like that when you need it. Finally I turned to my date, dropped her hand, looked her square in the eye, and said: "Um." Just like that: "Um." My brain absolutely loves to remember this. "Way to go, Dave!" it shrieks to me, when I'm stopped at red lights, 23-1/2 years later. Talk about eloquent! My brain can't get over what a jerk I was. It's always coming up with much better ideas for things I could have said. I should start writing them down, in case we ever develop time travel. I'd go back to the gym with a whole Rolodex file filled with remarks, and I'd read them to my date over the course of a couple of hours. Wouldn't she feel awful! Ha ha!

It just occurred to me that she may be out there right now, in our reading audience, in which case I wish to state for the record that I am leading an absolutely wonderful life, and I have been on the Johnny Carson show, and I hope things are equally fine with you.

Twice. I was on Carson twice.

MISC. BATHROOM NEWS

Denver. Sept. 29, 1993: "Portable potties at the construction site at Denver International Airport stink so much that someone has been setting them on fire. Five have been burned in the last month.

"One of the two burned on Monday bore a graffitti warning: 'If you don't fix the toilet paper dispenser, I'll burn down another one. Signed, The Flame Man.'

"Last week, a similar message on a charred toilet warned officials to 'Keep the toilets clean or they'll get burned.' "

COLORS

Colors have a lot more impact on our daily lives than you might think. Here are some things researchers have found out about people and color.

PINK

• Studies show that people almost always believe "pastries from a pink box taste better than from any other color box."

• People are willing to pay more for personal services (e.g., haircuts) performed by people wearing pink.

• Men believe pink products do the best job, but don't want to be seen buying them. If they think someone's watching, they'll choose something brown or blue.

ORANGE

• A quick attention-getter, it communicates informality.

• When it's used on a product, it "loudly proclaims that the product is for everyone."

PALE BLUE

• Pale blue can actually make people feel cooler. Designers often use it in places where men work, "because men feel 5° warmer than a woman in the same room temperature."

• Blue inhibits the desire to eat; in fact, researchers say "people tend to eat less from blue plates."

• Because blue is associated with eating less, marketers use it to sell products like club soda, skim milk, and cottage cheese.

BROWN

• Researchers say a brown suit "a symbol of informality that invites people to open up." It's recommended for reporters and marriage counselors.

GRAY

• Your eye processes gray more easily than any other color.

• Even so, people often become prejudiced against it, especially in areas with a bleak climate.

BRONZE

• This metallic hue gets a negative response. Researchers say it's "useful when rejection is desired."

GREEN

It's used to sell vegetables and chewing gum. But people avoid using it to sell meat, because it reminds consumers of mold.

Red is rarely used on ice cream packages, because it reminds people of heat.

FIRST FILMS

Stars like Madonna would probably just as soon you forgot about what they were doing before they hit it big. But Jami Bernard didn't. She wrote a book called First Films, *which we used as a reference to write this piece.*

TOM SELLECK

First Film: *Myra Breckinridge* (1970)

The Role: In his 17 seconds onscreen, Selleck plays an unnamed talent agent (listed as "The Stud" in the credits) opposite Mae West, the star of the film, who wants to help him find "a position." West discovered Selleck in a Pepsi commercial, and had him cast in the bit part.

HARRISON FORD

First Film: *Dead Heat on a Merry-Go-Round* (1966)

The Role: 24-year old Ford plays an unnamed bellhop who appears in only one scene, in which con man James Coburn gets some information from him and then refuses to give him a tip. The part is so small that Ford is not even listed in the credits.

Memorable Line: "Paging Mr. Ellis..."

MADONNA

First Film: *A Certain Sacrifice* (1979)

The Role: In this Super 8-mm student film, Madonna plays a minor character named Bruna, who shows her breasts, has "simulated" group sex, and gets smeared with a dead man's blood. The film is so bad that the home video version opens with a disclaimer warning the viewer of the film's "technical inconsistancies."

Memorable Line: "I'm a do-do girl, and I'm looking for my do-do boy."

JEFF GOLDBLUM

First Film: *Death Wish* (1974)

The Role: Goldblum plays "Freak #1," one of three unnamed punks who break into Charles Bronson's house, kill his wife, and rape his daughter. Bronson spends the rest of the film (and three se-

---

IRS workers suffer fewer assaults on the job than workers in any other govt. agency.

quels) gunning down punks on the streets of New York.

Memorable Line: "Don't jive, mother, you know what we want!"

KEVIN COSTNER

First Film: *Sizzle Beach, USA* (1974).

The Role: John Logan, a wealthy rancher. This film is about three big-breasted women who share a house in Malibu. The girls exercise and perform household chores while topless. One of them, Dit, falls in love with Costner's character (Costner also played a corpse in *The Big Chill*, but all of his scenes were cut out.)

Memorable Line: "L.A. women seem to be very impressed with money."

TOM CRUISE

First Film: *Endless Love* (1981).

The Role: Cruise plays Billy the teen arsonist, who gives the film's costar, Martin Hewitt, the idea of burning down Brooke Shield's house in order to act as a hero and win the respect of her parents.

Memorable Line: "When I was eight years old I was into arson."

SYLVESTER STALLONE

First Film: *A Party at Kitty and Stud's*, 1970 (Later renamed "The Italian Stallion" to cash in on Stallone's fame).

The Role: In this pre-Rocky soft-core porno flick, Stallone plays Stud, a frisky playboy with big hair (and small muscles) who spends much of the film entirely nude except for a medallion around his neck and a wristwatch...though he never actually engages in intercourse.

Memorable Line: "Mmmmm."

Can't Get No Respect

Stallone never lived his blue movie down. According to *Esquire* magazine, "Even when *Rocky* won the Oscar for best picture of 1976...the [only] Stallone movie in demand for the private screening rooms of Bel Air and Beverly Hills was the soft-core porn film he'd made when it was the only work he could get."

MYTH-PRONUNCIATION

It's surprising how many of our words are references to gods that we've never heard of. Here are some of the characters in Greek and Roman mythology we refer to daily.

Cereal: named after Ceres, the Roman goddess of grain and agriculture.

Atlas: One of the Greek Titans banished by Zeus when they sided with his son against him. Atlas was condemned to carry the world on his shoulders. That scene was popular with early map-makers, who regularly put it on the covers of their books of maps. The books themselves eventually became known as atlases.

Panic: Named after the Greek god Pan, who was believed to howl and shriek in the middle of the night. Greeks who heard these noises often *panicked*.

Hygiene: Inspired by Hygeia, the Greek goddess that brings good health.

Panacea: The Roman goddess that cures diseases.

Tantalize: Tantalus was a Greek God who was punished by the other gods. He was forced to stand in a pool of water up to his chin, but when he lowered his head to drink, the water receded just out of reach. The same was true with food: whenever he reached to pick a piece of fruit from a tree, the wind blew them just out of reach. The *tantalizing* food filled him with desire, but was completely unobtainable.

Siren: The Greeks believed the Sirens were women who called to passing sailors with their beautiful singing voices. Sailors couldn't resist them; in fact, men were driven mad by the songs, and dashed their ships on the nearby rocks in their frenzy to get closer.

Helium: This element, found in the gaseous atmosphere of the sun, is named after Helios, the Greek god of the sun.

Iridescent: Named after Iris, the Greek goddess of the rainbow.

Slow Learner: President Woodrow Wilson couldn't read until he was 11 years old.

Erotic: Named after Eros, the Greek god of...you guessed it: love.

Brownie: These cousins of the Girl Scouts are named after the Celtic *brownies*, small, brown-cloaked fairies that perform household chores while the family sleeps.

Aphrodisiac: named after Aphrodite, the Greek goddess of love. Her specialty: stirring up feelings of desire among the other gods.

Ghouls: From the Arabic word *ghul*, which was an evil spirit that robbed tombs and ate corpses. Today the name is given to anyone with an unhealthy interest in the deceased.

Lethargy: Named after the mythical Greek river of forgetfulness, *Lethe*.

Aegis: Originally the name of the shield of Zeus; today anything that's protected by someone else is said to be under its aegis.

Money: Named after Juno Moneta, the Roman goddess of money.

SPACE-FILLER: MONEY FACTS

• Ancient Sparta had a creative way of preventing capital flight: they made their coins so large and heavy that it was almost impossible to take them out of the country.

• The British Pound Sterling, originally composed of 240 silver pennies, really did weigh a pound.

• The Greek word *drachma* originally meant "handful."

• Why were gold and silver so widely used in coins? They were rare, valuable, and didn't deteriorate or rust. They were also pretty to look at—which historians say was no small consideration.

• U.S. law requires that the words "liberty," "United States of America," "E Pluribus Unum," and "In God We Trust" be inscribed on all coins.

• Biggest and smallest coins in history: the 1644 Swedish *ten-daler* coin (43.4 pounds), and the 1740 Nepalese silver *quarter-dam* (1/14,000 of an ounce).

• Biggest and smallest bills in history: the 14th-century Chinese *one-kwan* note (9 by 13 inches) and the 1917 Rumanian *ten-bani* note (1-1/2 square inches).

John Quincy Adams once said, "There never was a democracy yet that did not commit suicide."

3 WEIRD MEDICAL CONDITIONS

You never know what's going to happen to you, right? Like, you might get stuck on that seat, have to call 911 and wind up in the next edition of the Bathroom Reader*...Or you might find you've got one of these conditions. Don't laugh—it could happen to YOU!*

FOREIGN ACCENT SYNDROME

When: April, 1993
Where: Worcester, Mass
Headline: *Car Wreck Leaves American Speaking Like a Frenchman*
News Report: "A 46-year-old Massachusetts man walked away from a car accident with an unexpected problem: he spoke with a French accent.

"'At first it bothered me very much because I can't make myself well-understood,' said the man, who asked not to be identified, in a phone interview. He said he had no experience with a foreign language and had never even traveled farther than New Jersey from his home in Worcester."

MARY HART DISEASE

When: July 11,1992
Where: New York City
Headline: *TV Co-Host's Voice Triggers Seizures*
News Report: "A neurologist reports in today's *New England Journal of Medicine* that a woman got epileptic seizures by hearing the voice of 'Entertainment Tonight' co-host Mary Hart.

"Symptoms included an upset feeling in the pit of her stomach, a sense of pressure in her head, and mental confusion. 'It was very dramatic,' said her doctor, who studied the seizures. 'She would rub her stomach, hold her head, and then she would look confused and out of it.'

"The woman has not had any major seizures of this type since she stopped watching the syndicated TV show."

Q. Who designed Italy's national flag?   A. Napoleon.

VGE—VIDEO GAME EPILEPSY

When: April, 1991
Where: America and Japan
Headline: A Case of Nintendo Epilepsy
News Report: "On screen the aliens get zapped and enemy helicopters crash and burn. But people playing video games do not expect to get hurt. Most do not, but a few wind up with a case of video game epilepsy (VGE).

"A team of Japanese neurologists recently described the problem in an issue of Developmental Medicine and Child Neurology. They looked at five boys and two girls, ages 4 to 13, who suffered from headaches, convulsions and blurred vision while playing games. The convulsive responses lasted only a few minutes and, in some cases, happened only during a particular scene in a particular game.

"Parents can prevent VGE. A letter in the New England Journral of Medicine reports a similar incident of 'Nintendo epilepsy' in a 13-year-old girl. The doctor discussed the options with her and the parents: abstention from Nintendo or anti-convulsion drugs.

"The family chose the drugs, since they felt she would not be able to resist Nintendo's lure."

...AND NOW FOR SOME "STRANGE DEATHS"

February 30. When Augustus Caesar became emperor, February had 29 days in regular years and 30 days in leap years. Though the calendar had 365 days, leap years came every three years—which gradually threw it out of sync with the movement of the sun. Augustus fixed this, ordering that leap years come every four years instead. While he was at it, he decided to add a day to August, the month named after him. So he shortened February to 28 days, and lengthened August to 31 days.

Mauch Chunk, Pennsylvania. Jim Thorpe was one of the world's most famous athletes. But he was penniless when he died in 1953. His estate couldn't pay for the memorial his widow felt he deserved, so she asked his home state, Oklahoma, to foot the bill. When they refused, she offered to bury him in any U.S. town that would change its name to Jim Thorpe. The people of Mauch Chunk accepted the offer, and the town became Jim Thorpe, PA.

Q. What's the only animal on Earth with one ear?   A. The praying mantis.

DOROTHY PARKER SEZ...

*Wisecracks from one of America's
all-time sharpest female wits:*

"Hollywood money isn't money. It's congealed snow, melts in your hand, and there you are."

"You can lead a horticulture ...but you can't make her think."

"If all the girls who attended the Yale prom were laid end to end—I wouldn't be a bit surprised."

"Wit has truth in it. Wise-cracking is simply calisthenics with words."

"The only *ism* Hollywood believes in is plagiarism."

"The two most beautiful words in the English language are 'check enclosed.'"

"That would be a good thing for them to cut on my tombstone: 'Wherever she went, including here, it was against her better judgement.'"

"This is not a novel to be tossed aside lightly; it should be thrown with great force."

"Most good women are hidden treasures who are safe because nobody looks for them."

"I misremember who first was cruel enough to nurture the cocktail party into life. But perhaps it would be not too much to say, in fact it would be not enough to say, that it was not worth the trouble."

"Excuse me, everybody, I have to go to the bathroom. I really have to telephone, but I'm too embarrassed to say so."

"One more drink and I'd have been under the host."

"You can't teach an old dogma new tricks."

"The best way to keep children at home is to make the home atmosphere pleasant and let the air out of the tires."

"His voice was as intimate as the rustle of sheets."

"These young writers...are worth watching. Not reading; just watching."

CANDY BITS

It occurs to us that reading this stuff is sort of like getting a sugar rush from candy. An "info-rush." Empty calories of addictive information, which fill you up quick but still leave you craving more.

REESE'S PEANUT BUTTER CUPS. H. B. Reese was an employee of the Hershey Chocolate Company. In 1923 he quit and opened his own candy factory in the same town.

KRAFT CARAMELS. During the Depression, Joseph Kraft started making caramels. He didn't particularly like candy; he just needed another dairy product for cheese salesmen to carry on their routes. The product succeeded becasuse grocers needed a summer substitute for chocolate, which melted in the heat.

JUJUBES. Named after the jujube berry, which grows in the tropics. It isn't clear why—the jujube *isn't* an ingredient in the candy.

PEZ. Invented in 1927 by Eduard Haas, an Austrian anti-smoking fanatic who marketed peppermint-flavored PEZ as a cigarette substitute. The candy gets its name from the German word for peppermint, *pfefferminz*. Haas brought the candy to the U.S. in 1952. It bombed, so he reintroduced it as a children's toy, complete with cartoon heads and fruity flavors that kids liked. (One of the most secretive companies in the United States, PEZ doesn't have a company archivist or historian—and won't even disclose who currently owns the company.)

POP ROCKS. In 1956, William Mitchell, a General Foods chemist, was looking for a way to make instant carbonated soda pop by trapping carbon dioxide in hard candy tablets. One afternoon he popped some nuggets he was experimenting with into his mouth...and felt them pop. No one at General Foods could think of a use for the substance, so it was shelved for almost twenty years. But in 1975 it was introduced as Pop Rocks—and became the hottest selling candy in history. Between 1975 and 1980, more than *500 million* packets were sold... and then in 1980 they were suddenly withdrawn from the market. Reason: A pervasive urban myth—that "Mikey" of Life cereal fame had washed down a handful of pop rocks with a bottle of soda and exploded— turned concerned parents against the product. Pop Rocks were re-introduced in 1987, but sales have never reached 1970s levels.

21,203 Japanese citizens were arrested for "the illegal sale or abuse of paint thinner" in 1993.

EAT YOUR VITAMINS!

You've heard about vitamins since you were a little kid—but how much do you really know about them (besides the fact that they come in little pills)? Here's some food for thought, from BRI member John Dollison.

B ACKGROUND. The cells in your body are constantly converting digested fats, proteins, and carbohydrates into energy, new tissue and bone cells. Unfortunately, they can't perform this task alone—they need help from certain catalyst chemicals that your body can't produce (or can't produce in sufficient quantities). You have to get these chemicals—called *vitamins*— from your food.

VITAMIN HISTORY

• Long before scientists unlocked the chemical code of vitamins, it was generally understood that eating certain foods would prevent specific diseases. One example: In the 18th century people discovered that adding citrus fruits to their diet could prevent scurvy, a disease whose symptoms included internal hemorrhaging and extreme weakness. In the 19th century, it was proven that substituting unpolished rice for polished rice would prevent beriberi, whose symptoms included paralysis and anemia.

• No one understood the relationship between these foods and the diseases they cured until 1906, when the British biochemist Frederick Hopkins proved that in addition to proteins, carbohydrates, fats, minerals, and water, foods also contained what he called "accessory factors"—substances that the body needed to convert food into chemical forms that the body could use.

• In 1911 Casimir Funk, a Polish chemist, discovered that the beriberi-preventing substance in unpolished rice was an *amine*, a type of nitrogen-containing compound. Funk understood that the amine was vital to proper body function, so he named it "vitamine" (for "vital amine").

• A year later he and Hopkins proposed the Vitamin Hypothesis of Deficiency, which theorized that the absence of a particular vitamin in the diet could lead to certain diseases. By depriving animals of different types of foods in strictly controlled experiments, scientists identified numerous other similar substances.

48% of Americans say they'd donate the organs of deceased relatives *without* their permission.

• But they still didn't understand their chemical makeup, so they couldn't give the proper scientific names. Instead, they just called them all vitamines, and kept them separate by assigning a different letter of the alphabet to each new substance they discovered. They soon realized that many of the vitamins weren't amines at all—but by that time, the word "vitamine" had become so popular that they couldn't change it. So they just dropped the "e."

VITAMIN BASICS

• Scientists divide vitamins into two different types: water-soluble (the B-complex vitamins and vitamin C), and fat-soluble (A, D, E, and K).

• Your body can't store water-soluble vitamins very well, so if you eat more than your RDA, or Recommended Dietary Allowance, most of them pass out of your body in your urine. That's why it's important to eat them every day.

• Fat-soluble vitamins, however, are more easily stored: Your liver tissue can store large amounts of vitamins A and D, and vitamin E is stored in body fat and reproductive organs.

KNOW YOUR VITAMINS

Vitamin A (retinol).
Sources: Animal fats and dairy products, green leafy vegetables, and carrots.
Why it's needed: Because it is a component of the pigment in the retinas of your eyes, vitamin A is necessary for good vision. It also helps keep the immune system healthy, and is necessary for the proper functioning of most organs.

Vitamin B complex (B1 [thiamine], B2 [riboflavin], B3 [niacin and niacinamide], B5 [pantothenic acid], biotin, folacin, and B12 [cobalamin]).
Sources: All meats, cereals, grains, green vegetables, dairy products, and brewer's yeast.
Why it's needed: B vitamins are necessary for healthy skin, and for the normal operation of a number of cell processes, including digestion, respiration, blood cell and bone marrow production, and metabolism. They're also needed by the nervous system.

That's slow: The average drop of Heinz ketchup leaves the bottle travelling at 25 miles *per year.*

Vitamin C (ascorbic acid).

Sources: Fresh fruits and vegetables, especially citrus fruits and tomatoes.

Why it's needed: Your body uses vitamin C to heal wounds and bone fractures; build tendons, and other tissues; and it helps you absorb iron. It's also needed for healthy teeth, gums, and blood.

Vitamin D.

Sources: Your skin produces it when exposed to sunlight; also found in eggs, butter, and fish that have fat distributed through their tissue (salmon, tuna, sardines, oysters, etc).

Why it's needed: Your body uses it to regulate its absorption of calcium and phosphorus, which makes it essential for proper bone and cartilage formation.

Vitamin E.

Sources: Green, leafy vegetables, wheat germ oil, margarine, rice.

Why it's needed: Vitamin E is one of the least understood vitamins, but it is known to be necessary for proper reproduction and prevention of muscular dystrophy in laboratory rats. It may also impair neuromuscular functions.

Vitamin K.

Sources: Not made by the body itself, but by organisms that live in our intestinal tract. Also found in yogurt, egg yolks, leafy green vegetables, and fish liver oils.

Why it's needed: Enables your body to synthesize the proteins required for the proper clotting of blood. Also helps reduce excessive menstrual flow in women.

HEALTHY HINTS

• It's a good idea to wash your vegetables before you eat them—but don't soak them. You'll lose a lot of the water-soluable vitamins (B and C) if you do.

• If you don't eat fresh vegetables within a week of buying them, you're better off buying frozen vegetables. Fresh vegetables lose their vitamins over time, and after about a week in your refrigerator they have fewer vitamins than frozen ones. And they almost always have more vitamins than canned vegetables.

Male moths can smell female moths from as far as 7 miles away.

MYTH AMERICA

Some of the stories we recognize as Americans myths today were taught as history for many years. This one, about the "father of our country," was reverentially passed down for more than 150 years.

MYTH: Young George Washington chopped down a cherry tree. When his father found it and asked who was responsible, George stepped forward and said, "I cannot tell a lie, father—I did." The elder Washington was so moved by George's honesty that he didn't punish his son.

BACKGROUND: It's hard to believe today, but as late as the 1950s, this tale was still being taught in school as fact. It first appeared in a biography of Washington written by Parson Mason Locke Weems, called *The Life of George Washington with Curious Anecdotes: Equally Honorable to Himself and Exemplary to His Young Countrymen.* Here's the original version of the story:

> "George," cried his father, "do you know who killed this beautiful little cherry tree yonder in the garden?" This was a tough question: and George staggered under it for a moment; but quickly recovered himself: and looking at his father, with the sweet face of youth brightened with the inexpressible charm of all-conquering truth, he bravely cried out, "I can't tell a lie, Pa; you know I can't tell a lie, I did it with my hatchet." — "Run to my arms, you dearest boy," cried his father in transports, "run to my arms; glad am I, George, that you killed my tree: for you have paid me for it a thousand fold. Such an act of heroism in my son is more worth than a thousand trees, though blossomed with silver, and their fruits of purest gold."

THE TRUTH: Weems made it up. The book was first published in 1800—and was a huge best-seller in its time—but the story about the cherry tree didn't show up until the fifth edition, in 1806. Weems's only supporting documentation was his own statement that the tale was "too true to be doubted."

Weems didn't claim to be much of an historian to begin with; he was just capitalizing on an obvious market. "There's a great deal of money lying in the bones of old George," he reportedly told his publisher.

Heavy thought: Your skin accounts for 16% of your bodyweight.

SIBLING RIVALRY

Brothers who go into business together don't always stay close. In fact, going into business with a relative might be the best way to lose a family. Here are 4 classic cases.

ADIDAS / Adolf & Rudolf Dassler

Background: According to *Everybody's Business*, "Adolf and Rudolf Dassler were the sons of a poor laundress who grew up in the tiny Bavarian milltown of Herzogenerauch, near Nuremburg. Before World War II, they started a factory there to make house slippers, then branched to track shoes and soccer boots."

Rivalry: "They had a violent falling out and after the war went their separate ways. Rudolf left Adidas and started a rival athletic shoe company, Puma. Before long Adidas and Puma—both head-quartered in Herzogenerauch—were battling head-to-head all over the world. When Adolf died in 1978, the two brothers hadn't spoken to each other in 29 years."

GALLO WINE / Ernest, Julio & Joseph Gallo

Background: Ernest, Julio, and Joseph Gallo inherited the family vineyard in 1933 when their father murdered their mother and then committed suicide. 24-year-old Ernest and 23-year-old Julio used their inheritance to start the Gallo Winery. At the same time, they raised their teenage brother, Joseph—who went to work for them as a vineyard manager when he was old enough. After toiling for his brothers for 18 years, Joseph bought a nearby ranch. He grew grapes (which he sold to the Gallo Winery) and raised cattle.

Rivalry: In 1983, Joseph expanded his dairy operation to include Gallo cheese…but his brothers said he was infringing on their trademark, and in 1986 they sued him. Joseph retaliated with a countersuit, claiming that his 1/3 share of his father's inheritance entitled him to 1/3 of the winery. The fight was nasty. During the trial, the winemakers accused Joseph of "running a rat-infested cheese plant;" Joseph shot back that his brothers specialized in making cheap wine for drunks. Ernest and Julio won both suits.

The average American kid aged 5-17 has 3 cavities—down from 11 during the 1940s.

REVLON / Charles, Joseph & Martin Revson

Background: According to *Everybody's Business*: "The cosmetics giant was founded in 1932 by Charles Revson, his older brother Joseph, and Charles Lachman. A younger brother, Martin, joined the firm later. But it was Charles who led the company's drive to the top."

Rivalry: "Joseph left the company in 1955 because he didn't agree with Charles that Revlon should go public. He sold all his stock to the company for $2.5 million. (If he'd waited four years, the stock would have been worth $35 million.) Martin left in 1959 after bitter fights with his older brother. He sued the company, charging that his brother Charles 'engaged in a practice of mistreating executives and abusing them personally.' The brothers didn't speak to each other for 13 years. 'What brother?' Charles once said. 'I don't have a brother.' "

KELLOGG'S / John & William Kellogg

Background: In 1876, 25-year-old Dr. John Harvey Kellogg became head of the Battle Creek Sanitarium. His first official act was to hire his younger brother, William, as "chief clerk." To make the institution's vegetarian food more palatable, the brothers invented a number of foods—including corn flakes. Then they set up a company on the side, manufacturing and distributing their cereal around the country.

Rivalry: John, a world-famous doctor by 1900, insisted that Kellogg's cereals be "health foods." So he forbade the use of white sugar. William just wanted something that would sell...and when he added sugar to the flakes while John was out of the country, the partnership fell apart. "Will set out on his own...in 1906," writes William Poundstone in *Bigger Secrets*. "By 1909 the brothers weren't on speaking terms. Both spent much of the following decade suing each other. These complex legal actions resulted in the ruling that only Will's company could market cereal under the Kellogg's name, and in lifelong mutual enmity for the two brothers." When John Harvey died in 1942, the two hadn't spoken in 33 years.

Quickie: Robert, James & Edward Mead Johnson started *Johnson & Johnson* in an old wallpaper factory. Edward left and started Mead Johnson, which now competes with Johnson & Johnson.

Q & A:
ASK THE EXPERTS

More random questions and answers from America's trivia experts.

CRACKING THE CODE

Q: *How did phone companies assign area codes?*

A: It seems strange that 212 is for New York City, and 213 is for Los Angeles, across the country. But in 1948, assigning area codes had nothing to do with geography; it had to do with how fast people could dial them (not punch them on a touchtone phone, but *dial* them on a rotary phone). The faster numbers—1, 2, and 3—were called "low dial-pull" numbers. They were given to large cities for one simple reason: it saved the phone company money.

"Millions of people called those cities every day. The faster each caller was able to dial his number, the less time the phone company's switching machines would be tied up making the connection…[and] the fewer machines the phone company had to buy.

"Today, the only concern when assigning new area codes is to make them as different as possible form neighboring codes, so people won't confuse the numbers." (From *Know It All!*, by Ed Zotti)

BUG OFF!

Q: *How do flies walk upside down?*

A: A fly has six legs. On each leg there are two little claws that look sort of like a lobster's claws. "Underneath the claws [are] a pair of small web-like fuzzy pads called pulvilli. These are functional suction pads which the fly presses to the surface to squeeze out the air and create enough suction to hold itself up. Thus, with its claws and suction pads, the little pest can walk majestically upside down." (From *How Do Flies Walk Upside Down?*, by Martin M. Goldwyn)

STUMPED

Q: *Can you tell a tree's age by counting the rings on a stump?*

A: Not necessarily. "In temperate climates, a single ring of light and dark wood is usually added each year—but sometimes more than one ring is produced in a growing season, or sometimes no ring at all. If a tree loses most of its leaves from a severe insect attack or drought, it begins producing dense wood and thus completes a ring. Then if a new crop of leaves grows again that same season, another ring will be formed. In a very dry year the tree might not grow at all, and no ring would be added that year." (From *Do Elephants Swim?*, compiled by Robert M. Jones)

LOVE MATCH

Q: *Why is zero called Love in tennis?*
A: It has nothing to do with affairs of the heart. "Love is really a distortion of the French word *oeuf*, which means egg, as in goose egg." (From *The Book of Totally Useless Information*, by Don Voorhees)

ILLOGICAL

Q: *Where did the guys who created "Star Trek" come up with the name of Spock's home planet, Vulcan?*
A: Believe it or not, astronomers were sure there actually *was* a planet called Vulcan somewhere between the planet Mercury and the sun. "Its existence—first proposed by French astronomer Urbain Jean Joseph Leverrier in 1845—was hypothesized to explain a discrepancy in Mercury's orbit. Vulcan was even reported to have been observed once, but the observation was never confirmed. Einstein's general theory of relativity explained Mercury's odd orbit, and the existence of Vulcan was discredited." (From *The Book of Answers*, by Barbara Berliner)

DARK SECRETS

Q: *What is espresso?*
A: "Espresso is Italian for 'quick,' and it refers to a particular way of brewing coffee. Various espresso machines have been devised, but the basic idea always is to heat water under pressure above the boiling point and then force it rapidly through the ground coffee. The hotter the water, the more flavor is extracted from the coffee. The shorter the brewing time, the less bitter the coffee." Espresso also refers to dark-roasted types of coffee that make the best espresso brew. (From *Why Do Men Have Nipples*, by Katherine Dunn).

Crowd control: Purse-snatching is punishable by death in Haiti.

AUNT LENNA'S PUZZLES

More conversations with my puzzle-loving auntie. Answers are on page 226.

My Aunt Lenna is quite talkative. One day she took a cab and chattered on at the driver incessantly. Finally, the man apologetically explained that his hearing aid was off, and without it he wasn't able to make out a word she said. She stopped talking for the rest of the trip, but when she got to her destination, she realized she'd been tricked.

How did she realize this?

Aunt Lenna was chuckling.

"What's so funny?" I asked her.

"Just a silly little puzzle," she said.

"Tell me."

"Okay. See if you can write the number *one hundred* using six 9's."

"You mean, 9-9-9-9-9-9?"

"That's not how you do it, but those are the numbers."

How can I do it?

"Such a pity," said Aunt Lenna.

"What?" I asked.

"Oh, my friend's wife passed away. It was quite sudden. He kissed her before he left for work, shut the apartment door, walked to the elevator and pressed the ground-floor button. He immediately knew his wife had died. Very sad."

"Wait a minute," I stopped her. "How did he know she was dead? Is he psychic?"

Aunt Lenna shook her head.

"Well, then what happened?"

What did happen?

Forest Fact: A beaver can chop down as many as 216 trees per year.

Physics isn't my strong suit, so I was stumped when Aunt Lenna asked me this question: "Suppose there are three men on one side of a river, and someone fires a gun on the other side. One man sees the smoke from the gun; another hears the gunfire; and the third sees the bullet hit the water by his feet. Which of them knows the gun was fired first?"

Do you know the answer?

Aunt Lenna went for a walk by the water, and came back quite upset.

"What's the matter?" I asked.

"Oh, it was terrible! There was a woman standing on the pier. There were tears in her eyes. She was very angry, and she seemed indignant over some injury that had been inflicted upon her.

"I heard her cry, 'You monster of cruelty! I've stayed with you too long. You've hurt the very foundations of my being! I've endured your tortures day after day. The first time we met, your ease and polish attracted me to you... and when you became my own, my friends were quite envious. But now...take a look at what I've suffered for your sake! You keep me from advancing myself! My standing in society has been ruined by you! If we'd never met, I might have walked in peace...but now...now we part forever!' "

"And I declare, nephew, she threw something in the water. I rushed over and ..."

"Aunt Lenna! Did you call the police?!"

"Don't be silly."

"But I don't understand. Who...or what did she throw off the pier?"

Do you know?

"I went to a family reunion the other day," Aunt Lenna told me. There were 2 grandfathers, 2 grandmothers, 3 mothers, 3 fathers, 3 daughters, 3 sons, 2 mothers-in-law, 2 fathers-in-law, a son-in-law, a daughter-in-law, 2 brothers, and 2 sisters. Can you guess how many people there were?"

I thought for a moment. "Mm-m-m...I'd say, 10."

"That's right!" Lenna said, amazed. "How did you know?"

How did I get that number?

Fleas jump 130 times their own height—the equivalent of a human jumping a 65 story building.

FAMILIAR PHRASES

More origins of common phrases.

TO UNDERMINE

Meaning: To weaken, usually secretly and gradually.

Origin: "The term dates from the fourteenth century, when it was common practice for besiegers to tunnel under the foundations of a castle, either to enter it or to weaken the walls." The tunnels were called "mines," and the damaged walls were considered "undermined." By the fifteenth century, any underhanded method used to defeat an enemy had become known as "undermining." (From *Fighting Words*, by Christine Ammer)

THROW SOMEONE TO THE WOLVES

Meaning: Abandon someone; sacrifice someone to save yourself.

Origin: The term comes from the Victorian age, when it was popular for printmakers to depict horse-drawn sleighs at full gallop, chased by packs of wolves. "Traditionally, if the wolves got too close, one of the passengers was thrown out to lighten the sleigh, in hopes that the rest of the company could escape while the animals were devouring the victim." No one's sure if this really happened, but it resulted in a "durable metaphor." (From *Loose Cannons and Red Herrings*, by Robert Claiborne)

TO TURN OVER A NEW LEAF

Meaning: Get a fresh start; change your ways.

Origin: Believe it or not, the expression has nothing to do with leaves from a plant; it refers to the "leaves" (pages) in a *book*—"the turning to a blank page in a [journal or] exercise book where one can start one's work anew. Figuratively, such a fresh start gives the possibility of learning a new lesson in the book of life's principles: a chance to begin again and mend one's ways." (From *Getting to the Roots*, by Martin Manser)

Pigs and humans are the only animals that get sunburned.

PRIMETIME PROVERBS

TV comments about everyday life. From Primetime Proverbs, *by Jack Mingo and John Javna*

ON RAISING KIDS:

Fred Sanford: "Didn't you learn anything being my son? Who do you think I'm doing this all for?"
Lamont Sanford: "Yourself."
Fred:"Yeah, you learned something."

—Sanford and Son

Sophia: "She's always tellin' me what to do!"
Rocco: "Don't worry. My daughter treats me the same way."
Sophia: "Kids. Once they're over fifty, they think they know everything."

—The Golden Girls

ON PETS:

"He who lies down with dogs gets up with fleas."

—Herman Munster,
The Munsters

Morticia Addams: "Now Pugsley darling, who could be closer than a boy and his mother?"
Pugsley Addams: "A boy and his octopus?"
Morticia[smiling]: "Hmmm… Perhaps."

—The Addams Family

ON MAKEUP:

"City women is spoiled rotten. All they think about is smearin' themselves with beauty grease. Fancy smellin' renderin's. Why, if you was to hug one of 'em, she'd squirt out of yore arms like a prune pit!"

—Granny,
The Beverly Hillbillies

"I haven't worn makeup in years. It takes away that unnatural look that we girls like."

—Lily Munster,
The Munsters

ON SCIENCE:

"The roots of physical aggression found in the male species are in the DNA molecule itself. In fact, the very letters, dna are an acronym for 'Dames Are Not Aggressors.' "

—Cliff Claven,
Cheers

Aesop, Jr.: "There's no fuel like an old fuel!"
Aesop, Sr.: "Hmmm…I *gas* you're right."

—*The Bullwinkle Show*

Trap 40 fireflies in a jar and they'll generate enough light for you to read by.

FUN WITH ELVIS

*Imagine what a kick it would have been to hang out with the
King at Graceland. Well, it's too late now—but here
are some of the exciting moments you missed.*

AT THE POOL
Want to go for a dip? According to David Adler in *The Life
and Cuisine of Elvis Presley*, "Elvis enjoyed sitting around the
pool eating watermelon hearts. For entertainment while he ate, he
would float flashbulbs in the pool. Then he would take out a .22
and shoot at them. When they were hit, they would flash, and then
sink to the bottom."

ON THE 4th OF JULY
Every Independence Day at Graceland, Elvis had a "fireworks display." His Memphis Mafia split into two teams, put on gloves and
football helmets, and shot fireworks at each other. "They would
level arsenals of rockets and Roman candles at each other and blast
away at point-blank range for hours," says Steve Dunleavy in *Elvis:
What Happened.*

It was all laughs: "I've backed into burning rockets and had my
ass burned half off," laughs Elvis aide Red West. "I've seen Elvis
bending over a giant rocket and watched the thing go off while he
is leaning over it, nearly blowing his fool head off. [My brother]
Sonny carries a scar on his chest to this day where one of us tried to
blow a rocket through him. Roman candles would blow up in our
hands. The house caught fire twice."

DEMOLITION DERBY
When the King was bored, you never knew what might happen.
There was a beautiful little cottage in the corner of the Graceland
property. One day, Elvis decided to demolish it...so he put on a
football helmet and revved up his bulldozer. The only problem: his
father, Vernon Presley, was sitting on the cottage porch.

According to Red West, "[He yelled] 'You better move, Daddy.'
Vernon asks why and Elvis says, 'Because I'm gonna knock the god-
damn house down.' ...Vernon gives one of those looks like 'Oh,
Lordie,' but he doesn't say anything...he just gets up and Elvis

---

The average professional basketball player earned $1,208,000 in 1993.

starts roaring away." To make it more interesting, Elvis and Red set the house on fire while they battered it with heavy machinery.

AT THE MOVIES

The King couldn't just go out to the movies whenever he felt like it—he would have been mobbed. So he rented the whole theater instead. "Elvis had private midnight screenings at the Memphian Theater," writes David Adler. "They were attended by about a hundred of his friends. Admission was free, and so was the popcorn, but you had to watch the movie on Elvis's terms. Elvis made the projectionist repeat his favorite scenes. If the action got slow, such as during a love scene, the projectionist would have to skip to the next good part. Elvis once saw *Dr. Strangelove* three times straight, with a number of scenes repeated so he could figure out exactly what was going on."

"Elvis liked James Bond and *Patton*, and any movie with Peter Sellers. His favorite movie of all time was *The Party*."

WATCHING TV

And, of course, you could always stay home and spend a quiet evening watching TV...as long as Elvis liked the programs. If not, there was a good chance he'd pull out a gun and shoot out the screen. "Honestly," Red West says, "I can't tell you how many television sets went to their death at the hands of Elvis....He would shoot out television sets in hotel rooms and in any one of the houses he had. He shot out a great big one at Graceland, in Memphis, the one he had in his bedroom."

A classic example: One afternoon in 1974, the TV was blaring while Elvis was eating his breakfast. His least favorite singer, Robert Goulet, came on. As Red related: "Very slowly, Elvis finishes what he has in his mouth, puts down his knife and fork, picks up this big mother of a .22 and—boom—blasts old Robert clean off the screen and the television set to pieces....He then puts down the .22, picks up his knife and fork and says, 'That will be enough of that s---,' and then he goes on eating."

Elvis Trivia: On his way to meet Richard Nixon in 1970 (to pose for the famous photo), the King had a sudden craving. He insisted that his driver pull over to buy a dozen honey-glazed donuts; then he polished them off as they drove to the White House.

There are 3 colors of blood: Red, blue (lobsters), and yellow (insects).

MONEY FACTS

A few odds and ends about almost everyone's favorite subject.

T HE FDR DIME
Here's how FDR wound up on our 10¢ coin:
• Franklin D. Roosevelt, who was crippled by polio in 1921, escaped from his disability by swimming whenever he could. One of his favorite swimming holes: Warm Springs, Georgia, a natural spring. In 1926 the future president donated enough money to start a polio foundation at the site, so that other polio sufferers could enjoy the waters too.

• Despite the large donation, the foundation was always running out of money.

• Singer Eddie Cantor (a popular radio personality) knew about Roosevelt's concern for the foundation, and in 1937 he proposed to the president that he ask every American to send a dime to the White House to be used for polio research. Cantor suggested a name for the promotion: The March of Dimes.

• Roosevelt took his suggestion and made the appeal. The public response was enormous: on some days the White House was flooded with as many 150,000 letters containing dimes.

• The president became so closely associated with the March of Dimes that after his death in 1945, Congress voted to create the Roosevelt dime in his honor. The first ones were released to the public on January 30, 1946, Roosevelt's birthday—and the traditional start of the March of Dimes annual fund-raising campaign.

• The vaccine for polio was announced on April 12, 1955, on the ten- year anniversary of Roosevelt's death.

CATTLE CALL

• In about 2,000 B.C., man began trading bronze ingots shaped like cows (which had about the same value as a real cow). The value of these coins was measured by weighing them—which meant that any time a transaction was made, someone had to get out a scale to measure the value of the money.

• Around 800 B.C., the Lydians of Anatolia—who traded bean-shaped ingots made of a gold-silver alloy called *electrum*—began

---

A productive life: A queen ant can lay 30,000 eggs a month for up to 10 years.

stamping the ingot's value onto its face. This eliminated the need for a scale and made transactions much easier.

• But switching to countable coins from weighted ones increased the chances of fraud—precious metals could be chipped or shaved off the edges of the coins. One of the techniques designed to prevent this is still evident on modern U.S. coins—even though they no longer contain precious metals. What is it? Feel the edges of a dime or a quarter. Those grooves were originally a way to tell if any metal had been shaved off.

ARE YOUR BILLS REAL?

Here are some U.S. paper currency anti-counterfeit features you probably didn't know about:

√ The currency paper is fluorescent under ultraviolet light.

√ The ink is slightly magnetic—not enough for household magnets to detect, but enough for special machines to notice.

√ The paper has thousands of tiny microscopic holes "drilled" into it. Reason: when the money is examined under a microscope, tiny points of light shine through.

COIN FACTS

• The Director of the Mint gets to decide who appears on our coins, but the decisions have to be approved by the Treasury Secretary—and changes on any coin can't be made more than once every 25 years.

• Prior to the assassination of President Lincoln, it was a long-standing tradition *not* to have portraits on U.S. coins. Symbols of liberty were used instead. The only reason Lincoln's face got the nod: he was considered a human embodiment of liberty.

• If you design a portrait that gets used on a coin, you get to have your initials stamped in the coin alongside it. That's normally an innocuous addition to the coin, but there have been exceptions: When the Roosevelt dime was released in 1946, some concerned anti-communists thought the initials "JS" (for designer John Sinnock) stood for Joseph Stalin. And when the John F. Kennedy memorial half-dollar was issued in 1964, some conspiracy theorists thought the letters "GR" (for Gilroy Roberts) were a tiny rendition of the communist hammer and sickle. In both instances, the U.S. Mint refused to change the design.

What a kisser: A full-grown hippo's lips are about 2 feet wide.

OOPS! 2

More blunders to make you feel superior.

A SLIGHT MISUNDERSTANDING

"At the end of World War II, the Allies issued the Potsdam telegram demanding that the Imperial Japanese armies surrender forthwith. The Japanese government responded with an announcement that it was withholding immediate comment on the ultimatum, pending 'deliberations' by the Imperial government.

"Unfortunately, the official Japanese government news agency, in the heat of issuing this critical statement in English, decided to translate the Japanese word that means 'withholding comment for the time being' as 'deliberately ignore.'

"A number of scholars have suggested that if the ultimatum had not been so decisively rejected, President Truman might never have authorized the A-bomb attacks on Hiroshima and Nagasaki."

—From *David Frost's Book of the World's Worst Decisions*

CONTROL FREAKS

"The March 21, 1983 issue of *Time* magazine featured Lee Iacocca on the cover, along with a tease for Henry Kissinger's 'New Plan for Arms Contol.' After two hundred thousand of the covers had been printed, someone noticed a typographical error—the 'r' had been left out of 'Control.' It was printed as *Contol*.

"There had never been a misspelling on a *Time* cover in the history of the magazine. They stopped the presses, corrected the error, and withdrew all the *Contol* covers. The goof cost *Time* $100,000, and 40% of the newsstand copies went on sale a day late."

—From *The Emperor Who Ate the Bible*, by Scott Morris

THE WICKED BIBLE

In 1631, two London printers left one word out of an official edition of the Bible. The mistake cost them 3,000 pounds and nearly led to their imprisonment. The word was "not;" they left it out of the Seventh Commandment, which then told readers, "Thou shalt commit adultery." The book became known as "the Wicked Bible."

Mark Twain coined the phrase "gossip column" in 1893.

TRICK-OR-TREAT

"Two Illinois skydivers, Brian Voss, 30, and Alfred McInturff, 50, were tossing a pumpkin back and forth on their 1987 Halloween skydive when they accidentally dropped it from 2,200 feet. It crashed through the roof of Becky Farrar's home, leaving orange goo all over her kitchen walls and breaking the kichen table. Said Farrar: 'If this had happened an hour earlier, we would have been sitting at the table having lunch.' "

—From *News of the Weird*

NAKED TRUTH

PORTLAND, ORE. "Amtrak apologized and issued refunds to dozens of junior high students who took a train trip with a group of rowdy grown-ups playing strip poker.

"About half the 93 members of Portland's Robert Gray Middle School band and choir said they had to ride in a car with a smoking section and were subjected to rude comments from adults who took their clothes off in a poker game. The students were returning from a music competition in San Jose, California. Amtrak has promised to send the group a refund check for $4,830."

—AP, June 23, 1993

BACKFIRE

On August 7, 1979, a jet plane in the Spanish Air Force shot itself down when its own gunfire ricocheted off a hillside target, flew back, and hit the plane during field maneuvers.

GOOD LUCK?

"At a dinner party in the late 19th century, French playwright Victolen Sardou spilled a glass of wine. The woman sitting next to him poured salt on the stain, and Sardou picked up some of the salt and threw it over his shoulder for luck. The salt went into the eye of a waiter about to serve him some chicken. The waiter dropped the platter, and the family dog pounced on the chicken. A bone lodged in the dog's throat, and when the son of the host tried to pull it out, the dog bit him. His finger had to be amputated."

—John Berendt, *Esquire* magazine

President John Adams regularly referred to George Washington as "an old muttonhead."

READER'S ARTICLE OF THE YEAR

We get all kinds of articles and suggestions from readers, of course...some are very interesting, some are pretty weird...but this one is special. It's got a little bit of everything we look for in a Bathroom Reader *piece: an "origin" story, some gossip, pop history, the "gee whiz" factor, and so on. It was written by humorist Leo Rosten, and it's from his book* The Power of Positive Nonsense.

A MISCONCEPTION
"Any man who hates dogs and babies can't be all bad."

Sure, sure, I know: Umpteen anthologies of quotations credit this to W. C. Fields. But he did not say it. He may have said, "A woman drove me to drink, and I never even wrote to thank her," or "How do I like children? Boiled," or "Never give a sucker an even break." But he did not come up with "Any man who hates dogs and babies can't be all bad." The line was uttered *about* Fields.

ROSTEN IN HOLLYWOOD
The place was Hollywood. The time: 1939. I was working on a solemn sociological...study of the movie colony. One day, to my surprise, I received a telegram from the Masquers' Club, inviting me to be their guest at a banquet in honor of W. C. Fields.

I was delighted. I was transported. I revered Mr. Fields as the funniest misanthrope our land ever produced. And I knew that the Masquer dinners of homage were in fact "roasts" in which celebrated wits eviscerated the guest of honor with sparkling insults...and steamy boudoir revelations which, if uttered on any other occasion, could provide an airtight case for a lawsuit worth millions in damages for character assassination. I accepted the invitation.

THE MASQUERS' CLUB
I appeared at the Masquers with a wide grin and anticipatory chuckles. The lobby was packed with moviedom elite: stars, producers, directors, writers. All male, all famous, all treating me, as I circulated amongst them, the way princes of the blood treat a peas-

ant with anemia. I might have been made of glass, so easily did the glances of the celebrated go right through me. But I did not mind. I was very young, and felt lucky to be a guest on Parnassus. My heart thumped faster as I recognized noble Spencer Tracy, great Goldwyn, wonderful William Wyler, incomparable Ben Hecht. And was that Errol Flynn holding court in the corner?...I do not know. I was not sure, to tell you the truth, because I was so excited that my vision and my imagination were playing leapfrog.

TO THE STAGE

Suddenly I heard my name blaring, over and over, from loudspeakers, and an agitated voice pleading that I report to the desk "at once!"...I ploughed through the glittering assemblage to the distant desk, where I was told...that I was "damn late" for one who would be seated "on the dais!" A majordomo swiftly (and sourly) led me backstage. There I beheld Mr. Fields, already red-nosed from fiery waters, surrounded by illustrious roasters: Groucho Marx, Bob Hope, Jack Benny, George Burns, Edgar Bergen, Milton Berle....It was they, I assure you, in the flesh.

"Time to line up!" called a praetorian guard.

A hotel Hannibal began to recite name after hallowed name. Mine, unhallowed, was last.

"Proceed to the dais!" blared another....Someone flung heavy red draperies aside.

As we marched through the opening and across the stage, the glittering audience rose to its feet...applauding Marx, Benny, Hope, reaching a crescendo for Fields, hailing Berle, Bergen, Burns—until I appeared, last, certainly least, pale, brave, anonymous. The applause seeped away like sand in a net of gauze....Amidst the anticlimax of my reception, we all sat down to break bread.

THE NIGHTMARE

The dinner was excellent, the wines ambrosial, the brandy and cigars sublime. Then William Collier, Sr., rose to conduct the festivities. He received an ovation, which he deserved. A renowned M.C. and wit, he orated a barrage of dazzling, scathing yet affectionate ribs about our...guest of honor. The audience roared in counterpoint. And to each barbed line, Mr. Fields responded with

Jesse James Jr. played his famous father in two Hollywood films.

an evil grin, a leering grunt and another sip of alcoholic disdain.

Mr. Collier completed his backhanded eulogy. A tornado of applause. Then the masterful M.C. proclaimed: "Our first speaker to 'honor' Bill Fields is..." (he consulted his prep sheet and, there is no denying it, winced) "Dr. Leo Boston—no, I guess it's Rosten." It would be wrong to say that I could not believe my ears; the full measure of my horror lay in the fact that I did. I sat paralyzed. This could not be. It was a dream. It was a nightmare....It took the elbow of Red Skelton, jabbing into my ribs, to propel me to my feet.

"SAY SOMETHIN!" ?

The "applause" which had greeted Mr. Collier's garbled recitation of my name would not have awakened a mouse. Now, my erectness and visibility compounded my shame, for the faces of that auditorium broke into frowns of confusion and the many mouths uttered murmurs seeking enlightenment....I prayed for a trap door to open beneath me, or for lightning to strike me dead. Neither happened. Instead, I heard George Burns's hoarse sotto voice: "Say somethin'!" with unmistakable disgust. I gulped—then someone who was hiding in my throat uttered these words: "The only thing I can say about Mr. W. C. Fields, whom I have admired since the day he advanced upon Baby LeRoy with an icepick, is this: Any man who hates dogs and babies can't be all bad."

The appearance of Mae West in a G-string would not have produced a more explosive cachinnation. The laughter was so uproarious, the ovation so deafening, the belly-heavings and table-slapping and shoulder-punchings so vigorous, that I cleverly collapsed onto my chair.

I scarcely remember the rest of that historic night—except that the jokes and gags and needlings of Mr. Fields (who by now resembled a benign Caligula) put all previous celebrity "roasts" to shame. The next morning, the local papers led off their stories about the banquet with my ad lib. The AP and UP flung my remark around the world. CBS and BBC featured the quip on radio. Overnight, I was an international wit.

Alas, God put bitters in the wine of my enflatterment; for ever since then, "Any man who hates dogs and babies can't be all bad" has been credited to—W. C. Fields. Hardly a week passes in which I do not run across some reference to "Fields's immortal crack." But it was mine. Mine, I tell you, mine!

Casanova spent the last 13 years of his life working as a librarian.

OH NO, IT'S MR. BILL

*Comments from William F. Buckley, one of
America's best-known conservatives:*

"I get satisfaction of three kinds. One is creating something, one is being paid for it, and one is the feeling that I haven't just been sitting on my ass all afternoon."

"I would like to take you seriously, but to do so would affront your intelligence."

"Idealism is fine, but as it approaches reality the cost becomes prohibitive."

"I'd rather entrust the government of the United States to the first 400 people listed in the Boston telephone directory than to the faculty of Harvard University."

"Life can't be all bad when for ten dollars you can buy all the Beethoven sonatas and listen to them for ten years."

"I, for one, yearn for the days of the Cold War."

"One must bear in mind that the expansion of federal activity is a form of eating for politicians."

"Kennedy, after all, has lots of glamour. Gregory Peck with an atom bomb in his holster."

"...Any sign of weakness by the Free World increases the appetite of the enemy for more war and more conquest as surely as the progressive revelations of the stripteaser increase the appetite of the lecher."

"All civilized men want peace. And all truly civilized men must despise pacifism."

"In the wake of yet another disappearance of a teen-ager into the mortal coils of the flower world in Greenwich Village, where love is exercised through rape made tolerable by drugs and abstract declarations of fellowship with the North Vietnamese, one wonders anew about the pretensions of progress."

"What has détente done for us except provide a backdrop for the exchange of toasts between American presidents and Communist tyrants?"

THE LATEST THING

Nothing is sacred in the bathroom—go ahead and admit that you owned a pet rock or a mood ring...we understand...confession is good for the soul. And while you're pondering your follies, we'll tell you where they came from.

PAC-MAN. A Japanese import that hit American shores in late 1980, Pac-Man got its name from the word *paku,* which means "eat" in Japanese. The video game was so popular that Pac-Man was named *Time* magazine's "man" of the year in 1982. That year, Americans pumped $6 *billion* worth of quarters into Pac-Man's mouth, more than they spent in Las Vegas casinos and movie theatres combined.

MOOD RINGS. The temperature-sensitive jewelry that supposedly read your emotions, Mood Rings were the brainchild of Joshua Reynolds, a New Age heir to the R. J. Reynolds tobacco fortune. Reynolds envisioned them as "portable biofeedback aids" and managed to sell $1 million worth of them in a three-month period in 1975. Even so, the company went bankrupt—but not before it inspired a hoard of imitators, including "mood panties" (underwear studded with temperature-sensitive plastic hearts).

PET ROCKS. One night in 1975, an out-of-work advertising executive named Gary Dahl was hanging out in a bar listening to his friends complain about their pets. It gave him an idea for the perfect "pet": a rock. He spent the next two weeks writing the *Pet Rock Training Manual,* which included instructions for housetraining the rock. ("Place it on some old newspapers. The rock will know what the paper is for and will require no further instructions.") He had a friend design a box shaped like a pet carrying case—complete with air holes and a bed of straw—and then filled them with rocks he bought from a builder's supply store for a penny apiece. The rock debuted in August 1975 and sold for $3.95; by the end of October Dahl was shipping 10,000 a day. The fad encouraged a host of imitations as well as an entire Pet Rock "service industry," including dude ranches, "hair-care" products, and burials-at-sea. The fad died out in 1976.

EARTH SHOES. Earth Shoes were one of the best-selling shoes of the 1970s. Invented by a Danish shoe designer named Anne Kalsø, they were brought to the United States in 1969 by a woman who discovered them on a trip to Europe. She claimed they cured her back pains, but foot experts argued the shoes—which forced wearers to walk on the backs of their feet—were actually pretty bad for you. One study found that most wearers suffered "severe pain and cramping for the first two weeks of wear;" another expert predicted that the shoes would "cripple everyone who wears them." Still, they were a counterculture hit and sold thousands of pairs a year in their peak. The original Earth Shoes company went bankrupt in 1977, the victim of cheap knockoffs and changing times.

COATS OF ARMS. In the '60s, anyone with $20 could send away for a crest corresponding to their last name. At the fad's peak in 1969, status-seeking Americans spent $5 million a year displaying them on sport coats, ashtrays, bank checks, etc. Elitists were outraged. "People of good taste," one blue-blood sniffed, "don't use a coat of arms they're not entitled to." But by the early 1970s just about everyone had a crest—which defeated the purpose of having one in the first place. The fad died out soon afterwards.

SMILEY FACES. Introduced in 1969 by N. G. Slater, a New York button manufacturer. At first sales were slow, but by the spring of 1971 more than 20 million buttons had been sold—enough for one in every ten Americans—making it a craze as popular as the Hula Hoop of the 1950s. Pop-culture pundits called it the "peace symbol of the seventies," and presidential candidate George McGovern adopted it as his campaign logo. The fad died out after about a year, but in the mid-70s made a comeback—this time colored yellow and bearing the cheerful message, "Have a Happy Day!" By the late 1970s, however, Americans were completely sick of it.

Smiley Face Update

"Attorneys for a convicted killer asked yesterday that his death sentence be overturned because a judge signed the July 15, 1993 execution order with a 'happy face' sketch....The judge has said that he always signs his name that way as a symbol of his faith in God and that he does not plan to change it." —*The Associated Press*

WESTERN NICKAMES

Wild Bill...Black Bart...Billy the Kid...Butch and Sundance. Western heroes had colorful nicknames—but they weren't all as complimentary as they sound. Here's some info on a few of the names.

James Butler "Wild Bill" Hickok. Had a long nose and a protruding lip, and was originally nicknamed "Duck Bill."

William "Bat" Masterson. The famous sheriff of Ford County, Kansas, hit more lawbreakers over the head with his cane than he shot with his gun, and earned the nickname "Bat."

Robert LeRoy "Butch Cassidy" Parker. As a teenager, Parker idolized a criminal named Mike Cassidy, and eventually began using his friend's last name as an alias. He picked up the name "Butch" while working in a Rock Springs, Wyoming butcher shop.

Harry "The Sundance Kid" Longabaugh. As a teenager during the 1880s, Longabaugh spent 1-1/2 years in the Sundance Jail in Wyoming, serving out a sentence for horse stealing.

William "Billy The Kid" Bonney. Looked like a kid.

Henry "Billy The Kid" McCarty. Looked like a goat.

John "Doc" Holliday. A professional dentist by trade. He only became a gunslinger and professional gambler after a bout with tuberculosis forced him to move west in search of a drier climate. Even at the height of his criminal career, he practiced dentistry part-time. Holliday's girlfriend was a prostitute named "Big Nose" Kate Elder.

Charles E. "Black Bart" Boles. Came up with the name himself. He became a stagecoach robber by accident. Originally a schoolteacher in northern California's gold country, Boles had a friend who was a Wells Fargo stagecoach driver and decided to play a trick on him. One day in 1875, he covered his face with a scarf, found a stick about the size of a pistol, and jumped out in front of the coach hoping to scare his friend. To his surprise, the driver threw down the strongbox and rode off before Boles could tell him

It's against the law to play rock music on a Venitian gondola.

it was only a joke. Opening the strongbox, Boles discovered a fortune in gold coins and bullion. Realizing there was more money in stick-ups than there was in education, Boles quit his teaching job and began holding up stagecoaches full time. He robbed 28 stagecoaches between 1875 and 1883.

After each robbery, he penned a small poem and left it behind in the empty strongbox where he knew investigators would find it. He always signed it "Black Bart, Po-8." One read: "Blame me not for what I've done, I don't deserve your curses/and if for some cause I must be hung/Let it be for my verses." Boles was eventually caught and sentenced to 4 years in San Quentin prison, but returned to stagecoach robbing within a few weeks of his release. This time Wells Fargo detectives cut a deal with Boles behind the scene: according to legend, they offered Boles a lifelong pension of $200 a month in exchange for his agreement to give up crime. Whether or not the story is true, the robberies stopped immediately.

...And now, folks, we'd like you to meet the dumbest train robber in the West.

Al Jennings, a successful Oklahoma lawyer in the early 1890s, and his brother Frank, also a lawyer, gave up their chosen profession and began second career: sticking up trains—or at least trying to.

In 1897 they tried to rob a mail car on a Santa Fe train, but the conductor chased them away. Two weeks later the brothers tried to stop another train by blocking the track with railroad ties, but the train steamed right through the barrier. In another robbery attempt, they tried to dynamite open two safes, but only succeeded in blowing up the boxcar the safes were on.

The law eventually caught up with them; Frank got 5 years in prison and Al was sentenced to life in prison, but President Theodore Roosevelt granted him a "full citizenship" pardon in 1907.

Jennings returned to his law practice, and eventually ran for county attorney under the slogan, "When I was a train robber I was a good train robber, and if you choose me, I will be a good prosecuting attorney." He lost. In 1914 he ran for governor of Oklahoma (this time his slogan was "It takes the same sort of nerve to be an honest governor as to rob a train or bank") and lost that too.

HERE'S JOHNNY...

Quips from the archetypal late-night talk show host, Johnny Carson.

"I now believe in reincarnation. Tonight's monologue is going to come back as a dog."

"The only absolute rule is: Never lose control of the show."

[On Jimmy Carter] "I think he rented his family. I don't believe Lillian is his mother. I don't believe Billy is his brother. They're all from Central Casting."

"[Rona Barrett] doesn't need a steak knife. Rona cuts her food with her tongue."

"I like my work and I hope you do, too—but if you don't, I really couldn't care less. Take me or leave me—but don't bug me."

"The difference between divorce and legal separation is that a legal separation gives a husband time to hide his money."

"Never use a big word when a little filthy one will do."

"I don't know where my creativity comes from, and I don't want to know."

"The best things in life are free. And the cheesiest things in life are free with a paid subscription to *Sports Illustrated.*"

"The worst gift is a fruitcake. There is only one fruitcake in the entire world, and people keep sending it to each other."

"The difference between love and lust is that lust never costs over two hundred dollars."

"Married men live longer than single men. But married men are a lot more willing to die."

"Anytime four New Yorkers get into a cab together without arguing, a bank robbery has just taken place."

"Thanksgiving is an emotional holiday. People travel thousands of miles to be with people they only see once a year. And then discover once a year is way too often."

KITCHEN SCIENCE

In his book Kitchen Science, *Howard Hillman answers hundreds of questions about food. Here are some that the BRI editors thought were particularly enlightening.*

W **HICH HAS more caffeine, tea or coffee?**
"A pound of tea—on the average—has twice the caffeine of a pound of roasted coffee. However, since that weight of tea typically yields about 160 cups, whereas the pound of coffee brews about 40 cups, the net result is that the cup of tea has roughly half the caffeine of a cup of coffee.

"Parents who forbid their young children to drink coffee should be aware that a twelve-ounce bottle of a typical cola has approximately one-quarter the caffeine of an average cup of coffee—and many times more than is found in a cup of decaffeinated coffee."

IS CHOCOLATE milk a good way to get kids to drink milk?
"Though the chocolate flavoring is often an enticement, it is unsound from a nutritional standpoint. The oxalic acid in chocolate inhibits the digestive system's ability to absorb the milk's calcium, an essential mineral, especially for growing children."

HOW DOES milk become sour?
"About 5 percent of fresh milk's content is lactose, a milk sugar that gives the liquid a slight but noticeable sweet taste. As the milk ages, certain bacteria devour some of the lactose, converting it into lactic acid. Result: the milk sours."

WHICH IS better, iodized or plain salt?
"Iodine is essential in the diet because without it, your thyroid gland could not manufacture thyroxine—a hormone necessary for bodily functions such as growth, and the prevention of goiter....

"However, some medical authorities believe that if you eat a lot of seafood or food grown in iodine-rich soil (commonly associated with coastal areas), or drink water that has acquired the mineral from such soil, you may be overdosing on iodine if you also regularly use iodized salt. The iodine-fortified product makes more sense for people who live great distances from a seaboard."

President Andrew Jackson thought the world was flat.

ARE "PRAWNS" in restaurants really shrimp?

"In all probability, yes. A true prawn is biologically different from a shrimp; the prawn has lobster-like pincer claws. The best eating species are the Dublin Bay prawns of Ireland and the scampi of the northern Adriatic Sea. Both are larger than an average-sized shrimp but smaller than a lobster. When a restaurant serves you 'prawns' or 'scampi' in America, odds are a thousand to one that you're eating jumbo shrimp, a cheaper and less succulent substitute."

WHY DO I "cry" when I peel onions?

"Your eyes are very sensitive to the onion's volatile oils, and these oils easily escape into the air whenever you slice through an onion. When some of the oil comes wafting into your eyes, your body reacts defensively: Tears are produced to expel the irritant."

Note: "[If] your eyes [are] extremely sensitive to the onion's volatile oils, wear safety goggles...or — if you own one— a scuba diving mask. Skier's goggles will not serve your purpose because their ventilation holes allow the tear-producing fumes to penetrate the goggles and reach your eyes."

SHOULD coffee and tea drinkers avoid Styrofoam "hot cups?"

Yes. "The acid in coffee, and especially tea, dissolves some of the cup's polystyrene into the brew, a disintegration that doesn't benefit your taste buds or health. According to recent research, cup erosion is most pronounced when hot tea is flavored with lemon."

ARE PEOPLE really hungry an hour after eating chinese food?

"Yes and no....A typical American diner [may] receive hunger signals sooner than usual from his stomach because he has not eaten a genuine Chinese meal. A Chinese person from Canton, for example would eat a lot of rice complemented by smaller portions of vegetables (and even smaller portions of fish or meat, if any). [Americans] eat a lot of vegetables, while relegating the rice to a background role.

"Adding even more to the problem are the economics of some restaurant owners, who cut costs by serving a high proportion of watery vegetables (ingredients such as snow peas are expensive and therefore used sparingly, if at all). Since water quickly passes through the stomach, [diners] may indeed have that ol' empty feeling within an hour or two.

"Hunger pangs come about, too, because the average Chinese meal tends to be less rich in fats than the meals that Mr. Smith's stomach has come to accept as the norm. Since the digestive tract takes two or three hours longer to digest fat than it does carbohydrates and proteins, his stomach will start to rumble much sooner than if he had had his traditional high-fat American dinner."

WHY ARE the McDonald's and Burger King's french fried potatoes thinner than the norm?

"More than consumer preference is involved. Since the raw, precut potatoes are shipped and stored frozen, much of the starch in the vegetables converts to sugar. That extra sugar means that the french fries brown faster when cooked. If fast-food establishments served normal-sized American french fries, their product would either be too brown on the outside or undercooked on the inside."

WHY DO beans cause flatulence?

"Beans contain certain carbohydrates that humans cannot fully digest. When intestinal bacteria ferment these undigested substances, gas results. One way to minimize bean-induced flatulence is to discard the water in which they were soaked."

AND NOW A SPACE FILLER

Play Doh. Joseph McVicker's sister-in-law was a nursery school teacher in New Jersey. One day she happened to complain to him about how messy modeling clay was when her children played with it. McVicker, an employee at his father's soap company, set out to make something better. Using flour, water, and other ingredients (including, apparently, kerosene), he came up with "Play-Doh." More than 800 million cans of the stuff have been sold so far.

Money Fact: U.S. law requires that any coin minted after July 23, 1965 that's made of silver be inscribed with the year 1964—no matter what the year of coinage.

GREETINGS FROM OZ

The Wizard of Oz, *by Frank Baum, is on the BRI's list of recommended bathroom reading for adults. Here are a few random quotes taken from it.*

O## N COURAGE
"There is no living thing that is not afraid when it faces danger. True courage is in facing danger when you are afraid. "

—**The Wizard**

ON MONEY
"Money in Oz!…Did you suppose we are so vulgar as to use money here? If we used money to buy things, instead of love and kindness and the desires to please one another, then we should be no better than the rest of the world….Fortunately, money is not known in the Land of Oz at all. We have no rich, no poor: for what one wishes, the others all try to give him in order to make him happy, and no one in all of Oz cares to have more than he can use."

—**The Tin Woodsman**

ON EXPERIENCE
"Can't you give me brains?" asked the Scarecrow.
"You don't need them. You are learning something every day. A baby has brains, but it doesn't know much. Experience is the only thing that brings knowledge, and the longer you are on earth, the more experience you are sure to get."

ON THE VALUE OF BRAINS
"I realize at present that I'm only an imitation of a man, and I assure you that it is an uncomfortable feeling to know that one is a fool. It seems to me that a body is only a machine for brains to direct, and those who have no brains themselves are liable to be directed by the brains of others."

THE BEST THING IN THE WORLD
"Brains are not the best thing in the world," said the Tin Woodsman.
"Have you any?" enquired the Scarecrow.

"No, my head is quite empty," answered the Tin Woodsman. "But once I had brains, and a heart also; so, having tried them both, I should much rather have a heart...for brains do not make one happy, and happiness is the best thing in the world."

...And Now, Back to the World of Facts & Stats

• There are an estimated 5,000 foreign languages spoken throughout the world today—and nearly 100% of them have a dictionary translating them into English.

• The largest encylopedia of all time was a 16th-century Chinese encyclopedia; it was 22,937 volumes.

• Do you know what "unabridged" means when it refers to English dictionaries? It doesn't mean the work contains all the words in the English language; it just means that it contains all the words listed in earlier editions.

• The world's first Mongolian-English dictionary was published in 1953.

• What language has the most words? Mandarin Chinese, which has an estimated 800,000 words. English is believed to rank second.

• In English dictionaries, the letter "T" has the most entries.

• Few English dictionaries agree on which word is the longest in the language. Two contenders:

  √ *floccipaucinihilipilification* (OED), "the action of estimating as worthless."

  √ *pneumonoultramicroscopicsilicovolcanoconiosis* (Webster's Third International), "a lung disease common to miners."

• Many dictionaries do agree on the longest word *in common use:* it's *disproportionableness.*

• The oldest word in the English language that still resembles its earliest form is *land*, which is descended from *landa*, the Old Celtic word for "heath." It predates the Roman Empire (founded in 200 B.C.) by many hundreds of years.

UNEXPECTED ENCOUNTERS

"East is east, and west is west, and never the twain shall meet." When we were kids, that seemed to make sense—except the 'twain' part. That wasn't even a word, as far as we knew. Anyway, here are some examples of people you'd never expect to see together:

CHARLIE CHAPLIN & MAHATMA GANDHI

When: 1931, in London.

Who: Chaplin, the "Little Tramp," was the world's most famous comedian. Gandhi, a tiny figure in a loincloth, was one of the world most revered political and religious leaders.

What Happened: As they posed for photographers, Chaplin tried to figure out what to say. In his autobiography, he writes about his terror: "The room was suddenly attacked by flashbulbs from the camera as we sat on the sofa. Now came that uneasy, terrifying moment when I should say something astutely intelligent upon a subject I know little about...I knew I had to start the ball rolling, that it was not up to the Mahatma to tell me how much he enjoyed my last film...I doubted he had ever even seen a film." He finally got up the courage, and the two men politely exchanged political views. Then Chaplin stayed and watched Gandhi at his prayers.

GORGEOUS GEORGE & MUHAMMAD ALI

When: 1961, at a radio studio in Las Vegas.

Who: Gorgeous George, with his permed blonde hair and purple robes, was one of TV wrestling's original superstars. He sold out arenas wherever he played, and was named Mr. Televison in 1949; but by 1961 his career was almost over. Cassius Clay (aka Muhammad Ali) was a young boxer who'd just turned pro.

What Happened: In 1961 George made a wrestling appearance in Las Vegas. To promote it, he went on a local radio show, shouting "I am the greatest!" As it happened, the other guest on the program was a young Cassius Clay, who was so impressed with George's theatrics that he went to the wrestling match that evening. The place was packed. "That's when I decided I'd never been shy about talking," Ali remembers, "but if I talked even more, there was no

---

Americans say microwave ovens are the best recent change in their lives, infomercials the worst.

telling how much money people would pay to see me."

NICHELLE NICHOLS & MARTIN LUTHER KING, JR.

When: 1967, at a party.

Who: King was America's greatest civil rights leader, and the recipient of the Nobel Peace Prize. Nichols was playing Lt. Uhura in *Star Trek*'s first (low-rated) season. She was considering quitting the show because Paramount wouldn't give her a contract.

What Happened: According to one source: "A friend came up to Nichols at a party and said someone wanted to meet her. She expected a gushing Trekkie... but when she turned around, she was looking at Martin Luther King...who actually *was* a fan. He said he'd heard she was considering leaving *Star Trek*, and urged her not to; she was too important a role model for blacks—and the only black woman on TV with real authority. 'Do you realize that you're fourth in command on the *Enterprise*?' he asked. Nichols didn't. The next day she checked and found he was right.... She stayed with the show and finally got her contract the next season."

HARPO MARX & GEORGE BERNARD SHAW

When: 1931, at the Villa Gallanon in the south of France.

Who: Shaw was "the most important British playright since Shakespeare." Marx was part of the world's most popular slapstick team.

What Happened: Here's how Harpo described the meeting in his autobiography: "I went down the cliff to the little sheltered cove we used for nude bathing, took off my clothes, and went for a swim. I came out of the water and stretched out on a towel to sunbathe ....I was startled out of my doze in the sun by a man's voice, blaring from the top of the cliff. 'Halloo! Halloo! Is there nobody home?'

"I wrapped the towel around myself and scrambled up the cliff to see who it was. It was a tall, skinny, red-faced old geezer with a beard, decked out in a sporty cap and knicker suit. There was a lady with him. 'Who the devil are you?' I told him I was Harpo Marx. 'Ah, yes, of course,' he said. He held out his hand. 'I'm Bernard Shaw,' he said. Instead of shaking hands with me, he made a sudden lunge for my towel and snatched it away, and exposed me naked to the world. 'And this,' he said, 'is Mrs. Shaw.' From the moment I met him, I had nothing to hide from George Bernard Shaw." They became good friends.

ORIGIN OF THE "BIG THREE" NETWORKS

*They're a big part of your life...but we'll bet you
don't know how they got there. Let's correct that.*

T HE NATIONAL BROADCASTING COMPANY (NBC)
NBC is the oldest of the "Big 3" American broadcasting networks. It was founded on September 13, 1926, by the Radio
Corporation of America (RCA), the world's largest radio manufacturer, because they feared poor quality radio broadcasting was hurt-
ing sales.

Spurred on by RCA president David Sarnoff, NBC quickly became the most potent force in radio. The demand for programming
was so high that within a year NBC split its radio operations into
two divisions—the Red and Blue networks. The two continued
broadcasting side by side until 1943, when the U.S. Government
forced NBC to sell off the Blue network in an antitrust suit.

Meanwhile, RCA was experimenting with television (which
Sarnoff called "the art of distant seeing"). In 1931 NBC built its first
television transmitter, on top of the Empire State Building. Although development of TV was subsequently slowed by the Depression, regular TV service was started by NBC in 1939...and the first
TV network broadcast ever was on January 11, 1940, from NBC in
New York City to a GE-owned station in Schenectady, New York.

Because America was putting its resources into the war effort
from 1941 to 1945, NBC couldn't begin regular network TV broadcasts until 1945.

RCA was the sole owner of NBC until 1985, when GE—an original partner in 1926—bought RCA for $6.8 billion.

THE COLUMBIA BROADCASTING SYSTEM (CBS)

In the 1920s, Arthur Judson was a talent agent whose clients included the New York Philharmonic. When NBC pioneered TV broadcasting in 1926, Judson cut a deal with them to broadcast several of
his clients—but NBC reneged on its promise.

Judson was so angry that he started his own radio broadcasting network. He called it the United Independent Broadcasters, and began signing up independent radio stations around the country.

Judson was too broke to run the company alone, so he joined forces with the Columbia Phonograph and Records Co. and changed the network's name to the Columbia Phonograph Broadcasting System. It initially provided 10 hours of programming per week to 16 affiliates. But CPBS was losing money, and Columbia Phonograph pulled out. They sold their shares to Jerome Louchheim, a wealthy Philadelphia builder, who renamed CPBS the Columbia Broadcasting System. He, in turn, sold out to William S. Paley for $400,000 in 1929. Paley (whose father, owner of the Congress Cigar Co., was one of CBS's largest advertisers) turned the ailing network around almost overnight. By 1932 CBS was earning more than $3 million a year in profits—and in 1939 it was doing so well that it bought its former owner, Columbia Phonograph and Records.

THE AMERICAN BROADCASTING SYSTEM (ABC)

When the U.S. government forced NBC to sell off its Blue network in 1943, Lifesaver candy manufacturer Edward J. Noble bought it for $8 million and renamed it the American Broadcasting Company. Ten years later, ABC merged with United Paramont Theaters—a chain of movie theaters the government had forced Paramount Pictures to sell—and went into TV broadcasting.

A perpetual "weak sister" to its larger rivals, ABC remained a second-rate network until 1954, when its gavel-to-gavel coverage of the U.S. Senate's Army-McCarthy hearings made broadcasting history...and gave them newfound respectability.

ABC remained much smaller than its rivals, but made up for its lack of money and affiliate stations by producing more innovative TV shows than CBS and NBC. Some of its groundbreaking shows: "Disneyland," "The Mickey Mouse Club," and "Batman." ABC also revolutionized sports coverage with shows like "Monday Night Football," "Wide World of Sports," and its coverage of the Olympics. The network used the profits generated from sports and miniseries shows to strengthen its news and prime-time programming—and in 1975 its overall ratings shot ahead of its rivals for the first time. It has been on equal footing ever since.

America has 1,103 drive-in movie theatres, more than any other nation on earth.

THE GENUINE ARTICLE

*A random sampling of authentic articles,
dialogue, commentary. You are there.*

O UTRAGE OVER ELVIS
*In 1956, Elvis Presley appeared on the Ed Sullivan Show. We
think of it as a great moment in TV history, but critics (and other
grown-ups) didn't. These comments appeared in the* New York Times:

"Last Sunday on the Ed Sullivan Show, Mr. Presley made another of his appearances and attracted a record audience. In some ways, it was the most unpleasant of his recent three performances. Mr. Presley initially disturbed adult viewers with his strip-tease behavior on last spring's Milton Berle's program....On the Sullivan program he injected movements of the tongue and indulged in wordless singing that were singularly distasteful....

"Some parents are puzzled or confused by Mr. Presley's almost hypnotic power; some are concerned; [but] most are a shade disgusted and [will be] content to let the Presley fad play itself out."

CHARLIE CHAPLIN'S FAVORITE JOKE

At lunch one afternoon, Charlie Chaplin was asked to relate the funniest joke he'd ever heard. You'd think that "the world's greatest comic genius" would tell something hilarious. But...well...you decide.

"A man in a tea shop orders a cup of coffee and a piece of shortbread. On paying the bill, he compliments the manager on the quality of the shortbread and asks if it could be custom-made in any shape. 'Why, certainly.'

" 'Well, if I come back tomorrow, could you make me a piece shaped like the letter "e"?'

" 'No trouble,' says the manager. Next day, on returning to the shop, the man looks aghast.

" 'But you've made it a capital "E"!' He arranges to come back another day, and this time expresses himself completely satisfied.

" 'Where would you like me to send it?' asks the manager.

" 'Oh, I won't give you the trouble to send it anywhere,' says the customer. 'I'll sit down here, if I may, and eat it now.' And he does."

No one at lunch thought it was funny, either.

HISTORIC RECIPE

In 1770, American revolutionaries published these detailed directions for tarring and feathering, which was, at the time "a mob ritual."

How to Tar and Feather Someone

"First, strip a person naked, then heat the Tar until it is thin & pour it upon naked Flesh, or rub it over with a Tar brush.

"After which, sprinkle decently upon the Tar, whilst it is yet warm, as many Feathers as will stick to it.

"Then hold a lighted Candle to the Feathers, & try to set it all on Fire."

GREAT MOMENTS IN CENSORSHIP

In 1937, Mae West was barred from radio after she engaged in a slightly risqué dialogue on NBC's Edgar Bergen/Charlie McCarthy Show. The conversation was with McCarthy, a ventriloquist's dummy!

Mae West: "Why don't you come home with me now honey? I'll let you play in my woodpile."

Charlie McCarthy: "Well, I don't feel so well tonight. I've been feeling nervous lately...."

West: "You can't kid me. You're afraid of women. Your Casanova stuff is just a front, a false front."

McCarthy: "Not so loud, Mae, not so loud! All my girlfriends are listening...."

West: "You weren't so nervous when you came up to see me at my apartment. In fact, you didn't need any encouragement to kiss me."

McCarthy: "Did I do that?"

West: "You certainly did. I got marks to prove it. And splinters, too."

Protests poured in from church groups, ostensibly because the show had aired on Sunday (more likely reason: they objected to West's general "promiscuity"). The sponsor agreed it was "inappropriate," and apologized on the air; Hollywood disavowed both the skit and West; NBC declared she would never appear on radio again.

IMMACULATE CONCEPTION

On Nov. 4, 1874, this article appeared in The American Weekly. *It was quoted in an 1896 book,* Anomalies and Curiosities of Medicine. *It belongs in* Believe It or Not.

"During the fray [between Union and Confederate troops], a soldier staggered and fell to earth; at the same time a piercing cry was heard in the house nearby. Examination showed that a bullet had passed through the scrotum and carried away the left testicle. The same bullet had apparently penetrated the left side of the abdomen of a young lady...and become lost in the abdomen. The daughter suffered an attack of peritonitis, but recovered.

"Two hundred and seventy-eight days after the reception of the minie ball, she was delivered of a fine boy weighing eight pounds, to the surprise of herself, and the mortification of her parents and friends.

"The doctor concluded that...the same ball that had carried away the testicle of his young friend...had penetrated the ovary of the young lady and, with some spermatozoa upon it, had impregnated her. With this conviction, he approached the young man and told him of the circumstances. The soldier appeared skeptical at first, but consented to visit the young mother; a friendship ensued, which soon ripened into a happy marriage."

NIXONIA

You think Richard Nixon was "a little" stiff and formal? Here's a memo he sent to his wife on January 25, 1969.

To: Mrs. Nixon

From: The President

With regard to RN's room, what would be the most desirable is an end table like the one on the right side of the bed, which will accomodate two dictaphones as well as a telephone. RN has to use one dictaphone for current matters and another for memoranda for the file, which he will not want transcribed at this time. In addition, he needs a bigger table on which he can work at night. The table which is presently in the room does not allow enough room for him to get his knees under it.

Only 33% of people in the United Arab Emirates are women—the lowest percentage on Earth.

CARTOON NAMES

How did our favorite cartoon characters get their unusual names? Here are a few answers.

Bugs Bunny: In 1940 cartoonist Bugs Hardaway submitted preliminary sketches for "a tall, lanky, mean rabbit" for a cartoon called "Hare-um Scare-um"—and someone labeled the drawings "Bugs's Bunny." Hardaway's mean rabbit was never used—but the name was given to the bunny in the cartoon "A Wild Hare."

Casper the Friendly Ghost: Cartoonist Joe Oriolo's daughter was afraid of ghosts—so he invented one that wouldn't scare her. "We were looking for a name that didn't sound threatening," he says.

Chip an' Dale: Disney animator Jack Hannah was meeting with colleagues to pick names for his two new chipmunk characters. His assistant director happened to mention Thomas Chippendale, the famous furniture designer. "Immediately," Hannah remembers, "I said 'That's it! That's their names!' "

Mickey Mouse: Walt Disney wanted to name the character *Mortimer* Mouse—but his wife hated the name. "Mother couldn't explain why the name grated; it just did," Disney's daughter Diane remembers. Disney wanted the character's name to begin with the letter M (to go with Mouse)—and eventually decided on Mickey.

Porky Pig: According to creator Bob Clampett: "Someone thought of two puppies named Ham and Ex, and that started me thinking. So after dinner one night, I came up with Porky and Beans. I made a drawing of this fat little pig, which I named Porky, and a little black cat named Beans."

Rocky & Bullwinkle: Rocky was picked because it was "just a square-sounding kid's name;" Bullwinkle was named after Clarence Bulwinkle, a Berkeley, California used-car dealer.

Elmer Fudd. Inspired by a line in a 1920s song called "Mississippi Mud." The line: "It's a treat to meet you on the Mississippi Mud—Uncle Fudd."

Foghorn Leghorn: Modeled after Senator Claghorn, a fictional politician in comedian Fred Allen's radio show.

Best-selling children's book in history: *The Tale of Peter Rabbit*, by Beatrix Potter.

MORE LEFT-HANDED FACTS

Here's more info for lefties. Why devote two more pages to the subject? Okay, okay. We admit it—Uncle John is left-handed.

LEFT-HANDED STATS

• Lefties make up about 5-15% of the general population—but 15-30% of all patients in mental institutions.

• They're more prone to allergies, insomnia, migranes, schizophrenia and a host of other things than right-handers. They're also three times more likely than righties to become alcoholics. Why? Some scientists speculate the right hemisphere of the brain—the side left-handers use the most—has a lower tolerance for alcohol than the left side. Others think the stress of living in a right-handed world is responsible.

• Lefties are also more likely to be on the extreme ends of the intelligence scale than the general population: a higher proportion of mentally retarded people *and* people with I.Q.s over 140 are lefties.

LEFT OUT OF SCIENCE

• For centuries science was biased against southpaws. In the 1870s, for example, Italian psychiatrist Cesare Lombroso published *The Delinquent Male*, in which he asserted that left-handed men were psychological "degenerates" and prone to violence. (A few years later he published *The Delinquent Female*, in which he made the same claims about women.)

• This theory existed even as late as the 1940s, when psychiatrist Abram Blau wrote that left-handedness "is nothing more than an expression of infantile negativism and falls into the same category as...general perverseness." He speculated that lefties didn't get enough attention from their mothers.

LEFT-HANDED TRADITIONS

• Why do we throw salt over our left shoulders for good luck? To throw it into the eyes of the Devil, who of course, lurks behind us to our left.

Hmm: 61% of college women, but only 28% of college men, say they're in a "steady relationship."

• In many traditional Muslim cultures, it is extremely impolite to touch food with your left hand. Reason: Muslims eat from communal bowls using their right hand; their left hand is used to perform "unclean" tasks such as wiping themselves after going the bathroom. Hindus have a similar custom: they use their right hand exclusively when touching themselves above the waist, and use only the left hand to touch themselves below the waist.

• What did traditional Christians believe was going to happen on Judgement Day? According to custom, God blesses the saved with his right hand—and casts sinners out of Heaven with his left.

• Other traditional mis-beliefs:

> If you have a ringing in your left ear, someone is cursing you. If your right ear rings, someone is praising you.

> If your left eye twitches, you're going to see an enemy. If the right twitches, you're going to see a friend.

> If you get out of bed with your left foot first, you're going to have a bad day.

> If your left palm itches, you're going to owe someone money. If your right palm does, you're going to make some money.

LEFT-HANDED MISCELLANY

• Why are lefties called "southpaws"? In the late 1890s, most baseball parks were laid out with the pitcher facing west and the batter facing east (so the sun wouldn't be in his eyes). That meant left-handed pitchers threw with the arm that faced south. So Chicago sportswriter Charles Seymour began calling them "southpaws."

• Right-handed bias: Some Native American tribes strapped their children's left arms to the mother's cradleboard, which caused most infants to become predominantly right-handed. The Kaffirs of South Africa acheived similar results by burying the left hands of left-handed children in the burning desert sand.

• The next time you see a coat of arms, check to see if it has a stripe running diagonally across it. Most stripes are called *bends* and run from the top left to the bottom right. A stripe that runs from the bottom left to the top right, is called a "left-handed" bend or a *bend sinister*—and means the bearer was a bastard.

MORE STRANGE LAWSUITS

More bizarre doings in the halls of justice, from news reports.

THE PLAINTIFF: James Hooper, a 25-year-old student at Oklahoma State University.

THE DEFENDANT: The Pizza Shuttle, a Stillwater, Oklahoma pizza restaurant.

THE LAWSUIT: Hooper ordered an "extra cheese, pepperoni, sausage, black olive and mushroom pizza." Instead, he said, the Pizza Shuttle delivered "a pizza with something green on it, maybe peppers." He sued the restaurant for $7.00 in damages ($5.50 for the pizza, and $1.50 for the delivery boy's tip).

VERDICT: The court found in favor of the Pizza Shuttle—and ordered Hooper to pay $57 in court costs.

THE PLAINTIFF: Widow of Walter Hughes, who died in 1991.

THE DEFENDANTS: McVicker's Chapel on the Hill and Kevin Robinson, Hughes's son-in-law and former director of the Longview, Washington funeral home.

THE LAWSUIT: Mrs. Hughes sued the funeral home when she learned that it had buried her husband without his favorite cowboy hat.

VERDICT: She was awarded $101,000 in damages.

THE PLAINTIFF: Seven patrons of Charley Brown's, a Concord, California restaurant.

THE DEFENDANT: The restaurant.

THE LAWSUIT: In 1992, the restaurant hired an actor to stage a mock robbery as part of a dinner show called "The Suspect's Dinner Theater." The actor, dressed as a masked gunman, burst into the restaurant shouting "All you m------, hit the floor!" Dinner guests, thinking the robbery was real, cowered under their tables while the man shouted threats and fired several blank rounds from his .45-caliber pistol. (One patron, an investigator with the county district attorney's office, fought with the gunman until restaurant employees told him the robbery was part of the show.) "When the hostess said it was all just an episode of Mystery Theater," another diner told reporters, "I said, 'Mystery Theater, my a--. You're going to hear from my lawyer.'" He and six others sued the restaurant, claiming assault and intentional infliction of emotional distress.

VERDICT: The restaurant offered to settle the case by paying $3,000 to each of the plaintiffs—and later went out of business.

THE PLAINTIFF: Andrea Pizzo, a 23-year-old former University of Maine student.

THE DEFENDANT: The University of Maine.

THE LAWSUIT: Apparently, Pizzo was taking a class in livestock management, when a cow attacked her one afternoon in 1991. (It butted her into a fence.) She sued, claiming the school "should have known that the heifer had a personality problem."

VERDICT: Unknown.

THE PLAINTIFF: William and Tonya P., who booked a room at a Michigan Holiday Inn during their honeymoon in 1992.

THE DEFENDANT: The Holiday Inn.

THE LAWSUIT: William and Tonya claim that a hotel employee walked into their room on their wedding night while they were having sex. They filed a $10,000 lawsuit against the hotel, claiming the unannounced visit ruined their sex life. Holiday Inn does not dispute the charge but says they should have hung up a "Do Not Disturb" sign.

VERDICT: Unknown.

THE PLAINTIFF: John M., a 50-year-old Philadelphia teacher.

THE DEFENDANT: His wife Maryann K., a 46-year-old receptionist.

THE LAWSUIT: One day after her divorce from John became final, Ms. K. turned in a lottery ticket that was about to expire and won $10.2 million. Her lawyer claims that "Lady Luck" led her to find the ticket and turn it in two weeks before it expired—but Mr. M. thinks she deliberately waited until after the divorce was finalized to turn it in. He sued to get his share.

VERDICT: Still pending.

BLOTTO, LOOPED, FRIED

Most people know what sloshed, loaded and looped mean: being drunk, of course. But there are plenty of other words that mean the same thing. Here's a list of America's favorites that appear in I hear America Talking.

(The words are followed by the year they came into use.)

Stiff (1737)
Fuzzy (1770)
Half Shaved (1818)
Bent (1833)
Slewed (1834)
Stinking (1837)
Screwed (1838)
Lushy (1840)
Pixilated (1850)
Swizzled (1850)
Whipped (1851)
Tanglefooted (1860)
Spiffed (1860)
Frazzled (1870)
Squiffy (1874)
Boiled (1886)
Paralyzed (1888)
Pickled (1890)
Woozy (1897)
Pifflicated (1900)
Ginned (1900)
Ossified (1901)
Petrified (1903)
Tanked (1905)
Blotto (1905)

Shellacked (1905)
Jingled (1908)
Piped (1912)
Plastered (1912)
Gassed (1915)
Hooted (1915)
Have A Snoot Full (1918)
Jugged (1919)
Canned (1920)
Juiced (1920)
Fried (1920)
Buried (1920)
Potted (1922)
Dead To The World (1926)
Crocked (1927)
Busted (1928)
Rum-dum (1931)
Bombed (1940)
Feeling No Pain (1940)
Swacked (1941)
Sloshed (1950)
Boxed (1950)
Clobbered (1951)
Crashed (1950s)
Zonked (1950s)

Language barrier: 1 in 7 Americans don't speak English at home.

HELLMAN'S LAWS

Wisdom from Lillian Hellman, one of America's greatest playrights.

"Nothing, of course, begins at the time you think it did."

"Nobody can argue any longer about the rights of women. It's like arguing about the rights of earthquakes."

"I like people who refuse to speak until they are *ready* to speak."

"Nothing you write, if you hope to be any good, will ever come out as you first hoped."

"Cynicism is an unpleasant way of saying the truth."

"Callous greed grows pious very fast."

"God forgives those who invent what they need."

"People change...and forget to tell each other."

"Fashions in sin change."

"The convictions of Hollywood and television are made of boiled money."

"There are people who eat the earth and eat all the people on it, like in the Bible with the locusts. And [there are] other people who stand around and watch them eat it."

"It is a mark of many famous people that they cannot part with their brightest hour: what once worked must *always* work."

"It doesn't pay well to fight for what we believe in."

"Since when do you have to agree with people to defend them with justice?"

"I cannot, and will not, cut my conscience to fit this year's fashions."

"We are a people who do not want to keep much of the past in our heads. It is considered unhealthy in America to remember mistakes, neurotic to think about them, psychotic to dwell upon them."

"If I had to give young writers advice, I would say don't listen to writers talk about writing...or themselves."

Older and wiser: The average Ph.D. candidate spends 7 years on his or her dissertation.

AUNT LENNA'S PUZZLES

More conversations with my favorite aunt. Answers are on p. 227.

MONEY MINDED

My Aunt Lenna is a little unreliable when it comes to money. So I wasn't surprised when she came to me and asked, "Nephew, why are 1993 dollar bills worth more than 1992 dollar bills?"

"Aunt Lenna, don't be silly, they—"

"Tut, tut, Nephew. Think before you answer."

What's the answer to her question?

TRAIN OF THOUGHT

Aunt Lenna and I went down to the train station to pick up a friend. On the way, she came up with a little puzzle for me.

"Let's say that two sets of train tracks run right alongside one an-other...until they get to a narrow tunnel. Both tracks won't fit, so they merge into one track for the whole length of the tun-nel...then go back to being parallel tracks. One morning a train goes into the tunnel from the east end...and another goes into the tunnel from the west end. They're traveling as fast as they can go, in opposite directions, but they don't crash. Can you tell me why not?"

"Really, Aunt Lenna. I know I'm not the brightest guy in the world....But even I can figure this one out."

What's the story?

GREETINGS

"What have you got there, Aunt Lenna? "

"Oh, it's just the card I'm sending this year."

"Let's see." I looked at the card. It said:

ABCDEFGHIJKMNOPQRSTUVWXYZ

"Very cute, Aunt Lenna."

What did it say?

Food fact: If you're an average American, you eat 20.8 pounds of candy every year.

THE BLACK STONES

Aunt Lenna had a puzzle for me.

"Once there was a beautiful woman whose family owed money to an evil moneylender. 'I'll give you a chance to rid yourself of the debt,' the evil guy told her. 'How?' 'I'll put two stones in this bag,' he said—'one white, one black. You reach in and take one. If you pick the white one, your debt is wiped out. If you pick the black one, you marry me.' "

"I suppose he laughed maniacally at that point."

"Why, yes, how did you know? Where was I? Oh, yes—The girl agreed, and watched as the man put two stones in the bag. But she realized he had put two black stones in, and there was no chance of picking a white stone. How could she win the bet?"

How did she win?

QUICK CUT

Aunt Lenna loves to bake. One day she was busy rolling out dough for a cake when she turned to me and said, "Nephew, I've got a little puzzle for you. How is it possible to cut a cake into eight equal parts...with just three straight cuts with a knife?"

I thought for a minute. "It's not."

"Oh yes it is. Think about it awhile."

How can it be done?

TIME TO GO

Aunt Lenna was reminiscing. "When I was a teenager, there was a boy who kept coming around, asking me to the movies and such. I didn't want to hurt his feelings, but finally one day, I had to do something. So I asked him if he'd heard about the nine O's. He said no, so I drew nine O's, like this: O O O O O O O O O.

Then I added five vertical lines to the Os...and he got the message and stopped bothering me."

What did Aunt Lenna do with the lines?

Q & A:
ASK THE EXPERTS

More random questions…and answers from America's trivia experts.

VISIONARIES

Q: *Can animals see in color?*

A: "Apes and some monkeys [see] the full spectrum of color, as may some fish and birds. But most mammals see color only as shades of grey." (From *The Book of Answers*, by Barbara Berliner)

YOURS, MINE, AND HOURS

Q: *Why are there 24 hours in a day?*

A: "To the ancients, 12 was a mystical number. It could be evenly divided by 2, 3, 4, and 6 (that's one of the reasons we still use dozens today.) Twenty-four hours is made up of two 12s—12 hours before noon, and 12 hours after." (From *Know It All!*, by Ed Zotti)

GR-R-R

Q: *Why does your stomach rumble when you're hungry?*

A: "Every 75-115 minutes, your stomach's muscles contract. When no food is present, their rhythm is a wave-like stretching and contracting that molds the air, mostly digestive gases, in the stomach cavity. No one understands exactly why this makes the tummy-rumble noise, but it surely does." (From *Why Can't You Tickle Yourself?* by Ingrid Johnson)

FAR A-FIELDS

Q: Did W.C. Fields actually say, "Anyone who hates dogs and children can't be all bad?"

A: Nope, it was Leo Rosten. See page 141 for more info.

GOLD DISC

Q: *What was the first gold record?*

A: Glenn Miller got it for "Chattanooga Choo-Choo." The first certified million-selling album was the sountrack from *Oklahoma*.

Lobbyist's leverage: The average freshman U.S. Senator enters office $266,073 in debt.

ROCKIN' ROBIN

Q: *Why do birds sing?*

A: No, it's not because they're happy. "The vast majority of bird songs are produced by males and break down to two kinds: first, a call from male to male, proclaiming territory and warning other males away, and second, a call to females, advertising the singer's maleness...if he's not already committed." (From *Do Elephants Swim?*, compiled by Robert M. Jones)

OVER THE HUMP

Q: *How long can a camel go without water?*

A: "A camel can go for 17 days without drinking any water.... There is a secret to this: The camel carries a great deal of fat in its hump and has the ability to manufacture water out of this hump by oxidation. This is not to say that the camel doesn't get thirsty. When it gets the chance to drink after a long drought, it can suck down 25 gallons of water." (From *Science Trivia*, by Charles Cazeau)

BOXED RAISINS

Q: *Why don't the raisins in Raisin Bran fall to the bottom of the box?*

A: "Raisins are added to boxes only after more than half of the cereal has already been packed. The cereal thus has a chance to settle and condense. During average shipping conditions, boxes get jostled a bit...so the raisins actually sift and become evenly distributed throughout the box." (From *Why Do Clocks Run Clockwise, and Other Imponderables*, by David Feldman)

CHOCOLATE

Q: *Who brought chocolate from the New World to Europe?*

A: When the Spanish conquistador Hernan Cortés wrote to Emperor Charles V of Spain from the New World, he described a "divine drink...which builds up resistance and fights fatigue." Cortés was speaking of *chocolatl*, a drink the Aztecs brewed from a native *cacao* bean that was valued so highly that it was used as currency. He brought some home to Spain, and it became popular instantly.

Most-often earned Boy Scout merit badge in 1991: Swimming.

OTHER PRESIDENTIAL FIRSTS

We all know the first president (Washington), the first president to serve more than 2 terms (FDR), and so on. But who was the first to get stuck in a bathtub? Here's another BRI list of presidential firsts, with thanks to Bruce Fowler's book, One of a Kind.

THE PRESIDENT: Grover Cleveland (1885-89; 1893-97)
NOTABLE FIRST: First president to have hanged a man.
BACKGROUND: From 1871 to 1873, he was sheriff of Erie County, New York. When two men were sentenced to death there, Cleveland put the hoods over their heads, tightened the noose, and sprung the trap door himself. He explained later that he couldn't ask his deputies to do it just because he didn't want to. The experience affected him so deeply that he didn't run for re-election.

THE PRESIDENT: James Garfield (1881)
NOTABLE FIRST: First president who could write in two languages at once.
BACKGROUND: Garfield was ambidextrous; he could write in Greek with one hand while writing in Latin with the other.

THE PRESIDENT: William Howard Taft (1909-1913)
NOTABLE FIRST: First president entrapped by a White House plumbing fixture.
BACKGROUND: Taft weighed in at between 300 and 350 lbs. while he was president. He was so big that one morning he got stuck in the White House tub—and had to call his aides to help him get out. Taft subsequently ordered a tub large enough to hold four men. (He never got stuck again.)

THE PRESIDENT: James Madison (1809-1817)
NOTABLE FIRST: First president to weigh less than his I.Q.
BACKGROUND: Madison, the unofficial "Father of the U.S.

More Americans die in January than in any other month.

Constitution," was only 5'4" tall and never weighed more than 98 lbs. as president. One historian has called him "a dried-up, wizened little man"—and observed that when he went walking with his friend Thomas Jefferson, the two looked "as if they were on their way to a father-and-son banquet."

THE PRESIDENT: John Tyler (1841-1845)
NOTABLE FIRST: First president to elope while in office.
BACKGROUND: On June 26, 1844, the 54-year-old Tyler sneaked off to New York City with 24-year-old Julia Gardiner to tie the knot. They decided on a secret wedding because supporters were worried about the public's reaction to their 30-year age difference. It didn't matter—the press found out about it almost at once. Ironically, Julia turned out to be just about the most popular part of Tyler's presidency. (P.S.: They had 7 kids—the last one when Tyler was 70.)

THE PRESIDENT: Herbert Hoover (1929-1933)
NOTABLE FIRST: First president to have an asteroid named after him.
BACKGROUND: No, it's not in honor of his presidency. In 1920, Austrian astronomer Johann Palisa discovered an asteroid and named it *Hooveria*, to honor Hoover's humanitarian work as chairman of the Interallied Food Council, which was helping to feed starving people in post-WWI Europe. Said Palisa: "It is a pity we have only a middle-magnitude asteroid to give to this great man. He is worthy of at least a planet."

THE PRESIDENT: Jimmy Carter (1976-1980)
NOTABLE FIRST: First president to see a UFO.
BACKGROUND: One evening in 1969, Carter and a few companions saw a "bluish...then reddish" saucer-shaped object moving across the sky. "It seemed to move toward us from a distance," Carter later told UFO researchers, "then it stopped and moved partially away. It returned and departed. It came close...maybe three hundred to one thousand yards away...moved away, came close, and then moved away." He added: "I don't laugh at people anymore when they say they've seen UFOs."

COLD FOODS

The title doesn't really mean anything. We had a bunch of stories about food we wanted to use, and "cold" was the only thing we could think of that the foods had in common.

SWANSON TV DINNERS. When Carl Swanson stepped off the boat from Sweden in 1896, the only thing he owned was the sign around his neck that read, "Carl Swanson, Swedish. Send me to Omaha. I speak no English." Someone sent him to Omaha, where he started a grocery wholesale business that grew into the largest turkey processor in the United States. When his sons took over the company after his death, they began expanding their product line beyond turkeys. One of their first additions: frozen turkey and fried chicken meals they called "TV dinners," packaged in wood-grain boxes that simulated televisions. (Swanson never intended that the meals be eaten while watching TV—it just wanted to associate its "heat-and-eat miracle" with the magic of television.)

Swanson's first TV dinners bombed. The sweet potatoes in the turkey dinner were too watery, and customers complained that the fried chicken tasted like bananas—a problem caused by slow-drying, banana-scented yellow die that leached from the cardboard box onto the chicken. Swanson fixed the first problem by switching to regular potatoes; it solved the chicken problem by giving the boxes a longer time to dry. (What did it do with the chicken that had already been contaminated? It sold it to a Florida food chain that said its customers preferred the "new" banana taste.)

ESKIMO PIES. Christian Nelson owned a candy and ice cream store in Onawa, Iowa. One day in 1920, a kid came into the store and ordered a candy bar...and then changed his mind and asked for an ice-cream sandwich...and then changed his mind again and asked for a marshmallow nut bar. Nelson wondered for a minute why there wasn't any one candy-and-ice cream bar to satisfy all of the kid's cravings—and then decided to make one himself: a vanilla bar coated with a chocolate shell. Once he figured out how to make the chocolate stick to the ice cream, he had to think of a name for his product. At a dinner party, someone suggested "Eskimo," because it sounded cold. But other people thought it sounded too exotic—so Nelson added the word "pie."

MINUTE MAID ORANGE JUICE. In 1942 the U.S. Army announced that it would award a $750,000 contract to any company that could produce an orange juice "powder" cheap enough to send to troops overseas. After three years of intense research, the National Research Corporation (NRC) developed a way to concentrate and freeze orange juice, and was working out the bugs in the drying process. It won the contract—but just as it was lining up the financing for an orange juice plant, the U.S. dropped the A-bomb on Hiroshima, and World War II came to an end.

Convinced that powdered orange juice had a future, the NRC decided to forge ahead with its efforts to perfect the drying process. To raise money for the research, the company decided to unload some of its backlog of frozen concentrated orange juice. Marketed under the name Minute Maid, the stuff sold so well that NRC went into the frozen orange juice business instead.

ICE CREAM MISCELLANY

Ice Cream Sodas. In 1874, soda-fountain operator Robert M. Green sold a drink he made out of sweet cream, syrup, and carbonated water soda. One day he ran out of cream...so he used vanilla ice cream instead.

Ice Cream Sundaes. It seems ridiculous now, but in the 1890s, many religious leaders objected to people drinking ice cream sodas on Sunday. It was too frivolous. When "blue laws" were passed prohibiting the sale of ice-cream sodas on Sunday, ice-cream parlor owners fought back—they created the "Sunday," which was only sold on the Sabbath; it contained all of the ingredients of a soda *except* the soda water. A few years later the dish was being sold all week, so the name was changed to *sundae.*

Baskin-Robbins 31 Flavors. After World War II, Irvine Robbins and Burton Baskin built a chain of ice-cream stores in southern California. One day in 1953, Robbins says, "we told our advertising agency about our great variety of flavors and we said, almost in jest, that we had a flavor for every day of the month—thirty-one. They hit the table and said that was it, the thirty-one. So we changed the name of the company to Baskin Robbins 31. Like Heinz 57."

RUMORS

Why do people believe wild, unsubstantiated stories? According to some psychologists, "rumors make things simpler than they really are." And while people won't believe just anything, it's suprising what stories have flouished in the past. Many of these tales are stll in circulation today...

RUMOR: Wint-O-Green Lifesavers can kill you.
HOW IT SPREAD: In 1968 Dr. Howard Edward and Dr. Donald Edward wrote a letter to the *New England Journal of Medicine* warning that the eerie green sparks given off when you chomp on the Lifesavers could—under certain conditions—start a fire. Some possible conditions in which the Lifesavers could kill you: if you ate them in an oxygen tent, a space capsule, or in a room filled with flammable gas. (No word on whether anyone as ever actually *chewed* Wint-O-Greens under such conditions.)

WHAT HAPPENED: The letter inspired a number of researchers around the country to experiment with Wint-O-Green Lifesavers to see what made them spark, and to see if the sparks were indeed dangerous. Their findings: the sparks are caused by *methyl salicylate,* the synthetic crystalline substance that's used for flavoring instead of real wintergreen oil. The sparking effect is known scientifically as "triboluminescence," which is what happens when a crystalline substance is crushed. And since the spark is a "cold luminescence" and not a real spark, it can't cause an explosion. (Even so, researchers advise, if you are still nervous, just chew on them with your mouth closed.)

THE RUMOR: Silent screen starlet Clara Bow slept with the entire starting lineup of the 1927 USC football team.
HOW IT SPREAD: The story was started by Bow's private secretary, Daisy DeVoe, whom Bow fired after DeVoe tried to blackmail her. DeVoe got back at her by selling an "inside story" account of Bow's private life to *Graphic*, a notorious New York tabloid. The USC rumor was only part of the story; DeVoe also claimed that Bow had had affairs with Eddie Cantor, Gary Cooper, Bela Lugosi, and other celebrities.

WHAT HAPPENED: The surviving members of the 1927 team deny the story is true. Author David Stenn tracked them down while researching his biography *Clara Bow Runnin' Wild.* They admit that Bow often invited them to her parties, but they were entirely innocent—Bow didn't even serve alcohol. Even so, the tabloid story destroyed her career: Paramount Studios refused to renew her contract, and Bow "spent the greater part of the rest of her life suffering a series of nervous breakdowns in sanitariums."

THE RUMOR: Sesame Street is planning to "kill off" Ernie, the famous muppet of "Ernie and Bert" fame.

HOW IT SPREAD: The Children's Television Workshop believes the rumor started somewhere in New England after the 1990 death of muppet creator Jim Henson—who was Ernie's voice. CTW denied the rumor, but it quickly gained strength; according to Ellen Morgenstern, CTW's spokeswoman, "We've also heard that Ernie was going to die of AIDS, leukemia, a car crash.... Someone in New Hampshire even started a letter-writing campaign to save him. "

WHAT HAPPENED: Sesame Street, the Children's Television Workshop, and PBS have repeatedly denied the story. As Morgenstern puts it, "Ernie's not dying of AIDS, he's not dying of leukemia. Ernie is a puppet."

THE RUMOR: Corona Extra beer, imported from Mexico, is contaminated by workers at the brewery who regularly urinate into the beer vats.

HOW IT SPREAD: Corona Extra beer was introduced into the United States in 1981. It immediately became the brew of choice for southern California surfers. The fad quickly spread—and despite almost no advertising, by 1986 Corona had become the #2 imported beer in the nation. Less than a year later, however, the brand's importer, Barton Beers of Chicago, was inundated with rumors that Corona was contaminated with urine. Barton traced the rumor back to a competing wholesaler in Reno, Nevada.

WHAT HAPPENED: Barton Beers sued. In July 1987, the wholesaler settled out of court, and agreed to declare publicly that Corona "was free of any contamination."

THE RUMOR: In 1898 newspaper baron William Randolph Hearst sent the famous artist Frederic Remington to sketch the war in Cuba for the Hearst newspapers. The only problem: there was no war in Cuba—and Remington didn't think it would ever start. He cabled to Hearst, "Everything is quiet. There is no trouble here. there will be no war. I wish to return." Hearst cabled back: "Please remain. You furnish the pictures and I'll furnish the war"—and then single-handedly used his newspapers to generate enough pro-war public opinion to actually start the war.

HOW IT SPREAD: James Creelman, a Hearst reporter, first published the story in his memoirs.

WHAT HAPPENED: He never produced any evidence to support his charge, and Hearst denied the story in private. Many historians question whether the exchange ever took place...but no one knows for sure.

THE RUMOR: Cellular phones can give you brain tumors.

HOW IT SPREAD: In February 1993, according to a news report, "A Florida widower alleged on the CNN show 'Larry King Live' that the brain tumor which killed his wife in May, 1992 was caused by radio waves emitted by the cellular phone she used. His wife's monthly cellular bill was $150, roughly twice the national average. ...He contends the tumor was near the place the antenna of the phone pointed."

WHAT HAPPENED: Stock in some cellular phone companies dropped 6% overnight...but later recovered. Motorola, one of the country's largest cellular phone manufacturers, called a news conference to cite "thousands of studies" that showed the phones do not cause cancer. The Food and Drug Administration found that "there is no proof that there is a cancer threat from these phones." But the FDA conducted no independent tests before issuing the statement; instead it relied on information submitted by cellular phone manufacturers. All cellular phones on the market in 1993 tested well below federal guidelines for radio-frequency protection; nevertheless, Motorola advised customers "not to press body parts against the antennaes of cellular phones."

Irrelevant thought: "A man gazing at the stars is proverbially at the mercy of the puddles in the road." —*Alexander Smith*

THE TOUGHEST TOWN IN THE WEST

Think of a typical Western town in the 1870s. Saloons with swinging doors...horse manure all over the street...painted ladies waving at passersby...and gunfights. Lots of gunfights. It was such a popular image that Palisades, Nevada, decided to preserve it. Here's the story, with thanks to the People's Almanac.

A LEGEND IS BORN

By the late 1870s, the "Wild West" era was winding down. But it was such an entrenched part of American lore that many people hated to see it go.

One town, Palisade, Nevada, decided to keep it alive for as long as possible...by staging fake gunfights for unsuspecting train passengers on the Union Pacific and Central Pacific railroads, which regularly pulled into town for brief rest stops.

The idea got started when a train conductor suggested to a citizen of Palisade that "as long as so many easterners were travelling west hoping to see the Old West, why not give it to them?"

COMMUNITY ACTIVITY

The townspeople took the idea and ran with it: one week later they staged the first gunbattle in Palisade's history. The good guy was played by Frank West, a tall, handsome cowhand from a nearby ranch; Alvin "Dandy" Kittleby, a popular, deeply religious man (who also happened to look like a villain), played the bad guy.

Just as the noon train pulled into town for a 10 minute stop, Kittleby began walking down Main Street toward the town saloon. West, who was standing near a corral about 60 feet away, stepped out into the street and shouted at the top of his lungs: "There ya are, ya low-down polecat. Ah bin waitin' fer ya. Ah'm goin' to kill ya b'cause of what ya did ta mah sister. Mah pore, pore little sister." Then he drew his revolver and fired it over Kittleby's head. Kittleby fell to the ground kicking and screaming as if he had been shot, and the passengers immediatly dove for cover; several of the women fainted and some of the men may have too.

Ten minutes later when the train pulled out of the station, nearly every passenger was still crouched on the floor of the passenger compartment.

A MILESTONE

That was probably the first faked gunfight in the history of the Wild West, but it wasn't the last. Over the next three years, the Palisadians staged more than 1,000 gunfights—sometimes several a day.

To keep the townspeople interested and the train passengers fooled, the town regularly changed the theme of the gunfight, sometimes staging a duel, sometimes an Indian raid (in which real Shoshone Indians on horseback "massacred" innocent women and children before being gunned down themselves), and bank robberies involving more than a dozen robbers and sheriff's deputies.

Those who didn't directly participate in the gun battles helped out by manufacturing blank cartridges by the thousands and collecting beef blood from the town slaughterhouse. Nearly everyone within a 100-mile radius was in on the joke—including railroad workers, who probably thought the battles sold train tickets and were good for business. Somehow they all managed to keep the secret; for more than three years, nearly every passenger caught in the crossfire of a staged fight thought he was witnessing the real thing. The truth is, the town during these years was so safe that it didn't even have a sheriff.

NATIONAL OUTRAGE

One group of onlookers that weren't in on the joke were the metropolitan daily newspapers in towns like San Francisco, Chicago, and New York, which regularly reported the shocking news of the massacres on the front pages. Editorials were written by the dozens denouncing the senseless waste of human life and calling on local officials to get the situation under control. They even called on the U.S. Army to occupy the town and restore order...but since the Army itself was in on the joke, it never took action.

Over time Palisade developed a reputation as one of the toughest towns in the history of the West—a reputation that it probably deserved more than any other town, since it worked so hard to earn it.

Is it the cause or the result? Married men are twice as likely to be obese as single men.

FABULOUS FLOPS

*These products cost millions to invent. Their
legacy is a few bathroom laughs.*

The Studebaker Dictator. Not exactly "the heartbeat of America" when it was introduced in 1934. According to one auto industry analyst, "after Hitler and Mussolini came to power, a name like Dictator was downright un-American." Yet incredibly, the nation's #5 automaker stuck with it for 3 years.

Bic Perfume. The snazzy $5.00 perfume that looked like a cigarette lighter. Why wasn't it a hit with women? According to one industry expert, "It looked like a cigarette lighter." Bic lost $11 million.

Chilly Bang! Bang! Juice. The kiddie drink in a pistol-shaped package. Kids drank it by putting the barrel in their mouths and squeezing the trigger. Outraged parents—and complaints from officials in at least two states—got it yanked from the shelves.

Hop 'N' Gator. The inventor of Gatorade sold his original drink to a major corporation in 1966. Then, in 1969, he used the money to create another can't-miss product: a mixture of beer and Gatorade. The Pittsburg Brewing Company tried it out for a couple of years. Unfortunately, people didn't want Gatorade in their beer.

Zartan the Enemy action figures. Hasbro promoted the soldier doll as a "paranoid schizophrenic" that becomes violent under pressure. They pulled the product after mental health organizations complained.

Pepsi A.M. Why not get your morning caffeine from cola instead of coffee? The world's first breakfast soft drink didn't get far. Pepsi found out most consumers didn't *want* a breakfast soft drink—and people who *did* "still preferred the taste of plain old Pepsi."

Hands Up! Kids' soap in an aerosol can, introduced in 1962. Instead of a nozzle, there was a plastic gun mounted on top. You got soap out of the can by pointing the gun at a kid and squeezing the trigger. The Hands-Up slogan: "Gets kids clean and makes them like it."

EVERYDAY PHRASES

More origins of common phrases.

TOO MANY IRONS IN THE FIRE

Meaning: Working on too many projects at once.

Origin: "Refers to the blacksmith's forge, where if the smith had too many irons heating in the fire at the same time he couldn't do his job properly, as he was unable to use them all before some had cooled off." (From *Everyday Phrases*, by Neil Ewart)

THE NAKED TRUTH

Meaning: The absolute truth.

Origin: Comes from this old fable: "Truth and Falsehood went swimming. Falsehood stole the clothes that Truth had left on the river bank, but Truth refused to wear Falsehood's clothes and went naked." (From *Now I Get It!*, by Douglas Ottati)

TO GIVE SOMEONE THE COLD SHOULDER

Meaning: Reject, or act unfriendly toward, someone.

Origin: Actually refers to food. In England, a welcome or important visitor would be served a delicious hot meal. A guest "who had outstayed his welcome, or an ordinary traveler" would get a cold shoulder of mutton. (From *Rejected!* by Steve Gorlick)

READ SOMEONE THE RIOT ACT

Meaning: Deliver an ultimatum.

Origin: Comes from an actual Riot Act, passed by the British Parliament in 1714, that made it unlawful for a dozen or more people to gather for "riotous or illegal purposes." An authority would literally stand up and read out the terms of the Act, so that the rioters knew what law they were breaking: "Our Sovereign Lord the King chargeth and commandeth all persons assembled immediately to disperse themselves and peacefully to depart to their habitations or to their lawful business." If the crowd didn't disperse, they were arrested. (From *Why Do We Say It?*, by Nigel Rees)

Poll results: 40% of U.S. couples say they first discussed marriage in the back seat of a car.

PASS THE BUCK

Meaning: Blame someone else; avoid accepting responsibility.

Origin: "The original buck was a buckhorn knife passed around the table in certain card games. It was placed in front of the player whose turn it was to deal the cards and see that the stakes for all the players were placed in the pool." Someone who "passed the buck" literally passed that responsibility to the person next to him. (From *Everyday Phrases*, by Neil Ewart)

A BITTER PILL TO SWALLOW

Meaning: An experience that's difficult or painful to accept.

Origin: Refers to taking medicine in the time before doctors had any way to make pills more palatable. "The bark of a New World tree, the cinchona, was effective in fighting malaria. But the quinine it contains is extremely bitter. Widely employed in the era before medications were coated, cinchona pellets caused any disagreeable thing to be termed a bitter pill to swallow." (From *Why You Say It*, by Webb Garris)

HE'S TIED TO HER APRON STRINGS

Meaning: A man is dominated by his wife.

Origin: In England several hundred years ago, if a man married a woman with property, he didn't get title to it, but could use it while she was alive. This was popularly called *apron-string* tenure. A man tied to his wife's apron strings was in no position to argue; hence, the phrase came to stand for any abnormal submission to a wife or mother." (From *I've Got Goose Pimples*, by Marvin Vanoni)

Credit Where Credit Is Due

The name "credit card" was coined in 1888 by futurist author Edward Bellamy, who wrote a fictional account of a young man who wakes up in the year 2,000 and discovers that cash has been dumped in favor of "a credit corresponding to his share of the annual product of the nation...and a credit card is issued to him with which he procures at the public storehouses...whatever he desires, whenever he desires it." 60 years later, his vision (in slightly altered form) came true.

Atlantic coast seals aren't afraid of most boats—but they're scared to death of kayaks.

PRIMETIME PROVERBS

TV comments about everyday life. From Primetime Proverbs, *by Jack Mingo and John Javna*

ON DOCTORS:

Henry Blake: "I was never very good with my hands."

Radar O'Reilly: "Guess that's why you became a surgeon, huh, Sir?"

—*M*A*S*H*

Sophia: "How come so many doctors are Jewish?"

Jewish Doctor: "Because their mothers are."

—*The Golden Girls*

ON GOD:

"It's funny the way some people's name just suits the business they're in. Like God's name is just *perfect* for God."

—Edith Bunker,
All in the Family

ON FRIENDS:

"I've never felt closer to a group of people. Not even in the portable johns of Woodstock."

—Reverend Jim Ignatowski,
Taxi

"A friend, I am told, is worth more than pure gold."

—*Popeye*

ON GREED:

"Oh, yes indeedy, it doesn't pay to be greedy."

—Popeye,
The Popeye Cartoon Show

Robin [*anguished*]: "The Bat-diamond!"

Batman: "What about it, Robin?"

Robin: "To think it's the cause of all this trouble!"

Batman: "People call it many things, old chum: passion, lust, desire, avarice….But the simplest and most understandable word is greed."

—*Batman*

ON SEX:

Sam Malone: "I thought you weren't going to call me stupid now that we're being intimate."

Diane Chambers: "No, I said I wasn't going to call you stupid *while* we were being intimate."

—*Cheers*

ON DEATH:

"Death is just nature's way of telling you, 'Hey, you're not alive anymore.'"

—Bull,

The Canadian Mounties haven't mounted horses since 1938.

A WILD & CRAZY GUY

Observations from Steve Martin, one of America's biggest hams:

"Sex is one of the most beautiful-natural things that money can buy."

"I gave my cat a bath the other day....He sat there, he enjoyed it, it was fun for me. The fur would stick to my tongue, but other than that..."

"What? You been keeping records on me? I wasn't so bad! How many times did I take the Lord's name in vain? One million and six? Jesus CH—!"

"A celebrity is any well-known TV or movie star who looks like he spends more than two hours working on his hair."

"In talking to girls I could never remember the right sequence of things to say. I'd meet a girl and say, 'Hi was it good for you too?' If a girl spent the night, I'd wake up in the morning and then try to get her drunk..."

"I learned about sex watching neighborhood dogs. The most important thing I learned was: Never let go of the girl's leg no matter how hard she tries to shake you off."

"Boy, those French, they have a different word for *everything.*"

"I believe you should place a woman on a pedestal, high enough so you can look up her dress."

"I like a woman with a head on her shoulders. I hate necks."

"What is comedy? Comedy is the art of making people laugh without making them puke."

"There is something going on now in Mexico that I happen to think is cruelty to animals. What I'm talking about, of course, is cat juggling."

"I believe that Ronald Reagan can make this country what it once was—an arctic region covered with ice."

"I started a grease fire at McDonald's—threw a match in the cook's hair."

"I have a new book coming out. It's one of those self-help deals; it's called *How to Get Along with Everyone.* I wrote it with this other asshole."

Q. What's the most common language spoken by New York City cabdrivers? **A.** Urdu.

GONE, BUT
NOT FORGOTTEN

You can see them in museums or in books—but you won't see them
on the road, because no one makes them anymore. Here's
some info about 5 automobile legends.

THE PIERCE-ARROW (1901-1938). One of the most prestigious cars of its day, the Pierce Arrow set the standards for luxury and performance. According to one auto critic, "Even a massive limousine could whisper along at 100-mph—uniformed chauffeur up front; tycoon, cigar, and *Wall St. Journal* in the rear. (Some cars had speedometers back there so the owner could keep an eye on the chauffer's lead-foot tendencies.)" Pierce Arrow was the car of choice for rumrunners—who liked its quiet engine and reliability—and presidents: Woodrow Wilson rode in a customized Pierce Arrow limousine; so did FDR and J. Edgar Hoover (theirs were bulletproof).

Fate: When the Depression hit, the company kept building expensive cars, thinking the business downturn was temporary. Sales dropped from a high of 10,000 cars in 1929 to only 167 in 1937. The company was sold at auction a year later.

THE REO (1905-1936). In 1904, Ransom Eli Olds left the Olds Motor Co. and began a new one. The Olds Motor Company wouldn't let him use his last name—but couldn't stop him from using his initials, so he called it the Reo Motor Car Co. By 1907 it had become the 3rd largest auto manufacturer, after Ford and Buick. Five years later Olds announced his retirement and introduced his last car, Reo the Fifth (the company's fifth model).

Fate: Olds retired from day-to-day operations, but retained enough veto power to make himself a nuisance. As a result, Reo began to lag behind its competitors. Olds finally gave up control in 1934, but it was too late: two years later the company became yet another victim of the Great Depression.

THE STUTZ BEARCAT (1911-1935). Grandfather of the American muscle car, it was built for speed. According to legend,

---

Hi, Mom: 60% of Americans call their mother at least once a week.

founder Harry Stutz designed his clutches with "springs so stiff that a woman couldn't operate them." It was a teenager's dream car in the 'teens and 'twenties, because it won so many races. In 1912 it won 25 of the 30 national races it entered, and in 1915 Cannonball Baker drove a 4-cylinder Bearcat from San Diego to New York in less than 12 days, shattering the transcontinental record.

Fate: Another casualty of the Depression. Stutz couldn't slash costs and prices fast enough to stay competitive. In January 1935 it got out of the passenger-car business, and went bankrupt 2 years later.

THE DUESENBERG (1920-1937). To the driver of the 1920s, the name Duesenberg meant the top of the line: "The Duesenberg was more than a status symbol; it was status pure and simple, whether the owner was a maharajah, movie star, politician, robber baron, gangster or evangelist....'He drives a Duesenberg' was the only copy in many company advertisements." The first passenger cars rolled off the assembly line in 1920; for the next 17 years the phrase "It's a Duesy" meant the very best.

Fate: Duesenberg was the best carmaker of its day—but it was probably also the worst-run. The Duesenberg brothers were notoriously bad administrators. Chronic mismanagement, combined with the stock market crash of 1929, pushed the ailing company permanently into the red. It collapsed in 1937.

KAISER (1946-55). When World War II ended in 1945, shipbuilding magnate Henry J. Kaiser decided to start his own car company. The U.S. government wasn't buying ships anymore, and the auto industry hadn't released new models since the beginning of the war. Kaiser thought he could beat existing carmakers to market with flashy new models, and change the Big Three to the Big Four.

Kaiser's 1946 models *did* make the Big Three's cars look dowdy and old-fashioned in comparison. The company's sales hit 70,000 in 1947—but it soon ran into trouble.

Fate: Ford, GM, and Chrysler shed their pre-war image in 1947-8, and began beating Kaiser on price. The situation became desperate: some years Kaiser's sales were so bad that rather than introduce a new model, the company just changed the serial numbers on unsold cars and introduced *them* as the new models. In 1954 the company merged with the Willys-Overland (forerunner of the Jeep company); one year later the Kaiser model line was discontinued.

Explosive fact: 12,000 Americans are injured by fireworks every year.

CHILDHOOD WISDOM

Quotes from classic children's books.

"We are all made of the same stuff, remember, we of the Jungle, and you of the City. The same substance composes us—the tree overhead, the stone beneath us, the bird, the beast, the star—we are all one, all moving to the same end....Bird and beast and stone and star—we are all one, all one—Child and serpent, star and stone—all one."

—**The Hamadryad,** *Mary Poppins*

"If I can fool a bug, I can fool a man. People are not as smart as bugs."

—**Charlotte,** *Charlotte's Web*

"Money is a nuisance. We'd all be much better off if it had never been invented.What does money matter, as long as we all are happy?"

—**Dr. Doolittle,** *Dr. Doolittle*

"Winter will pass, the days will lengthen, the ice will melt in the pasture pond. The song sparrow will return and sing, the frogs will awake, the warm wind will blow again. All these sights and sounds and smells will be yours to enjoy, Wilbur—this lovely world, these precious days."

—**Charlotte,** *Charlotte's Web*

"Don't be angry after you've been afraid. That's the worst kind of cowardice."

—**Billy the Troophorse,** *The Jungle Books*

"Time flies, and one begins to grow old. This autumn I'll be ten, and then I guess I'll have seen my best days."

Pippi Longstocking, *Pippi Goes on Board*

Are you lonesome tonight? In a recent survey, 1% of Americans said they have no friends.

LOOK IT UP!

Every bathroom reader knows the value of a good record book, or a volume of quotes, in a pinch. Here are the stories of the originals.

B ARTLETT'S FAMILIAR QUOTATIONS.
John Bartlett was 16 years old when he left school in 1836 and got a job as a clerk at the University Bookstore across the street from Harvard.

Over the next 13 years he saved enough money to buy the store—and in that time managed to read nearly every book it contained. He became so well-known as a "quotation freak" that whenever someone asked where a familiar saying came from, or needed a quote to dress up a term paper, the answer would be, "Ask John Bartlett." By the mid-1850s, his reputation had grown beyond even his own remarkable abilities; no longer able to recite everything from memory, he began writing things down.

In 1855 he printed up 1,000 copies of his 258-page list of quotes, and began selling them at the store. "Should this be favorably received," he wrote in the preface, "endeavors will be made to make it more worthy of the public in a future edition." Sixteen editions and nearly 140 years later, *Bartlett's Familiar Quotations* is the most frequently consulted reference work of its kind.

THE GUINNESS BOOK OF WORLD RECORDS.
In 1954 Sir Hugh Beaver, an avid sportsman and managing director of Arthur Guinness, Son and Company (brewers of Guinness Stout beer), shot at some game birds in the Irish countryside...but they all got away. Looking for an excuse, he exclaimed that he'd missed because the breed of birds—plovers— were "the fastest game bird we've got" in the British Isles. But were they? He had no idea, and no reference he consulted could tell him.

He never found out for sure about the plovers. But the experience *did* give him the idea for a book of world records. He commissioned two researchers, Norris and Ross McWhirter, to write it for Guinness. Four months later they were finished, and four months after that the first *Guinness Book of World Records* was #1 on the British best seller list.

More collect calls are made on Father's Day than on any other day.

DONKEY KONG

Some people are so addicted to Nintendo that they've got it set up in the bathroom. Really? No. We made that up as an intro to this tale of Donkey Kong's origin. Interesting idea, though.

BACKGROUND. In 1977, a young artist named Sigeru Miyamoto asked his father to get him an interview with Hiroshi Yamauchi, a friend who owned a small electronics company called Nintendo.

Yamauchi liked the young man, and hired him as Nintendo's first staff artist—even though they didn't really need one.

Then in 1980, Yamauchi called Miyamoto into his office...and told him that he was looking for a video game. Here's David Scheff's account of what happened, from *Game Over:*

THE CHALLENGE

"Miyamoto had played many video games at college in Kanazawa. He loved them. In video games, cartoons came to life. He boldly told the Nintendo chairman that he would enjoy creating a game. However, he said, the shoot-'em-up and tennis-like games that were in the arcades at that time were unimaginative, simply uninteresting to many people. He had always wondered why video games were not treated more like books or movies. Why couldn't they draw on the great stories: some of his favorite legends, fairy tales, and fiction—*King Kong, Jason and the Argonauts,* even *Macbeth?*

"Nodding impatiently, Yamauchi rushed to the point: A Nintendo coin-operated video game called *Radarscope* was a disaster. There was no one else available to come up with a new game design. Miyamoto had to...convert *Radarscope* to something that would sell."

A NEW GAME

Miyamoto decided Radarscope was too boring. He threw it away and began designing his own game....

"...He thought about *Beauty and the Beast,* but simplified the story. He came up with his own beast, a King Kong-like ape, a humorous bad guy, 'nothing too evil or repulsive,' Miyamoto recalls. The ape would be the pet of the main character, 'a funny, hang-loose kind of guy' who was not especially nice to the gorilla....At his first opportunity, the gorilla escaped and kidnapped the guy's beautiful girlfriend.

"The gorilla didn't take the woman to hurt her—an important point in Miyamoto's mind—but to get back at the little man. The man, of course, then had to try to save the girl.

"Miyamoto wanted the main character to be goofy and awkward. He chose an ordinary carpenter, neither handsome nor heroic... someone anyone could relate to....The engineers had taught Miyamoto that it was important to distinguish the body so it would be visible on a video-game screen. Therefore he clothed his chubby character in bright-colored carpenter's overalls. In order to make the movement obvious in the simple animation of video games, it was important that characters' arms moved, so he drew stocky arms that swung back and forth. The engineers said it was difficult to accurately represent hair in a video game because...when a character fell, logically his hair would have to fly up. To avoid the problem, Miyamoto added a red cap. 'Also,' he adds, 'I cannot come up with hairstyles so good.' "

NAMING THE GAME

"...When the game was complete, Miyamoto had to name it. He consulted the company's export manager, and together they mulled over some possibilities. They decided that *kong* would be understood to suggest a gorilla....*Donkey*, according to their Japanese/English dictionary, was the translation of the Japanese word for stupid or goofy, [so] they combined the words and named [it] 'Donkey Kong.'

"Later, when the American sales managers...heard the name, they looked at one another in disbelief, thinking Yamauchi had flipped. 'Donkey *Hong?*' '*Konkey Dong?*' '*Honkey Dong?*' It made no sense. Games that were selling had titles that contained words such as *mutilation, destroy, assassinate, annihilate.* When they played 'Donkey Kong,' they were even more horrified. The salesmen were used to battle games with space invaders, and heroes shooting lasers at aliens. One hated 'Donkey Kong' so much that he began looking for a new job.

"Yamauchi heard all the feedback but ignored it. 'Donkey Kong,' released in 1981, became Nintendo's first super-smash hit."

Pet lovers: 21% of cat owners and 27% of dog owners include their pets in their wills.

MORE PEOPLE WATCHING

Here are the results of more studies, reported in
Bernard Asbell's The Book of You.

STUDIES ABOUT MARRIAGE SHOW THAT...

• *If you're talking with your spouse:* The more comfortable you are with your marriage, the less you...look at each other as you talk. If you are a poorly adjusted couple...you glance often, each of you seeming to monitor the other's reactions, particularly after a criticsm or barb."

• *If you think you're starting to look alike:*

√ You may be right. Robert B. Zajonc of the University of Michigan randomly collected photographs of two dozen couples, taken when they were just married....The researchers then... collected relatively fresh photos of the subjects, who were generally 50-60 years old. [Students] were then asked to pair up the married couples, both then and now. With the younger faces, they did no better than chance at linking husbands with wives. But they did significantly better with the more recent photos.

√ How does Zajonc explain the results? Over time, husbands and wives deepen in their habit of mimicking one another, especially in facial expressions. This...imitation, says Zajonc, "would leave wrinkles around the mouth and eyes, alter the bearing of the head, and the overall expression. Eventually it would produce... changes that make spouses appear more similar than they...were."

STUDIES ABOUT ROMANCE SHOW THAT...

• *If you want to do the most romantic thing for your lover that you can imagine:* You'd probably say "I love you."

• *If you want your lover to do the most romantic thing for you that you can imagine:* Well, when you put it *that* way—the answer comes out much different. Hearing "I love you" ranks only as twelfth most desirable in this survey of students. First choice, by far, is "Lying

Clear priorities: More than 50% of teenage boys say they'd "rather be rich than smart."

about in front of a fire." The runners-up: "Walking on the beach," and "taking a shower together." (The study's subjects were 787 college students who were asked to rate various activities on a scale from "very romantic" to "not romantic at all.")

STUDIES ON THE WAY WE FEEL ABOUT BODIES & WEIGHT SHOW THAT...

If you're a woman:
> √ [You think of yourself as fatter than you think men would prefer you to be.] The surprising fact, according to this study of 500 college age men and women, is that men prefer women fatter than what most women think men like, and certainly fatter than what most women think is ideal.

If you're a man:
> √ In constrast to women, you tend to think better of your body than others do.... You're apt to feel little or no discrepancy between the way you feel your body looks, and what your notion is of an ideal body weight—or, for that matter, what you think women prefer in a man's body.
> √ You're happily deluding yourself. Women in a study prefer men lighter than your notion of an ideal—and lighter than what you think women like.

STUDIES ABOUT THE WAY PEOPLE REACT TO EACH OTHER SHOW THAT...

• *If you're talking to someone you just met, and the person lightly touches you at the end of the conversation:*
> √ If you're both men, you're more likely...to give the other person a high rating as a "nice guy" if he patted you on the back than if he touched you on the arm.
> √ If you're both women—or if one of you is a woman and the other a man—you'll probably rate the other person more likeable if he or she touched you on the arm rather than patted you on the back.

• *If you talk loudly:* The impression given others...is that you are assertive, aggressive, and possibly not too desireable to work with. But your loud voice...causes people to pay more attention to what you say than they do voices of lower volume.

76% of teenagers say they believe in angels. That's up from 64% in 1978.

THE MONA LISA

It's the most famous painting in the world—even Uncle John has heard of it. But what else do you know about this mysterious lady?

BACKGROUND. Sometime between 1501 and 1506—no one is sure exactly when—Leonardo da Vinci, the great Renaissance artist, scientist, and thinker, painted his masterpiece "La Joconde," better known as the Mona Lisa. Hardly anything is known about the painting. Da Vinci kept extensive records on many of his *other* paintings, but none on the Mona Lisa. He never once mentioned it in any of his notebooks, and never made any preliminary studies of it.

However, historians believe the painting was one of Leonardo's favorites. Unlike most of his other paintings, which he painted on commission and turned over to their owners as soon as they were finished, da Vinci kept the Mona Lisa for more than 15 years—and still had it in his possession when he died in 1519.

WHO'S THAT GIRL?

No one knows who really modeled for the Mona Lisa—but some of the popular candidates are:

• **Mona Lisa Gherardini,** wife of Francesco del Giocondo, a Florentine silk merchant. After da Vinci's death, Gherardini was so widely believed to have been the model for the painting that it was named after her. But art historians now doubt she was the model, because the source of this rumor was Giorgio Vasari, da Vinci's biographer—who never even saw the painting in person.

• **Another Noblewoman** da Vinci knew—or perhaps a composite painting of two or more of them.

• **No one.** Some historians think the painting was a *finzione* or "feigning"—a fictional woman not based on any particular person.

• **Himself.** The painting is a feminine self-portrait. This theory is strange but surprisingly plausible. In 1987, computer scientists at AT&T Bell Laboratories took da Vinci's 1518 Self-Portrait, reversed the image (it faces right, not left like the Mona Lisa), enlarged it to the same scale, and juxtaposed it against the Mona Lisa, the similarities were too striking to be accidental...or so they say.

Poll results: 7% of Americans say they have a radio in their bathroom.

MONA LISA FACTS

• The Mona Lisa is considered one of the most important paintings of the Renaissance period—but King Francis I of France, who took possession of the painting after da Vinci died, hung it in the palace bathroom.

• Napoleon, on the other hand, was a big fan of the painting; he called it "The Sphinx of the Occident" and kept it in his bedroom.

• Why is Mona Lisa wearing such a strange smile? Some art historians suspect that this most famous feature may actually be the work of clumsy restorers who tried to touch up the painting centuries ago. Da Vinci may have intended her to wear a much more ordinary expression. Dozens of other theories have been proposed to explain the strange grin, including that Mona Lisa has just lost a child, has asthma or bad teeth, or is really a young man. Sigmund Freud theorized that da Vinci painted the smile that way because it reminded him of his mother.

• Mona Lisa may be "in the family way." According to writer Seymour Reit, "the lady is definitely pregnant, as shown by the slightly swollen hands and face, and her 'self-satisfied' expression." Other historians disagree—they think that Mona Lisa is just chubby.

THE THEFT

• According to a 1952 Paris study, there are at least 72 excellent 16th- and 17th- century replicas and reproductions of the Mona Lisa in existence—leading conspiracy theorists to speculate that the painting in the Louvre is itself a replica.

• One of the most interesting forgery theories has to do with a theft of the painting that occurred in 1911. On August 21 of that year, the Mona Lisa vanished from the Louvre in what was probably the biggest art heist of the century. French authorities conducted a massive investigation, but were unable to locate the painting. Two years later, an Italian carpenter named Vincenzo Perugia was caught trying to sell the masterpiece to an Italian museum.

The official story is that Perugia wanted to return the work to Italy, da Vinci's (and his) birthplace...But Seymour Reit, author of *The Day They Stole The Mona Lisa*, theorizes that the plot was the work of Marqués Eduardo de Valfierno, a nobleman who made his living selling forged masterpieces to unsuspecting millionaires. He wanted to do the same with the Mona Lisa—but knew that no one would buy a forgery of such a famous painting unless the original were stolen from the Louvre first. So De Valfierno paid a forger to paint half a dozen fakes, and then hired Perugia to steal the real Mona Lisa.

Reit argues that De Valfierno had no plans for the original masterpiece—he didn't want to sell it or even own it himself—and was only interested in selling his forgeries. He never even bothered to collect the original from Perugia, who hid it in the false bottom of a dirty steamer trunk for more than two years waiting for De Valfierno to come and get it. But he never did, so Perugia finally gave up and tried to sell the Mona Lisa to an Italian museum. As soon as he handed over the painting, he was arrested and the painting was returned to France. Perugia was tried and convicted for the theft, but spent only 7 months in prison for his crime. De Valfierno was never tried.

PROTECTING THE PAINTING

• The Mona Lisa isn't painted on canvas—it's painted on a wood panel made from poplar. This makes it extremely fragile, since changes in the moisture content of the wood can cause it to expand and shrink, which cracks the paint.

• Because of this, the Louvre goes to great lengths to protect the Mona Lisa from the elements—and from vandals. Since 1974 the painting has been stored in a bulletproof, climate-controlled box called a *vitrine* that keeps the painting permanently at 68° Fahrenheit and at 50-50% humidity.

• Once a year, the painting is removed from its protective case and given a checkup. The process takes about an hour and requires almost 30 curators, restorers, laboratory technicians, and maintenance workers.

• Despite nearly 500 years of accumulated dust, dirt, and grime, the risks associated with cleaning the masterpiece are so great that the museum refuses to do it—even though the filth has changed the appearance of the painting dramatically. Pierre Rosenberg, the Louvre's curator, says: "If we saw the Mona Lisa as da Vinci painted it, we would not recognize it....Da Vinci actually painted with bright, vivid colors, not the subdued tones that are visible today." But he's adamant about leaving the painting in its present state. "The Mona Lisa is such a sacrosanct image that to touch it would create a national scandal."

WHAT IS HYPNOTISM?

You are getting sleepy...sleepy...you will do anything we tell you. Now listen carefully: When you leave the bathroom, you will experience an irresistible urge to give everyone you know copies of Uncle John's Sixth Bathroom Reader. Do you understand? Good. When you emerge from the bathroom, you won't remember anything we've said. Now resume reading.

BACKGROUND. The history of hypnotism—drawing someone into an "altered state of consciousness" in which they are more susceptible to suggestion than when fully conscious—dates back thousands of years and is as old as sorcery, medicine, and witchcraft. The first person in modern times to study it was Franz Mesmer, an 18th-century Viennese physician. In 1775 he devised the theory that a person could transmit "universal forces," known as *animal magnetism*, to other people.

Critics derisively named this practice "Mesmerism," and chased him out of Vienna for practicing witchcraft. He then resettled in Paris, where a royal commission dismissed Mesmerism's "cures" as the product of his patients' imaginations.

Viewed as a crackpot science by the entire medical establishment, Mesmerism might have died out, except for one thing: anesthesia hadn't been invented yet, and physicians were desperately looking for something to kill the pain in surgical procedures. Mesmer himself had performed surgery using mesmerism as anesthesia as early as 1778, and other doctors soon began trying it.

One of the most successful was John Elliotson, a London surgeon who used it successfully on thousands of patients—but at great personal cost: he was booted out of his professorship and became a laughing stock of English medical society. John Elsdaile, a medical officer with the East India Company, had better luck: he performed hundreds of operations, including amputations, "painlessly and with few fatalities" using mesmerism. At about the same time another English physician experimenting with the procedure, James Braid, renamed it "hypnosis" after Hypnos, the Greco-Roman god of sleep.

In the 1880s Sigmund Freud visited France and decided to experiment with hypnosis in the fledgling field of psychology. He used it to treat neurotic disorders by helping patients remember events in their past that they had either forgotten or repressed. But as he developed his method of psychoanalysis, he lost interest in hypnosis and eventually dumped it entirely.

Despite Freud's rejection, hypnotism continued to grow in popularity. By the mid-1950s the British and American Medical Associations had approved its use. Although hypnotism is seldom used as an anesthetic in surgery today—except in combination with pain-killing drugs—it is widely used to prepare patients for anesthesia; ease the pain of childbirth; lower blood pressure; combat headaches; ease the fear associated with dentist appointments; and a variety of other applications. More than 15,000 physicians, dentists, and psychologists currently incorporate hypnotherapy into their practices.

BENEFITS

According to *US News and World Report*, as many as 94% of hospital patients who are hypnotized as part of their therapy "get some benefit" from it. Some examples cited by the magazine:

• "Cancer patients can undergo chemotherapy without the usual nausea if they are first hypnotized."

• "Burn patients recover faster and with less medication if they are hypnotized within two hours of receiving their burns and told they will heal quickly and painlessly. Researchers think hypnotherapy gives them the ability to will the release of anti-inflammatory substances that limit the damage."

• "J. Michael Drever, a cosmetic surgeon, finds that postsurgical hypnotic suggestions can see his patients through breast reconstructions and tummy tucks with less bleeding, fewer complications and quicker recovery."

NONBELIEVERS

One of hypnotism's most outspoken critics is Las Vegas performer "The Amazing Kreskin," who dismisses it as "just a figment of the imagination." Kreskin worked as a hypnotherapist under the supervision of a New Jersey psychologist in the 1960s. But he ultimately became a skeptic: "Anything I ever did with a patient who was supposedly under hypnosis I was able to do without putting them in the slightest trance—by persuading them, encouraging them, threatening them, browbeating them or just giving them an awful lot of confidence....All that's happening is what Alfred Hitchcock does every time he terrifies you and changes the surface of your skin with goosebumps. You're using your imagination."

HYPNOSIS FACTS

• It is impossible to hypnotize someone against their wishes.

• A hypnotized person, even when they appear to be asleep or in a trance, is physiologically awake at all times. Unlike sleepwalkers, their brain waves are identical to those of a person who's fully awake.

• A hypnotized person is always completely aware of his or her surroundings—although they can be instructed to ignore surrounding events, which creates the appearance of being unaware of their surroundings.

ANOTHER FORM OF HYPNOSIS?

Here's some background on America's most pervasive credit cards:

American Express. Formed by American Express in 1958 to complement its lucrative travelers check business. According to *American Heritage* magazine, "American Express came to dominate the field partly because it could cover the credit it was extending with the float from its traveler's checks, which are, after all, a form of interest-free loan from consumers to American Express."

Visa. California's Bank of America began issuing its BankAmericard in 1958. At first it was intended to be used at stores near Bank of America branches, but it was so profitable that the bank licensed banks all over the country to issue it. However, other banks hated issuing a card with B of A's name on it. So in 1977 the card's name was changed to *Visa.*

MasterCard. Originally named Master Charge, the card was formed in 1968 by Wells Fargo Bank and 77 other banks, who wanted to end BankAmericard's dominance of the credit card business. They succeeded: thanks to mergers with other credit cards, it became the biggest bank card within a year. Can you remember why it changed its name to MasterCard in 1979? According to company president Russell Hogg, they wanted to shed the card's "blue collar" image.

JFK's PRESIDENTIAL AFFAIRS

You've heard about his liaison with Marilyn Monroe. But there's more. A lot more. Here's some of the gossip you probably haven't heard.

BACKGROUND
Rumors of marital infidelity have plagued a number of Presidents, but perhaps none as much as John F. Kennedy.

According to books like *JFK: A Question of Character*, many of the rumors are true. While he was president, Kennedy's youth and charisma proved irresistible to scores of attractive young women who found themselves in his company—and JFK made the most of the opportunity. One member of the administration remembers: "it was a revolving door over there. A woman had to fight to get into that line."

As Traphes Bryant, a White House employee who served under the Kennedys and other first families, says, "Despite all the stories I've heard about other past presidents, I doubt we will ever have another one like Kennedy."

Here are a few of the *tamer* details that have surfaced since JFK's infidelities became public in 1977.

A LITTLE HELP FROM HIS FRIENDS

• The White House staff were directly involved in Kennedy's womanizing. Top aides such as Evelyn Lincoln, the President's personal secretary, were responsible for sneaking women in and out of the White House unobserved by Mrs. Kennedy or the press.

• According to Bryant, "there was a conspiracy of silence to protect his secrets from Jacqueline and to keep her from finding out. The newspapers would tell how First Lady Jacqueline was off on a trip, but what they didn't report was how anxious the President sometimes was to see her go. And what consternation there sometimes was when she returned unexpectedly."

• The Secret Service was also in on the act. They helped remove traces of JFK's affairs from White House bedrooms, and were responsible for ferrying Kennedy to and from "love nests" undetected

---

Dieter's nightmare: The baby blue whale gains 10 lbs. *per hour.*

during presidential trips. Charles Spaulding, one of Kennedy's closest friends, remembers one such trip when the president was staying at the Carlyle Hotel in New York. He and Kennedy traveled to their mistresses' nearby apartments via a network of underground tunnels beneath the hotel. "It was kind of a weird sight," Spaulding remembers. "Jack and I and two Secret Service men walking in these huge tunnels underneath the city streets alongside those enormous pipes, each of us carrying a flashlight. One of the Secret Service men also had this underground map and every once in a while he would say, 'We turn this way, Mr. President.'"

• On occasions when Kennedy felt he couldn't trust his Secret Service detachment with his affairs—or simply didn't want them around—he just ditched them. Once he even became separated from the Army officer carrying the "football," the briefcase containing the nation's nuclear launch codes—and went to a party unescorted. "The Russians could have bombed us to hell and back," one aide remembered, "and there would have been nothing we could have done about it."

JFK's 1,000 POINTS OF LIGHT

• JFK liked to sleep with famous women—Marilyn Monroe and actor David Niven's wife among them. According to one story, a White House staffer once asked Kennedy what he wanted for his birthday. According to another staffer's diary entry, the President "named a TV actress from California....His wish was granted."

• In addition to actresses and models, Kennedy had relationships with numerous female employees on the White House staff. He also slept with female reporters in the White House Press Pool. He even had an affair with Judith Campbell Exner, the girlfriend of a reputed mob boss Sam Giancana. And according to some accounts, the Mafia recorded the President's lovemaking sessions and used the tapes to blackmail the White House into going easy on them.

• Kennedy loved to frolic nude with girlfriends in the White House pool and let his mistresses streak through the White House corridors. Once Bryant was riding in an elevator when it stopped on the President's floor. "Just as the elevator door opened, a naked blonde office girl ran through the hall. There was nothing for me to do but get out fast, and push the button for the basement."

DANGEROUS LIAISONS

On at least one occasion, Kennedy's romances came close to destroying his presidency. Not long after being elected president, he
talked his wife into hiring Pamela Turnur, a striking 23-year-old
brunette with whom he was having an affair, as her press secretary.
"That way [Pamela would] be right there close at hand when he
wanted her," one friend remembers.

Although Jacqueline apparently knew about their relationship
from the beginning and seemed to grudgingly accept it, Turnur's
landlady, Mrs. Leonard Kater, did not. She waited and snapped a
picture of Kennedy leaving Turnur's apartment early one morning.
Determined to expose the President as a "debaucher of a girl young
enough to be his daughter," Kater contacted the media and told
them her story.

But luckily for JFK, the photo she took didn't actually show Kennedy's face (he was covering it with his hands)—so nobody could
be sure it was really the President. When the reporters refused to
cover the story, Mrs. Kater wrote a letter to the Attorney General
(Bobby Kennedy)—and when that failed, she marched up and
down Pennsylvania Avenue carrying a sign that said, "Do you want
an adulterer in the White House?", giving away copies of her photograph. Kater was dismissed as a crackpot.

KEEPING SECRETS

No matter how hard he and the White House staff tried, Kennedy
couldn't prevent his wife from finding out about his numerous affairs. Mrs. Kennedy apparently became aware of JFK's extracurricu-
lar activities soon after their marriage in 1953. And according to
one close friend, she took the discovery hard. "After the first year
they were together, Jackie was wandering around looking like the
survivor of an airplane crash."

But as time went on she became resigned to Jack's womanizing,
and even a bit cynical. Once when she discovered a pair of panties
stuffed into a pillowcase on their bed, she confronted him with the
evidence. One witness remembers, "She delicately held it out to
her husband between thumb and forefinger—about the way you
hold a worm—saying, 'Would you please shop around and see who
these belong to? They're not my size.' "

Edgar Allen Poe's *The Murders in the Rue Morgue* was the first detective story ever written.

STAR WARS

"There's a whole generation growing up without any kind of fairy tales. And kids need fairy tales—it's an important thing for society to have for kids." —George Lucas

BACKGROUND. In July, 1973 George Lucas was an unknown director working on a low-budget 1950s nostalgia film called *American Graffiti*. He approached Universal Studios to see if they were interested in a film idea he called *Star Wars*. Universal turned him down.

It was the biggest mistake the studio ever made.

Six months later, Lucas was the hottest director in Hollywood. *American Graffiti*, which cost $750,000 to make, was a smash. It went on to earn more than $117 million, making it the most profitable film in Hollywood history—even today.

While Universal was stonewalling Lucas, an executive at 20th Century Fox, Alan Ladd, Jr., watched a smuggled print of *American Graffiti* before it premiéred and loved it. He was so determined to work with Lucas that he agreed to finance the director's new science fiction film.

Star Wars opened on May 25, 1977, and by the end of August it had grossed $100 million—faster than any other film in history. By 1983 the film had sold more than $524 million in ticket sales worldwide—making it one of the 10 best-selling films in history.

MAKING THE FILM

• It took Lucas more than two years to write the script. He spent 40 hours a week writing, and devoted much of his free time to reading comic books and watching old Buck Rogers and other serials looking for film ideas.

• Lucas insisted on casting unknown actors and actresses in all the important parts of the film—which made the studio uneasy. Mark Hamill had made more than 100 TV appearances, and Carrie Fisher had studied acting, but neither had had much experience in films. Harrison Ford's biggest role had been as the drag racer in *American Graffiti*, and when he read for the part of Han Solo he was working as a carpenter.

THE CHARACTERS

Luke Skywalker. At first Lucas planned to portray him as an elderly general, but decided that making him a teenager gave him more potential for character development. Lucas originally named the character Luke Starkiller, but on the first day of shooting he changed it to the less violent Skywalker.

Obi-Wan Kenobi. Lucas got his idea for Obi-Wan Kenobi and "the Force" after reading Carlos Castaneda's *Tales of Power,* an account of Don Juan, a Mexican-Indian sorcerer and his experiences with what he calls "the life force."

Darth Vader. David Prowse, a 6' 7" Welsh weightlifter, played the part of Darth Vader. But Lucas didn't want his villain to have a Welsh accent, so he dubbed James Earl Jones's voice over Prowse's. Still, Prowse loved the part. "He took the whole thing very seriously," Lucas remembers. "He began to believe he really was Darth Vader."

Han Solo. In the early stages of development, Han Solo was a green-skinned, gilled monster with a girlfriend named Boma who was a cross between a guinea pig and a brown bear. Solo was supposed to make only a few appearances in the film, but Lucas later made him into a swashbuckling, reckless human (allegedly modeled after film director Francis Ford Coppola).

Chewbacca. Lucas got the idea for Chewbacca one morning in the ealy 1970s while watching his wife Marcia drive off in her car. She had their Alaskan malamute, Indiana, in the car (the namesake for Indiana Jones in *Raiders of the Lost Ark*), and Lucas liked the way the large shaggy mutt looked in the passenger seat. So he decided to create a character in the film that was a cross between Indiana, a bear, and a monkey.

Princess Leia. Carrie Fisher was a beautiful 19-year-old actress when she was cast to play Princess Leia, but Lucas did everything he could to tone down her femininity. At one point, he even ordered that her breasts be strapped to her chest with electrical tape. "There's no jiggling in the Empire," Fisher later joked.

R2-D2. Lucas got the name R2-D2 while filming *American Graffiti*. During a sound-mixing session for the film, editor Walter Murch asked him for R2, D2´(Reel 2, Dialogue 2) of the film. Lucas liked the name so much that he made a note of it, and eventually found the right character for it.

C-3PO. Inspired by a robot character in Alex Raymond's science fiction novel, *Iron Men of Mongo*. Raymond's robot was a copper-colored, polite robot who was shaped like a man and who worked as a servant. Lucas intended that C-3PO and R2-D2 be a space-age Laurel and Hardy team.

SPECIAL EFFECTS
• The spaceship battles were inspired by World War II films. Before filming of the special effects began, Lucas watched dozens of war movies like *Battle of Britain* and *The Bridges of Toko-Ri*, taping his favorite air battle scenes as he went along. Later he edited them down to a 10 minute black-and-white film, and gave it to the special effects team—which re-shot the scenes using X-wing and T.I.E. fighter models.

• None of the spaceship models ever moved an inch during filming of the flight sequences. The motion was an optical illusion created by moving the cameras around motionless models. The models were so detailed that one of them even had Playboy pinups in its cockpit.

MISCELLANEOUS FACTS
• The executives at 20th Century Fox hated the film the first time they saw it. Some of the company's board of directors fell asleep during the first screening; others didn't understand the film at all. One executive's wife even suggested that C-3PO be given a moving mouth, because no one would understand how he could talk without moving his lips.

• The underwater monster in the trash compactor was one of Lucas's biggest disappointments in the film. He had planned to have an elaborate "alien jellyfish" in the scene, but the monster created by the special-effects department was so poorly constructed that it reminded him of "a big, wide, brown turd." Result: The monster was filmed underwater during most of the scene—so that moviegoers wouldn't see it.

Q & A:
ASK THE EXPERTS

More random questions…and answers from America's trivia experts.

HIC!

Q: *What are hiccups…and why do we have them?*

A: "Hiccups… involve an involuntary contraction of the diaphragm, the muscle separating the abdomen and chest. When the diaphragm contracts, the vocal chords close quickly, which is what makes the funny 'hiccuping' sound." Hiccups seem to be induced by many different circumstances. No one's sure *why* people hiccup, but in some circumstances, hiccups are predictable: for example, eating or drinking too fast, nervousness, pregnancy, alcoholism.

"Most of the time hiccups…stop in a few minutes whether you do anything about them or not.…There was, however, one case of hiccups listed in the *Guinness Book of World Records* that lasted for sixty years. Charles Osborne of Anthon, Iowa started hiccuping in 1922 after slaughtering a hog, and he must have hiccuped at least 430 million times. He said he was able to live a fairly normal life during which he had two wives and eight children. He did have some difficulty keeping his false teeth in his mouth." (From *Why Doesn't My Funny Bone Make Me Laugh?*, by Alan Xanakis, M.D.)

BIRD POOP

Q: *What's the black dot in the middle of bird droppings?*

A: "The black dot is fecal matter. The white stuff is urine. They come out together, at the same time, out of the same orifice. The white stuff, which is slightly sticky, clings to the black stuff." (From *Why Do Clocks Run Clockwise, and Other Imponderables*, by David Feldman)

ONCE IN A BLUE MOON

Q: Is there really a such thing as a blue moon?

A: Yes, occasionally it *looks* blue "because of dust conditions in the atmosphere. The most famous widely observed blue moon of recent times occurred on September 26, 1950, owing to dust raised by Canadian forest fires." (From *The Book of Answers*, by Barbara Berliner)

A BIRD ON THE WIRE

Q: *Why don't birds get electrocuted when they perch on electric wires?*

A: Because they're not grounded. "There must be a completed circuit in order for the current to go through its body. If the bird could stand with one leg on the wire, and one on the ground, the circuit would be completed. In all cases where a person has been electrocuted, part of the body touched the wire and another part touched an uninsulated object, such as the ground, or something touching the ground." (From *How Do Flies Walk Upside Down?*, by Martin M. Goldwyn)

GRIN AND BEAR IT

Q: *Do bears really hibernate?*

A: Some bugs, reptiles, amphibians, and mammals do hibernate, but though the bear is known for it, it's not a "true" hibernator. "It does gain fat and, when winter arrives, sleeps for long periods, but not continuously. At irregular intervals, it arouses and wanders about, but doesn't eat much." (From *Science Trivia*, by Charles Cazeau)

ABOUT FIBER

Q: *What is fiber, and why is it good for you?*

A: Fiber—the 'roughage' found in fruits, vegetables, grains and beans, helps food move through the body. It's been credited with a long list of preventative health benefits, including lowering blood cholesterol levels, and reducing the risk of colon cancer.

There are two types of fiber: Insoluble fiber is found mainly in whole grains and the outside, or skin, of seeds, fruits, and beans. Studies show that this fiber may help prevent colorectal cancer. It absorbs food like a sponge and moves it through the bowel—decreasing the amount of cancer-causing substances that come in contact with the bowel wall. Soluble fiber is found in fruits, vegetables, seeds, brown rice, barley, and oats. It may lower cholesterol by adhering to fatty acids and reducing the amount of fat absorbed into the bloodstream.

83% of Hawaiians have cable TV—more than in any other state.

THE KING OF FARTS

Just when you think you've heard it all...someone comes up with something like this. It's from a little book called It's a Gas, *by Eugene Silverman, M.D., and Eric Rabkin, Ph.D. It's required reading for BRI history buffs.*

I n all fairness to the farters of the world, the greatest of them all was not by his passing of gas also passing a judgment. His completely conscious control of his abilities was confirmed by numerous chemical examinations, including two in published form. This man, a hero at bottom, was a gentle and loving father, a noble and steadfast friend, a successful and generous businessman, and a great stage entertainer. This unique individual, a phenomenon among phenomena, this explosive personality and credit to our subject, was christened Joseph Pujol, but invented for himself the name by which all history knows him: Le Petomane!

THE ART OF THE FART
Le Petomane could fart as often and as frequently as he wished. His farts were odorless. As other people use their mouths, Le Petomane had learned to use his anus. Furthermore, by constricting or loosening his anus he could vary the pitch of the air he expelled and by controlling the force of abdominal contraction he could control its loudness. With these two fundamental tools, simple enough but rarely seen, Le Petomane contrived to imitate not only a variety of farts, but to make music.

He headlined at the Moulin Rouge in Paris, the most famous nightclub in the world at that time, and brought in box office receipts more than twice as high as those of the angelic Sarah Bernhardt. He was one of the greatest comedians of the turn of the century. The manager of the Moulin Rouge kept nurses in the theater to tend to female customers whose uncontrolled laughter in tight corsets often caused them to pass out as Le Petomane passed gas. Here was not a court fool at all, but the toast of civilized society.

DISCOVERING HIS GIFT
As a boy, Joseph had had a frightening experience in the sea. Holding his breath and ducking underwater, he suddenly felt a rush of

cold water enter his bowels. He went to find his mother but was embarrassed to see water running out of himself. Although he recounted this in later years, apparently as a child he tried to keep his terrifying experience a secret.

Early in his married life he was called to military service and in the all-male atmosphere of the barracks he recounted for the first time his strange experience in the sea. When asked for a demonstration, he agreed to try again. On their next furlough, he and his unit went to the sea. He did succeed in taking water in and then letting it out. This might have been viewed as mere freakishness, but combined with Joseph's gentleness and good humor, it struck the soldiers as a delightful feat.

Pujol, using a basin, practiced this art in private with water and, once able to control the intake and outflow by combined exertions of his anal and abdominal muscles, he soon began to practice with air as well. This, of course, was only for his own amusement and the occasional amusement of his fellow soldiers.

A STAR IS BORN

When he returned home, he resumed his life as a baker and father but added to it his newfound love of entertainment. He began to work part-time in music halls as an ordinary singer, as a trombone player, and soon as a quick-change artist with a different costume for each song. He began to add comic routines of his own writing to his singing and playing acts, and was quite popular locally.

At the same time, he began to turn his special ability into an act, learning to give farts as imitations. Soon his friends urged him to add this to his act but he was diffident about the propriety of such a thing. In order to give it a try, he rented a theater of his own. He was an almost instant success. He left the bakery in care of his family and went to a number of provincial capitals, and at each stop Le Petomane played to packed houses. Finally, in 1892, he blew into Paris.

HIS FART'S DESIRE

The Moulin Rouge was his aim—and he went right for it. The manager of the Moulin Rouge, one Oller, on hearing of Le Petomane's specialty, was astounded at Pujol's audacity but agreed to give him an audition. In Paris as in Marseille, the act was an instant success.

HIS ACT

Le Petomane would begin by walking out dressed quite elegantly in silks and starched white linen, a thorough swell.

After his opening monologue Le Petomane leaned forward, hands on knees, turned his back to the audience, and began his imitations. "This one is a little girl," he would say and emit a delicate, tiny fart. "This one is a mother-in-law," he'd say, and there would be a slide. "This is a bride on her wedding night," very demure indeed, "and this the morning after," a long, loud one. Then he would do a dressmaker tearing two yards of calico, letting out a cracking, staccato fart that lasted at least ten seconds, and then cannonfire, thunder and so on. The public loved the act and the Moulin Rouge gave him an immediate contract. In a short time, he was their headliner.

A PATRON OF THE FARTS

His act grew with his popularity. Among other feats he could mix in to the performance were those dependent upon inserting a rubber tube in his rectum (very decorously passed through his pocket). With this tube he could amiably chat away while at the same time smoking a cigarette. Sometimes he would insert a six-stop flute into the tube and accompany his own singing. A few simple nursery tunes he could play without recourse to the tube at all. And finally, he would almost always end his acts by blowing out a few of the gas-fired footlights. All that was left, before rising and bowing out, was to invite the audience to join him—and they did with gusto, their own convulsed abdomens insuring that many of the patrons could indeed participate in the group farting at the appropriate moment.

SPECIAL PERFORMANCES

The management of the Moulin Rouge wanted Le Petomane to submit to a medical examination so that his authenticity would be even more accepted, and this he did. For similar reasons of believability, Oller allowed Pujol to give private performances for all-male audiences at which he could perform wearing pants with an appropriate cut-out.

Before these events, and before his regular performances as well, he thoroughly washed himself by drawing water in and then shooting it out. In the smaller groups he would extinguish a candle at the distance of a foot and demonstrate his water jet over a range of four or five yards. These distances are also corroborated by medical observation.

FARTING IN EUROPE

The Moulin Rouge, acting as Le Petomane's agent, also encouraged him to travel abroad. In other European countries, and especially in Belgium, he was a star attraction. At his private performances in France, where no admission was charged, Pujol would finish by passing the hat. At one of these gatherings a man leaned forward and put a 20 louis gold piece in the hat and told him to keep it, that the show was worth it although he had had to travel from Brussels to see it. He had heard so much about Le Petomane but could not see him in his own country because his own movements were so closely watched there. So he had come to Paris that night incognito to see and hear the great Le Petomane. He was King Leopold II of Belgium.

FINAL PASSING

The Medical Faculty at the Sorbonne offered Pujol 25,000 francs for the right to examine his body after his death. He was a vigorous man, a proud patriarch, and, knowing what such a sum could mean to his children and grandchildren, he accepted. But, despite the fact that he had distinguished himself by publicly displaying himself for so many years, he was held in such regard by those around him that, on his peaceful demise in 1945 at the age of 88, the family refused the offer. And so, having made flatulence a subject not for aggression but for pleasantry, Joseph Pujol, the greatest farter in history, came to his proper end.

A PAUSE FOR POETRY

A profound poem by Sir John Suckling, 17th-century cavalier poet:
> Love is the fart
>   of every heart
>   For when held in,
>   doth pain the host,

FAMOUS TRIALS: HENRY FORD VS. *THE TRIBUNE*

Here's an episode that's been forgotten by most historians: In 1916 Henry Ford sued The Chicago Tribune *for libel after it called him "ignorant" in an editorial.*

BACKGROUND
On march 9, 1916, just before World War I, the United States was "invaded" by Mexican revolutionary Pancho Villa. He led a 1,500-man raid on Columbus, New Mexico and killed 17 people—including 8 U.S. soldiers.

President Woodrow Wilson's response: He mobilized the National Guard to patrol the Mexican-American border. As a part of its coverage of the story, *The Chicago Tribune* asked the Ford Motor Company whether employees called up for the Guard would be paid by Ford while they served on the Mexican border. *The Tribune* wanted to talk to Henry Ford himself, but he wasn't available, so they talked to company treasurer Frank Klingensmith instead.

THE CONFLICT
Without checking with his superiors, Klingensmith told the reporters that not only was Ford not going to pay employees who left their jobs to fulfill their reserve duties, it was also not going to reinstate them when they returned from patrolling the border.

Actually, Ford employees who were called up to serve in the National Guard were given special badges that guaranteed them their jobs back when they returned, plus the company set up a special program to assist the families of reservists while they were away. But *The Tribune* ran the story without double-checking the information, and on June 23, 1916, it printed a scathing editorial titled *Ford Is An Anarchist*, attacking Ford for being "not merely an ignorant idealist, but an anarchistic enemy of the nation which protects him in his wealth"—and suggested that "a man so ignorant as Henry Ford may not understand the fundamentals of the government under which he lives."

THE LAWSUIT

Ford, no stranger to criticism, initially dismissed *The Tribune's* assault on his character. But his lawyer, Alfred Lucking, wanted him to sue the paper for libel. Ford reconsidered the matter, and agreed.

It would have been easy to prove the libel charge against *The Tribune* if Ford's legal team had sued the newspaper specifically for using the word "anarchistic"—which in earlier cases had been proven to be a libelous term. But instead the lawyers made their complaint against the entire editorial, which gave *The Tribune* more room in which to maneuver: Instead of having to prove that Ford was an anarchist, they had only to prove that he was "ignorant." And they set out to do just that.

EDUCATING HENRY

The son of a farmer, Henry Ford had left school at the age of 15. To make matters worse, he rarely if ever found time to read the newspaper, and had only a superficial understanding of what was going on in the world. So Ford's lawyers tried to give him a crash course on U.S. history, current events, and other topics, but Ford was a less-than-perfect student.

In the end the task proved too great; try as they might, Ford's lawyers couldn't fill his head with facts quickly enough, and when he arrived to testify at the trial on July 16, 1919, he was forced to admit "ignorance of 'most things.' " Here are some quotes from the transcript of *The Tribune's* lawyer, Elliot G. Stevenson, questioning Henry Ford:

On Ignorance
Q: Mr. Ford, have you ever read history?
A: I admit I am ignorant about most things.
Q: You admit it?
A: About most things.

On The Military
Q: Did you understand what a mobile army was?
A: A large army mobilized.
Q: A large army mobilized. Is that your notion of a mobile army?
A. An army ready to be mobilized.
Q: What is your understanding about a mobile army?

7% of men and 61% of women say they agree: "The way to a partner's heart is through their stomach."

A: I don't know.

On History

Q: Have you ever heard of a revolution in this country?

A: There was, I understand.

Q: When?

A: In 1813.

Q: In 1813, the revolution?

A: Yes.

Q: Any other time?

A: I don't know.

Q: You don't know of any other?

A: No.

Q: Don't you know there wasn't any revolution in 1813?

A: I don't know that; I didn't pay much attention to it.

Q: Don't you know that this country was born out of a revolution—in 1776—did you forget that?

A: I guess I did.

Q: Do you know when the United States was created?

A: I could find it in a few minutes.

Q: Do you know?

A: I don't know as I do, right offhand.

Q: Did you ever hear of Benedict Arnold?

A: I have heard the name.

Q: Who was he?

A: I have forgotten just who he is. He is a writer, I think.

Q: What subjects do you recall he wrote on?

A: I don't remember.

Q: Did you ever read anything that he wrote?

A. Possibly I have, but I don't know.

Q. Would you be surprised to be informed that Benedict Arnold was a general in the American army who was a traitor and betrayed his country?

A: I don't know much about him.

On Government

Q: Mr. Ford, have you heard of the Declaration of Independence?

A: Oh, yes. that is based on justice.

Q: Did you ever read it?

A: Yes, I have read it.

Q: Have you in mind any of the significant things in that?

U.S. city with the most skyscrapers: New York, with 130. Chicago is 2nd with 53.

A: No, I have not.

On Reading

Q: Mr. Ford, I think the impression has been created by your failure to read one of these that have been presented to you that you could not read; do you want to leave it that way?

A: Yes, you can leave it that way. I am not a fast reader, and I have the hay fever, and I would make a botch of it.

Q: Are you willing to have that impression left here?

A: I am not wiling to have that impression, but I am not a fast reader.

Q: Can you read at all?

A: I can read.

Q: Do you want to try it?

A: No, sir.

THE VERDICT

After hearing testimony from dozens of witnesses on both sides of the case for more than 14 weeks, the jury—composed of 11 local farmers and one public roads inspector—met to decide on a verdict. A short time later they found the *Chicago Tribune* guilty of libeling Henry Ford. But Ford's own testimony had damaged his case severely—the jury agreed that he was not an anarchist, but they weren't convinced he wasn't ignorant—and in the end they awarded the automaker a whopping 6¢ in damages.

THE PUBLIC RESPONSE

The public and the press began taking sides on the issue almost immediately. The *Nation* dismissed Ford as a "Yankee mechanic... with a mind unable to 'bite' into any proposition outside of his automobile business;" the *New York Times* editorialized that Ford had not "received a pass degree" in the case.

But the general public was more forgiving. According to Robert Lacey in *Ford: The Men and the Machine*, "His very nakedness when subjected to the city-slicker cleverness of *The Tribune* attorneys struck a chord with thousands who were equally hazy on their knowledge of the American Revolution, and who would have been even more reluctant to read aloud in public."

The trial was big news in its day, but in the long run—like Ford's isolationism, his anti-Semitism, and his early admiration of Adolf Hitler—it had almost no impact on the way he is remembered.

---

5 most popular garden veggies: tomatoes, peppers, onions, cucumbers, and beans.

THE DEATH OF MARILYN

Ever wondered what really happened to Marilyn Monroe? You're not alone. Here's a version that appeared in It's A Conspiracy, *by the National Insecurity Council. It's great bathroom reading; be sure to pick up a copy for yourself.*

At 4:25 a.m. on August 5, 1962, Sergeant Jack Clemmons of the West Los Angeles Police Department received a call from Dr. Hyman Engelberg. "I am calling from the house of Marilyn Monroe," he said. "She is dead."

When Clemmons arrived at 12305 Helena Drive, he found the body lying face down on the bed. The coroner investigating the case ruled that Monroe, 36, had died from "acute barbiturate poisoning due to ingestion of overdose...a probable suicide."

THE OFFICIAL STORY
• The night before, Monroe had gone to bed at about 8:00 p.m., too tired to attend a dinner party at actor Peter Lawford's beach house. A few hours later, Monroe's housekeeper, Eunice Murray, knocked on the star's bedroom door when she noticed a light was on inside, but got no response. Assuming that Monroe had fallen asleep, Murray turned in.

• When Murray awoke at about 3:30 a.m. and noticed the light still on in Monroe's room, she went outside to peek into the window. She saw Monroe lying nude on the bed in an "unnatural" position. Alarmed, Murray called Dr. Ralph Greenson, Monroe's psychiatrist, who came over immediately and broke into the bedroom. She also called Dr. Engelberg, Monroe's personal physician. After Engelberg pronounced her dead, they called the police.

SUSPICIOUS FACTS
From the start, there were conflicting versions of what had happened.

When Did Monroe Die?
Although Murray told the police she'd found the body after 3:30 a.m., there's evidence that Monroe died much earlier.

• Murray first told the police that she'd called Dr. Greenson at midnight; she later changed her story and said it had been 3:30

a.m. Sgt. Clemmons claims that when he first arrived on the scene, Engelberg and Greenson agreed that Murray had called them at about midnight. But in their official police statements, the doctors said they were called at 3:30 a.m.

• According to Anthony Summers in his book *Goddess*, Monroe's press agent, Arthur Jacobs, may have been notified of Monroe's death as early as 11:00 p.m., when he and his wife were at a Hollywood Bowl concert. According to Jacob's wife, Natalie, "We got the news long before it broke. We left the concert at once."

• In 1982, Peter Lawford admitted in a sworn statement that he learned of Monroe's death at 1:30 a.m., when her lawyer, Milton Rudin, called from the house to tell him about it.

• The ambulance crew summoned by the police noticed that Monroe's body was in "advanced rigor mortis," suggesting that she had been dead for 4 to 6 hours. That would mean she died about midnight.

Where Did Monroe Die?

Monroe supposedly died in her bedroom. But did she?

• Monroe's body was stretched out flat on the bed, with the legs straight—not typical for a person who had overdosed on barbiturates. According to Sgt. Clemmons, barbiturate overdoses often cause a body to go into convulsions, leaving it contorted: "You never see a body with the legs straight. And I've seen hundreds of suicides by drug overdose." He speculated that she had been moved. (*The Marilyn Conspiracy*)

• William Shaefer, president of the Shaefer Ambulance Service, insists that "in the very early morning hours"—well before 3:00 a.m.—one of his ambulances was called to Monroe's house. She was comatose; the ambulance took her to Santa Monica Hospital, where she died. "She passed away at the hospital. She did not die at home." And he was certain it was Monroe: "We'd hauled her before because of [earlier overdoses of] barbiturates. We'd hauled her when she was comatose." (ibid.)

How Did Monroe Die?

• Though Deputy Medical Examiner Thomas Noguchi speculated that Monroe had swallowed roughly 50 Nembutal pills, a common barbiturate, he found "no visual evidence of pills in the stomach or

---

Yecch! 3% of American households keep a supply of anchovy paste in the kitchen.

the small intestine. No residue. No refractile crystals." Yet, as Noguchi recounted in his book *Coroner*, toxicological reports of Monroe's blood confirmed his suspicions of an overdose.

• Why was there no pill residue in Monroe's body? Noguchi said that some "murder theorists" have suggested that an injection of barbiturates would have killed her without leaving pill residue. Other theorists have suggested that a suppository with a fatal dose of barbiturates would also leave no residue in her stomach. Or, at some point after the overdose, Monroe's stomach may have been pumped.

MISSING EVIDENCE
Why has so much evidence pertaining to Marilyn Monroe's case disappeared or been destroyed?

Phone Records
• Did Monroe try to call anyone the night she died? When a reporter for the *Los Angeles Herald Tribune* tried to get her phone records and find out, a phone company contact told him, "All hell is breaking loose down here! Apparently you're not the only one interested in Marilyn's calls. But the tape [of her calls] has disappeared. I'm told it was impounded by the Secret Service....Obviously somebody high up ordered it." (*Goddess*)

• In 1985, a former FBI agent claimed: "The FBI did remove certain Monroe records. I was on a visit to California when Monroe died, and became aware of the removal of the records from my Los Angeles colleagues. I knew there were some people there, Bureau personnel, who normally wouldn't have been there—agents from out of town. They were there on the scene immediately, as soon as she died, before anyone realized what had happened. It had to be on the instruction of somebody high up, higher even than Hoover...either the Attorney General or the President." (ibid.)

Monroe's Diary
• Monroe supposedly kept a detailed diary. According to Robert Slatzer, a longtime friend of the actress, "For years, Marilyn kept scribbled notes of conversations to help her remember things." What things? Slatzer said the diary included her intimate discussions with people like Robert Kennedy. Monroe supposedly told Slatzer, "Bobby liked to talk about political things. He got mad at

me one day because he said I didn't remember the things he told me." (*The Marilyn Conspiracy*)

• After Monroe's death, Coroner's Aide Lionel Grandison claimed that the diary "came into my office with the rest of Miss Monroe's personal effects" during the investigation. But by the next day the diary had vanished—and, according to Grandison, someone had removed it from the list of items that had been brought in for investigation. (ibid.)

The Original Police Files

• In 1974, Captain Kenneth McCauley of the Los Angeles Police Department contacted the Homicide Department to ask about the files. They wrote back that the department had no crime reports in its files pertaining to Monroe's death. Even the death report had vanished.

• The files on Monroe may have disappeared as early as 1966. That year, Los Angeles Mayor Sam Yorty requested a copy of the files from the police department. The police declined, saying that the file "isn't here."

• What happened to the files? Lieutenant Marion Phillips of the Los Angeles Police Department claimed that he was told in 1962 that a high-ranking police official "had taken the file to show someone in Washington. That was the last we heard of it."

MONROE AND THE KENNEDYS

• As part of his research for *Goddess*, the most authoritative book on Marilyn Monroe, Anthony Summers interviewed more than 600 people linked to her. He quotes friends, acquaintances, reporters, and politicians who confirm what many Americans already suspected—that Monroe had affairs with both John and Robert Kennedy.

• Apparently, John Kennedy met her through his brother-in-law, Peter Lawford. According to Lawford's third wife, Deborah Gould, "Peter told me that Jack...had always wanted to meet Marilyn Monroe; it was one of his fantasies." Quoting Lawford, Gould says "Monroe's affair with John Kennedy began before he became president and continued for several years." (*Goddess*)

• According to Gould, JFK decided to end his affair with Monroe early in 1962. He sent his brother Robert to California to give her

---

the news. "Marilyn took it quite badly," says Gould, "and Bobby went away with a feeling of wanting to get to know her better. At the beginning it was just to help and console, but then it led into an affair between Marilyn and Bobby." (ibid.)

• It didn't last long. By the summer of 1962, RFK began having second thoughts and decided to break off the affair. Monroe, already severely depressed, began acting erratically after being dumped by Bobby. She began calling him at home; when he changed his unlisted phone number to avoid her, she began calling him at the Justice Department, the White House, and even at the Kennedy compound in Hyannisport. When Bobby still refused to take her calls, Monroe threatened to go public with both affairs.

WAS IT A CONSPIRACY?

THEORY #1: Monroe was distraught about her affairs and committed suicide. To protect the Kennedys from scandal, someone tried to cover up the suicide and cleaned up Monroe's house.

• Monroe may have become frantic when Robert Kennedy cut her off, perhaps—as some theorists guess—because she was pregnant.

• Fred Otash, a Hollywood private detective, claimed that a "police source" told him that weeks before her death Monroe had gone to Mexico to have an abortion. According to Otash, "An American doctor went down to Tijuana to do it, which made Monroe safe medically, and made the doctor safe from U.S. law," since at that time abortion was illegal in the U.S. But author Summers disagrees, noting: "There was no medical evidence to support the theory that Monroe had been pregnant." (*Goddess*)

• In any event, if Monroe was threatening to embarrass the Kennedys by going public about their affairs, it was cause for alarm. According to several reports, Robert Kennedy—who was vacationing with his family near San Francisco—flew to Los Angeles on August 4 to meet with Monroe and try to calm her down. It didn't work.

• Terribly depressed, Monroe took a massive dose of sleeping pills, but not before calling Peter Lawford and saying, in a slurred voice, "Say goodbye to Pat [Lawford's wife], say goodbye to Jack [JFK], and say goodbye to yourself, because you're such a nice guy."

• The call may have frightened Lawford so badly that he—and perhaps RFK—drove to Monroe's home. There he may have found her comatose and called an ambulance. (This would explain the Shaefer Ambulance claim of having taken Monroe to the hospital that night.) If Monroe had been taken to a hospital emergency room because of an overdose, her stomach would almost certainly have been pumped—which would account for the coroner's finding no "pill residue" in her stomach. When even the hospital's best attempts could not save Monroe, perhaps her body was returned to her bedroom in an effort to avoid controversy.

The Cleanup

• No suicide note was ever found, nor was Monroe's personal phone book. Someone had probably "sanitized" her bedroom before the police came. The most likely person was Peter Lawford. His wife Deborah claimed, "He went there and tidied up the place, and did what he could, before the police and the press arrived." She also claimed Lawford had found a suicide note and destroyed it.

• Lawford may also have hired detective Fred Otash to finish the cleanup. According to a security consultant who worked with Otash, Lawford hired him on the night of the death to "check her house, especially for papers or letters, that might give away her affairs with the Kennedys."

THEORY #2: The Mob killed Monroe to embarrass—or even frame—Attorney General Robert Kennedy.

• The Mob almost certainly knew of Monroe's affairs with the Kennedys: in fact, several reputable accounts claim that the star's house had been bugged by the Mob. By recording intimate moments between Monroe and Robert Kennedy, the syndicate may have hoped to blackmail the attorney general and thus end his prosecution of Teamsters boss Jimmy Hoffa and other gangsters.

• In their book *Double Cross*, Chuck and Sam Giancana—the brother and godson of Mob godfather Sam "Mooney" Giancana—allege that the Mafia eventually decided to kill Monroe and make with RFK, they figured, the public would decide that Monroe had killed herself over him. They figured a sex and suicide scandal would force him to resign. So, the Mob waited for Kennedy to visit Monroe, in response to her desperate phone calls.

• Finally, Kennedy took the bait. According to the authors of *Double Cross*, when Sam Giancana learned that Bobby would be in

California the weekend of August 4, he arranged the hit on Marilyn. The authors allege he chose Needles Gianola, an experienced killer, for the mission. Needles selected three men of his own to help him. Together they traveled to California "under Mooney's orders, to murder Marilyn Monroe."

• According to *Double Cross*, the mob had already bugged Marilyn's home, and the hit men were waiting at their secret listening post nearby when Kennedy arrived late Saturday night. They heard Bobby and another man enter the home and begin talking to Marilyn, who was extremely upset. Marilyn, the authors report, "became agitated—hysterical, in fact—and in response, they heard Kennedy instruct the man with him, evidently a doctor, to give her a shot to 'calm her down.' Shortly afterwards, RFK and the doctor left."

• *Double Cross* claims that the four killers waited until nightfall and then sneaked into Monroe's home to make the hit. Marilyn resisted, but was easily subdued because of the sedatives: "Camly, and with all the efficiency of a team of surgeons, they taped her mouth shut and proceeded to insert a specially 'doctored' Nembutal suppository into her anus. According to the authors, the killers waited for the lethal combination of barbiturates and chloral hydrate to take effect. Once she was totally unconscious, the men carefully removed the tape, wiped her mouth clean, and placed her across the bed. Their job completed, they left as quietly as they had come."

• Unfortunately for the conspirators, however, Kennedy's close friends and the FBI so thoroughly cleaned up Monroe's house and commandeered her phone records that any proof of the romance was eliminated. The Giancanas say that J. Edgar Hoover protected the Kennedys because, after keeping their secrets, he knew that they'd never fire him. *Double Cross* also alleges that the CIA was also in on the hit, but its reasoning is not convincing.

FOOTNOTE

In 1982, after reinvestigating Marilyn Monroe's death, the Los Angeles District Attorney's Office released the following statement: "Marilyn Monroe's murder would have required a massive, in-place conspiracy covering all of the principals at the death scene on August 4 and 5, 1962; the actual killer or killers; the Chief Medical Examiner-Coroner; the autopsy surgeon to whom the case was fortuitously assigned; and almost all of the police officers assigned to

ANSWERS

Here are the solutions to our brain teasers, quizzes, etc.

WHAT DOES IT SAY?, PAGE 16

1. *John Underwood, Andover, Mass.* (JOHN under WOOD, and over MASS)

2. I thought I heard a noise outside, but it was *nothing after all.* (0 after ALL)

3. Let's have *an understanding* (AN under STANDING)

4. *Look around you.* (LOOK around U)

5. "Remember," she said to the group, "*united we stand, divided we fall.*" (United WESTAND, divided WE FALL)

6. "Why'd he do that?" Jesse asked. "Well, son," I said, "he's a *mixed-up kid.*" (DKI = kid)

7. Texas? I love *wide-open spaces.* (S   P   A   C   E   S)

8. "Drat! My watch broke. Time to get it *repaired.*" (RE paired)

9. "I remember the 1960s," she said, *looking backward:* (GNIKOOL = "looking" spelled backward)

10. No, we're not living together anymore. It's a *legal separation.* (L   E   G   A   L)

11. Haven't seen him in a while. He's *far away from home.* (FAR away from HOME)

12. Careful, I warned my sister. He's a *wolf in sheep's clothing.* (WOLF inside WOOL)

13. "How do I get out of here?" he asked. I said, "Just calm down and put the *car in reverse.*" (R A C = car spelled backward)

14. I tried to teach her, but no luck. I guess she's a *backward child.* (DLIHC = *child* spelled backward)

15. When it's raining, *she meets me under an umbrella.* (SHE meets ME under AN UMBRELLA)

The FBI has more than 200 million fingerprints on file—and 40% are people with no convictions.

THE GODZILLA QUIZ, PAGE 36

1. C) They added Raymond Burr, casting him as Steve Martin, a reporter who remembers the whole incident as a flashback. It starts off with Burr in a hospital bed, recalling the horror he's seen. Then, throughout the film, footage of Burr is cleverly inserted to make it seem as though he's interacting with the Japanese cast.

2. C) *Gigantis*; it was illegal to use the name Godzilla. Warner Brothers brought the film into America, but they forgot to secure the rights to the name Godzilla, so they couldn't legally use it. In this film, by the way, Godzilla crushes Osaka instead of Tokyo, and begins his long tradition of monster-fighting (he takes on a giant creature called Angorus).

3. B) A giant cockroach and a robot with a buzz saw in his stomach. The seatopioans, stationed under the sea, are using a metal bird monster with a buzz saw (Gaigan) and a giant cockroach (Megalon)—described as a "metal monster insect with drill arms"— to fight Godzilla on the surface. Godzilla can't take them on alone. He teams up with Jet Jaguar, a cyborg who can change size to fight monsters.

4. B) A giant moth. The thing is Mothra, who starred in his/her own film a few years earlier. Godzilla kills Mothra—but a giant egg on display at a carnival hatches, and two "junior Mothras" emerge. They spin a cocoon around Godzilla and dump him in the ocean.

5. A) He fought a Godzilla robot from outer space. The film was originally called *Godzilla vs. the Bionic Monster*, presumably to cash in on the popularity of the "Six Million Dollar Man" TV show. But the owners of that TV show sued, and the title was changed to *Godzilla vs. the Cosmic Monster*.

6. C) A three-headed dragon. To defeat them, Godzilla takes a partner again—this time Angorus, his foe from *Gigantis*.

7. A) The Smog Monster—a 400-foot blob of garbage. The smog monster flies around, leaving a trail of poisonous vapors that cause people to drop like flies, especially at discos where teens are danc-

---

Nearly 40% of the people who get plastic surgery are between 35 and 55 years old.

ing to anti-pollution songs. Don't miss the smash tune, "Save the Earth."

8. B) To show a little kid how to fight bullies. The boy falls asleep and dreams he travels to monster Island, where Godzilla and his son teach him how to defend himself.

9. C) A giant lobster. Actually, he might be a giant shrimp. It's hard to tell. His strength: he can regenerate a limb every time one is torn off.

10. C) It was Godzilla's son. Imagine that—Godzilla's a parent!

AUNT LENNA'S PUZZLES, PAGE 92

1. The accountant and lawyer were women. Steve is a man's name.

2. The answers are WHOLESOME and ONE WORD.

AUNT LENNA'S PUZZLES, PAGE 131

1. He couldn't have heard where she was going if he was deaf.

2. 99-99/99

3. His wife was on a life-support system. When he pushed the elevator button, he realized the power had gone off.

4. The first man, who saw the smoke, knew first; the second man, who heard it, knew second; the third man, who saw the bullet, knew last. The speed of light travels faster than the speed of sound, and the speed of sound travels faster than a bullet.

5. Her shoes. Check it out against the woman's laments—it makes sense.

6. Let's start with the grandmothers and grandfathers. That's four. They're all mothers and fathers, so if there are three mothers and three fathers, we have two new people—one mother, one father—for a total of 6.

The two mothers-in-law and fathers-in-law are the grandparents, so we don't count them again. The son-in-law and daughter-in-law are the two additional parents, so we don't count them again, either. The two sons and two daughters are their children—which makes 10 people.

AUNT LENNA'S PUZZLES, PAGE 169

1. She's talking about the amount of bills, not the year. 1,993 bills are worth exactly $1 more than more than 1,992 bills.

2. They were traveling at different times.

3. Noel (No "L").

4. She grabbed one of the stones and quickly let it "slip" from her hands. Then, because she "couldn't find" the stone she'd dropped, she just looked in the bag to see what was left. It was a black stone, of course…which meant she'd won the bet.

5. Cut them into quarters with two cuts…then stack the quarters on top of each other and cut once. Eight pieces, three cuts.

6. She wrote:

THE LAST PAGE

F ELLOW BATHROOM READERS:
The fight for good bathroom reading should never be taken loosely—we must sit firmly for what we believe in, even while the rest of the world is taking pot shots at us.

Once we prove we're not simply a flush-in-the-pan, writers and publishers will find their resistance unrolling.

So we invite you to take the plunge: "Sit Down and Be Counted!" by joining The Bathroom Readers' Institute. Send a self-addressed, stamped envelope to: B.R.I., 1400 Shattuck Avenue, #25, Berkeley, CA 94709. You'll receive your attractive free membership card, a copy of the B.R.I. newsletter (if we ever get around to publishing one), and earn a permanent spot on the B.R.I. honor roll.

ᇮ   ᇮ   ᇮ

UNCLE JOHN'S *SEVENTH* BATHROOM READER IS IN THE WORKS

Don't fret—there's more good reading on its way. In fact, there are a few ways you can contribute to the next volume:

1) Is there a subject you'd like to see us cover? Write and let us know. We aim to please.

2) Got a neat idea for a couple of pages in the new Reader? If you're the first to suggest it, and we use it, we'll send you a free copy of the book.

3) Have you seen or read an article you'd recommend as quintessential bathroom reading? Or is there a passage in a book that you want to share with other B.R.I. members? Tell us where to find it, or send a copy. If you're the first to suggest it and we publish it in the next volume, there's a free book in it for you.

Well, we're out of space, and when you've gotta go, you've gotta go. Hope to hear from you soon. Meanwhile, remember:
Go With the Flow.